WHAT OTHERS ARE SAYING /
GREEN CHINA, GREEN ECONOMY

There is a deep tension between a beautiful, healthful, and sustainable environment and rapid growth of industrial civilization. The Chinese people want both. What is astonishing is the extent to which China is finding ways to continue growing that are not so costly to the environment. The problems are still enormous, and many of them are growing worse. But the efforts made to curb the destruction are also enormous and there are even prospects for reversing the deterioration while continuing to grow. China is struggling to find its way to an industrialized ecological civilization.

I hope the world will begin to emphasize increasing the carbon absorption by plants and soil as much as reducing carbon emissions. this report indicates that China is reforesting, an immensely positive move. Whereas industrial farming continues to poison the land and lose soil, organic farms absorb carbon and build up the soil. May Chinese farmers return to organic methods before it is too late. - *John B. Cobb, Jr.*

Global emission reduction and aggressive continued progress in reaching 2 centigrade climate target is of first importance for everyone, everywhere. China's role is obvious. - *Roy Morrison*

Environmentalists in the United States greet this report with enthusiasm. It records the concrete steps that the Chinese people are taking to reduce China's carbon footprint and to correct the practices of the past, which have harmed China's air, ground, and water. Although we advocate for even stricter standards, we are excited to see real advances towards the "greenization" of China. - *Philip Clayton*

The depth and breadth of China's efforts on the environment, as documented in this excellent report from Xinhua News, is both impressive and inspiring. China can be a role model for other countries in the developing world by demonstrating what is possible despite significant economic and social challenges. The best way for China to be a role model is to ensure it reports its progress in achieving its stated goals with complete honesty and transparency. China's integrity and credibility will be enhanced measurably if all progress is disclosed even if some goals are missed. No one expects perfection: periodic self-evaluation, mid-course corrections when needed and the desire for continuous improvement are much more important.

Despite the success in Paris, many participants remain skeptical that the goals agreed to will be adequate in avoiding volatile weather patterns (hurricanes, floods, drought etc.), species extinction and other natural disasters. It is, therefore, essential that countries not only do their utmost to fulfill the pledges made in Paris but increase their greenhouse gas emission reduction targets over time. This will not be easy, but China knows firsthand that the environment must be a top priority or the inevitable consequences will be severe. *~ David Schwerin*

This report covers a wide and important range of subjects and the important progress China appears to be making. *~ Mark Anielski*

Green China

Green Economy

Green China
Green Economy

China Ecological Civilization
Annual Report & Outlook
(2015-2016)

Xinhua News Agency

PROCESS
CENTURY
PRESS
ANOKA, MINNESOTA 2016

Green China, Green Economy: China Ecological Civilization Annual Report & Outlook (2015-2016)

© 2016 Process Century Press

Process Century Press
RiverHouse LLC
802 River Lane
Anoka, MN 55303

Process Century Press books are published in association with the International Process Network.

Cover design: Jing Wang

ISBN 978-1-940447-19-3
Printed in the United States of America

Contents

ACKNOWLEDGMENTS, *i*

INTRODUCTION, *iii*

PART 1: SLOWER GROWTH, BUT GREENER ECONOMY

1.1   China unveils new, ambitious climate goals, *1*

1.1.1   China growing green economy under
        new climate pledges, *4*

1.2   China unveils proposals for formulating
        13th five-year plan, *6*

1.2.1   What China's "medium-high" growth
        means to the world, *8*

1.2.2   Green shoots of growth to meet China's
        climate-change promises, *10*

1.2.3   China shapes green economy for next 5
        years: leading U.S. ecological expert, *12*

1.3.   Chinese leaders push for "greenization", *13*

1.3.1   Xi's eco-protection footprint, *14*

1.3.2   China faces unprecedented environment,
        development conflict: minister, *17*

1.4   A new course of growth for China, *18*

1.4.1   Bright spots in China's slowing economy, *21*

1.4.2   China identifies priority sectors
         for industrial upgrades, *25*

1.4.3   China sees 10,000 new firms every day, *25*

1.4.4   Consumption, services push China
         toward sustainable growth, *26*

**PART 2:   ENVIRONMENTAL PROTECTION
             A KEY GROWTH DRIVER**

2.1   China promotes greener industry, *30*

2.1.1   China finds new engines as economy slows down, *31*

2.1.2   China to spend 6.7 trillion USD on low-
         carbon industries by 2030, *33*

2.1.3   Green finance booming among Chinese banks, *35*

2.1.3.1 Chinese banks lend more to green sector, *36*

2.1.4   China environment protection firms
         enjoy sunny outlook, *37*

2.1.5   China's national emissions trading system plan
         is "a very important signal": WB V.P, *39*

2.1.6   China's green economy could create
         enormous business opportunities, *41*

2.1.6.1 Water pollution treatment open for trillions
         yuan of private investment, *43*

2.1.6.2 China lends huge fund to battle
         heavy metal pollution, *44*

2.2   China's economic downturn "vastly
         overstated": report, *45*

2.2.1   China 2014 growth revised down to 7.3%, *48*

2.2.2   Power consumption reveals China's
         economic transition, *49*

2.2.3   IMF confident about China's GDP growth
        expectations at 6.5-7.5% this year, *51*

2.2.4   China transitions to slower but better growth—IMF, *52*

2.3   China moves forward in developing
        circular economy, *54*

2.3.1   Multi-billion dollar recycling project targets
        industrial waste around Beijing, *55*

2.3.2   Chinese researchers help paper plant
        realize zero waste discharge, *56*

2.4   High-speed trains make China smaller,
        give tourists better mobility, *57*

2.4.1   "High-speed train tribe" grows with
        China's expanding rail network, *59*

**PART 3:   CHINA CARBON EMISSIONS EXPECTED TO PEAK
            WELL AHEAD OF 2030: NGO**

3.1   China's carbon growth rate in decline: report, *63*

3.1.1   China's energy use slows in 2014, *64*

3.1.2   China on bold move to build low-
        carbon energy system, *65*

3.1.3   China's sustainable energy competitiveness
        tops global ranking, *66*

3.1.3.1 Renewable energy to lead world power
        market growth: IEA report, *68*

3.1.3.2 UNEP hails China's leadership in
        renewable energy investment, *69*

3.2.   China tops global list of clean energy investment, *71*

3.2.1   China's installed wind power capacity
        hit record high in 2014, *72*

3.2.1.1 Wind power helps clean China's air, *72*

3.2.1.2   Northern China looks to wind
          power for winter heating, *75*

3.2.2   China's PV power capacity to hit
          150 gigawatts by 2020, *76*

3.2.2.1   China's largest solar power tower
          plant starts construction, *76*

3.2.2.2   China builds PV power base in desert, *77*

3.2.2.3   600,000 Tibetans have access to solar power, 78

3.2.2.4   Apple to build first international solar
          project in SW China, *79*

3.2.3   China to lower on-grid price of
          wind power, PV power, *82*

3.2.4   China eyes huge solar-thermal power project, *83*

3.2.5   China's first biomass-solar power plant
          begins initial operation, *84*

3.3   China unveils new energy micro-
          power grid guidelines, *85*

3.4   China gives fresh support for new-energy cars, *86*

3.4.1   China slashes tax to promote green vehicles, ships, *87*

3.4.1.1   New perks for green car buyers, *88*

3.4.1.2   Beijing residents to buy foreign new
          energy vehicles more easily, *89*

3.4.2   China's new energy vehicle output surges, *89*

3.4.2.1   China's electric car production grows in 2014, *90*

3.4.2.2   Electric car sales accelerate in Beijing, *91*

3.4.2.3   BYD represents influence in clean green vehicles, *92*

3.4.3   China to build 12,000 NEV chargers by 2020, *93*

3.4.3.1   Beijing to double charging stations before 2016, *94*

3.4.3.2   Electric car chargers installed on Beijing-
          Shanghai expressway, *95*

3.4.3.3   Expressways in Beijing and neighboring
          region to add electric charging posts, *96*

3.4.3.4   Beijing pilots street lamp chargers for electric cars, *97*

3.4.3.5   Tesla teams with property developer
          to expand charging poles, *98*

3.4.4   Chinese firm to produce solar-powered cars, *99*

3.5   China's first electricity-powered aircraft
          gets production approval, *99*

3.6   China raises consumption tax on oil products, *100*

3.7   China to cap coal consumption, *101*

3.7.1   Slump in Shanxi's coal industry, *102*

3.7.2   Top Chinese coal mining company
          reports sharp profit drop, *103*

3.7.3   China's most polluted province cuts coal use, *104*

3.7.4   Coal-rich China sees shift in power mix: Fitch, *104*

3.7.5   China pays power stations to cut emissions, *105*

3.8   China's crude steel output in landmark dip, *106*

Case Study: Gloom for Hebei as steel loses shine, 107

**PART 4:   INTERNET TECHNOLOGY RESHAPES
           CHINA'S ECONOMY**

4.1   China's online population reaches 648 MLN, *114*

4.1.1.   China to give whole nation 4G coverage by 2018, *114*

4.2   Internet-led consumption boom almost unnoticed
          amid China's stock market jitters, *115*

4.3   China to deliver 50 bln express
          parcels by 2020: Official, *117*

4.4   When the Internet meets agriculture, *118*

4.4.1   Chinese farmers turn to e-commerce
        to rid poverty, *120*

4.4.2   China's rural areas to benefit more
        from e-commerce, *122*

4.5   E-books overtake paper in China, *123*

4.5.1   China's e-book revenues surge in eight years, *123*

**PART 5:   CHINA TO BOOST SUSTAINABLE GROWTH IN
           AGRICULTURE**

5.1   China strives for eco-friendly farming, *125*

5.1.1   China's farmland well above "red line", *126*

5.1.2   China adjusts subsidy policy to help farmers, *127*

5.1.3   China to strengthen financial support to agriculture, *128*

5.1.3.1 China's 2014 loan for agriculture hits 23.6 TRLN yuan, *129*

5.1.4   Xinjiang civil servants boost rural development, *130*

5.2   China to curb farm pollution, *132*

5.2.1   China caps fertilizer, pesticide use, *132*

5.2.2   Maps reveal extent of China's antibiotics pollution, *134*

5.2.3   Washing away soil erosion worries, *136*

5.3   Producers hope potatoes takes root in China, *141*

**PART 6:   CHINA VOWS TO PROMOTE LOW CARBON URBAN
           DEVELOPMENT**

6.1   Growth in farmer-turned-laborers slows, *146*

6.2   Beijing to shift city admin to ease "urban ills", *148*

6.3   Embracing green construction on a local level, *151*

6.4   More than 97% of China's household
        garbage treated properly, *153*

6.5   Industrial city faces pollution control conundrum, *154*

Case Study: China eyes infrastructure projects to relieve poverty, power economy, 155

PART 7: CHINA'S ECOLOGICAL FOOTPRINT EXPECTED TO PEAK IN 2029: REPORT

7.1   China to stop commercial logging of natural forests in key zones by 2020, *159*

7.1.1   China to keep on greening, *160*

7.2   China to spend 1.6 bln on wetlands protection, *161*

7.2.1   Beijing to expand green spaces, wetland, *162*

7.3   China to further protect desertified land, *163*

7.3.1   Desertification in China reversed over past decade, *163*

7.4   China's nature reserves flourishing, *164*

7.4.1   Who pays for wildlife "crime"?, *164*

7.4.2   China's wild tiger, leopard population in recovery, *167*

Case Study: Protecting Yangtze River at source, 168

PART 8: NEW ENVIRONMENTAL PROTECTION LAW SHOWS ITS TEETH

8.1   Tougher penalties for China's air polluters, *172*

8.1.1   Chinese court accepts first lawsuit from environmental organization, *172*

8.1.1.1   China NGOs win landmark environmental lawsuit, *174*

8.1.2   China prosecutors file lawsuit against environmental department, *175*

8.1.3   Prosecutors fast-track pollution case in east China, *176*

8.1.3.1   Oil giants sued over Bohai spill, *177*

8.1.3.2   China arrests four for dumping industrial waste water, *179*

8.1.3.3   Chinese firm punished for polluting desert, *179*

8.1.3.3.1 Another Chinese firm punished
          for polluting desert, *181*

8.1.4   China imposes greater fines for
          environmental violations in 2014, *182*

8.1.4.1   China rules that all polluters held
          accountable regardless of fault, *183*

8.1.5   China cleans up 1,790 environment
          crimes from January to July, *184*

8.1.5.1   Environmental violations seen in China
          in first half of 2015: 25,164, *185*

8.1.5.2   China Focus: 8,500 arrested for
          environmental crimes in 2014, *185*

8.1.6   China passes law to control air pollution, *188*

8.2   Environment tax law on fast track, *190*

8.2.1   China Focus: China proposes double
          taxes on excess emissions, *192*

8.2.2   China levies consumption tax on batteries, paint, *193*

8.3   China pushes hard for cleaner environment;
          tougher requirement on officials, *194*

8.3.1   Lifelong liability for polluting officials
          in China: regulation, *197*

8.3.2   Ministry names and shames northern
          city for pollution, *197*

8.3.3   China's all provincial regions reach
          pollutants emission cut target, *198*

8.4   Extra efforts needed to battle smog: minister, *199*

8.4.1   China sees less acid rain in the first of 2015, *200*

8.4.2   Ministry plans five-year air pollution control project, *201*

8.4.2.1   China environment communique exposes
          poor air, groundwater quality, *202*

8.4.3   Beijing PM2.5 level down 20%, *203*

8.4.3.1   Beijing breathes cleaner air in first half 2015, *204*

8.4.3.2   Beijing shut down nearly 400 polluting
          factories in 2014, *204*

8.4.3.3   Over 300 furnaces dismantled
          around Beijing in one day, *205*

8.4.3.4   Beijing closes 185 firms to fight pollution, *206*

8.4.3.5   Beijing fights pollution through regional
          cooperation, plant closures, *206*

8.4.3.6   Beijing to charge emitters of PM2.5-
          forming pollutants, *208*

8.4.4   Pollution control slashes GDP growth
          in Beijing's neighbor, *209*

8.4.4.1   China's Hebei to close 2,500 brick
          kilns to cut pollution, *210*

8.4.5   Industrial firms around Shanghai Disney
          scheduled for closure, *211*

8.4.6   60% of high-emission vehicles removed
          from China's roads, *212*

8.4.6.   China speeds up fuel quality
          upgrading for better air, *212*

8.4.6.2   Beijing upgrades diesel buses to cut air pollution, *213*

8.5   China to inspect water pollution
          prevention, control, *214*

8.5.1   Cooperation between government, citizens
          encouraged on water pollution prevention, *215*

8.5.2   Water pollution plan to bring long-term gain, *216*

8.5.2.1   Beijing conserves more water in 2014, *219*

8.5.2.2 Social capital encouraged in water pollution control, *219*

8.5.3   Cleaning up China's big rivers, *220*

8.6   China to deploy space-air-ground sensors for environment protection, *222*

8.6.1   UAVs bring new trends in environmental protection, *223*

8.6.2   Drones detect environment violations, *224*

8.7   China records 471 environment emergencies in 2014, *225*

8.7.1   Reducing China's air pollution may prevent about 900,000 cardiovascular deaths by 2030: study, *226*

8.8   Green volunteer alliance launched, *227*

8.9   Chinese man invents "green firecracker" to fight smog, *228*

PART 9: POVERTY RELIEF HIGH ON CHINA'S 2016-2020 GOVERNMENT AGENDA: OFFICIAL

9.1   More than 10 mln Chinese overcome poverty in 2014, *231*

9.2   China's rich-poor gap narrows in 2014, *232*

9.3   China realizes universal power access, *232*

PART 10: CHINA PLEDGES 3 BILLION USD FOR DEVELOPING COUNTRIES TO FIGHT CLIMATE CHANGE

10.1   Climate change mainly caused by human activities: climate report, *238*

10.1.1   Top meteorological official warns of climate change risks, *239*

10.1.2   Tibet's glaciers retreat, even as protection advances, *240*

10.2   China's environmental protection experience
         could benefit world: Group, *242*

10.3   Sustainable development agenda pursues
         economic, social progress while highlighting
         environment protection: UN official, *243*

10.4   Renewable energy sources cost-
         competitive: IRENA report, *245*

APPENDIX

I.   Full Text: Integrated Reform Plan for
         Promoting Ecological Progress, *248*

II.   Full Text: Enhanced Actions on Climate Change: China's
         Intended Nationally Determined Contributions, *280*

Acknowledgments

Without the hard work of Xinhua reporters who cover the economic, social and ecological developments in China, there would not be this Annual Report & Outlook which reflected the great effort of Chinese people toward a more sustainable future. There would not be the *China Ecological Civilization* e-newsletter either, which has been edited and released by Xinhua News Agency Los Angeles Bureau since 2013 with the support from Xinhua's headquarters in Beijing and the North American Branch.

As a product to introduce the latest sustainable development policy and effort in China to the world, *China Ecological Civilization* always gets support from many friends and organizations, including the Institute for Postmodern Development of China led by Dr. John Cobb, Jr., Dr. Philip Clayton, Dr. Zhihe Wang and Dr. Meijun Fan. They provided valuable thinking which inspired the Xinhua journalists who edited the e-newsletters and the Annual Report & Outlook.

Roy Morrison, David Schwerin and Mark Anielski, who have been doing related research for many years, kindly provided their comments on this book. Their words are encouraging, not only for the effort to make *China Ecological Civilization* e-newsletter and this book available, but also for the vital transformation in China.

i

Jeanyne B. Slettom, publisher and editor of Process Century Press, provided great help and the opportunity to make this book formally published.

All the efforts of Xinhua reporters and the help of friends have a common goal — for a better world and an ecological civilized future shared by all mankind.

Introduction

2015 was the second year we published the *China Ecological Civilization* e-newsletter. In the past year, the COP21 was held in Paris, China saw fewer smoggy days, and the Chinese economy was turning greener.

This dynamic world changes fast. As more people are talking about the need for action on climate change, China, the biggest developing country in the world, is steadfastly pursuing its green economic and social policies.

2016 will be the first year for the implementation of China's 13th Five-Year Development Plan. The next five years will be critical, not only to China's sustainable growth, but also to the joint efforts by all nations to keep our planet a good place to live for many generations to come. We hope to show our readers what happened in China in 2015 and what will happen next through this book.

All the facts and figures in this book have come from stories released in 2015 by Xinhua News Agency, the biggest media outlet in China.

For further information about China's latest ecological civilization development, please subscribe to the China Ecological Civilization e-newsletter by sending an email to econews@xinhua.org, visit www.xinhuacec.com, or follow us on Twitter by @Xinhuacec and like us on Facebook.

Part 1

Slower Growth, but Greener Economy

1.1 CHINA UNVEILS NEW, AMBITIOUS CLIMATE GOALS

http://news.xinhuanet.com/english/2015-07/01/c_134369901.htm

China on July 1 made fresh pledges on fighting climate change, setting out ambitious targets beyond 2020 in what it calls its "utmost efforts" in tackling the global challenge.

The world's largest greenhouse gas emitter aims to cut carbon dioxide emissions per unit of gross domestic product (GDP) by 60 percent to 65 percent from the 2005 level by 2030, according to China's intended nationally determined contributions (INDC), an action plan submitted to the Secretariat of the UN Framework Convention on Climate Change.

That goal will be a big step further from China's previous emission control target, which eyes a decrease of 40 percent to 45 percent from the 2005 level by 2020.

In 2014, carbon emissions per unit of GDP was 33.8 percent lower than the 2005 level.

The enhanced actions "represent its (China's) utmost efforts in addressing climate change," the INDC said.

Acting on climate change is driven by China's domestic needs to ensure economic and ecological security, as well as by its sense of responsibility to fully engage in global governance, according to the document.

BOOST FOR GLOBAL ACTIONS

China's new climate goals will provide strong support for global emission reduction and push more countries to adopt concrete climate actions, said Li Junfeng, director of the National Center for Climate Change Strategy and International Cooperation (NCSC).

China intends to achieve the peaking of carbon dioxide emissions around 2030 and will make best efforts to peak early, the INDC said, reiterating a goal set in a joint statement between China and the United States—also a big carbon emitter—in November 2014.

That promise will make it much more likely to realize the peaking of global greenhouse gas emissions between 2020-2030, an important condition for controlling global warming, Li commented. "China's pledges are very forceful if compared with those of some developed countries," he said.

With the carbon target it sets for 2030, China has to reduce carbon emissions by an average annual rate of 3.6 percent to 4.1 percent between 2005 and 2030, a faster decrease than the United States and EU, Li estimated.

The United States has announced a target of cutting its emissions by 26 to 28 percent from its 2005 level by 2025, while the EU eyes a reduction of at least 40 percent by 2030 on the basis of the 1990 level.

Those targets demand an average annual emission decrease of 3.5 percent to 3.6 percent for the United States and 3.2 percent for the EU, according to Li's calculations.

In its INDC, China called on developed countries to "undertake ambitious economy-wide absolute quantified emission reduction targets by

2030" in accordance with their historical responsibilities. It reiterated its stance that climate talks should follow the principles of common but differentiated responsibilities, equity and respective capabilities.

China has reached out to other developing countries to help them cope with climate change. Since 2011, China has accumulatively invested around 44 million U.S. dollars in South-South cooperation and provided assistance to other developing countries through low-carbon products, training and capacity building.

CATALYST FOR GREEN ECONOMY

As a developing country with a population of more than 1.3 billion, China is among those countries that are most severely affected by the adverse impacts of climate change, according to China's INDC.

Chinese leaders have "declared war" on the pollution that has taken a heavy toll on its air, water and soil after a three-decade dash for economic growth.

Apart from the emission target, China also lays out plans to expand the share of non-fossil fuels in its primary energy consumption to around 20 percent by 2030 from the 11.2-percent ratio in 2014, and increase the forest stock volume by 4.5 billion cubic meters from the 2005 level.

To realize that goal, China's non-fossil fuel use is expected to increase by about 800 million tons in next 16 years, cutting carbon emissions by nearly 2 billion tons every year, Li Junfeng said.

More non-fossil fuels make it necessary to boost investment in clean energy such as nuclear, hydro and solar power, providing new engines for China's economy as its growth slows.

To fulfill its climate pledges, China's total investment in low-carbon industries in the coming 16 years will exceed 40 trillion yuan (6.45 trillion U.S. dollars), according to NCSC estimates.

"None of the developed countries had to cope with the challenge of transforming to low-carbon economy while in the midst of industrialization and urbanization, which is what China has to do now," Li said. "If China successfully creates a new path of green development, it will set good examples for other developing countries."

1.1.1 CHINA GROWING GREEN ECONOMY UNDER NEW CLIMATE PLEDGES

http://news.xinhuanet.com/english/2015-07/01/c_134373390.htm

It's hard to imagine that China, the world's largest greenhouse gas emitter, could one day lead the world in going green, but the country is nurturing a new competitive edge through environmentally friendly growth.

China submitted a plan with ambitious goals to reduce carbon emissions and develop a green economy to the Secretariat of the UN Framework Convention on Climate Change by the end of June, underscoring that going green will be a new focus for China as its economy plateaus.

From financial policies supporting green development to growing green businesses and promotion of less polluting lifestyles, the Chinese economy is gaining new momentum from stimulus measures based on environmental concerns.

GREEN FINANCING

China is aiming to effectively curb carbon dioxide emissions by 2030, when it will have cut such emissions per unit of GDP by 60 to 65 percent from 2005 levels, according to the "Intended Nationally Determined Contributions (INDC)".

Capital is crucial to meeting the targets, and China is working on channeling more money into environmentally friendly projects.

A financial system will be built to channel funding through loans, private equity, bonds, securities and insurance to the green industry, agreed senior Chinese officials at a summit in southwest China's Guizhou Province in June.

"A financial mechanism is the decisive top-down design for green growth. It might be difficult to invest in a green manner at the beginning, but it pays in the long run," said Ma Jun, chief economist with the research bureau under China's central bank.

Chinese banks have been lending more to the green sector. Loans to low-carbon projects reached 7.59 trillion yuan (1.24 trillion U.S. dollars) at the end of 2014, according to the China Banking Association.

"Green finance only accounts for about 2 percent of the world's total investment, but it has certainly helped many countries adjust their economic models," Ma said, pointing to China's potential in this area.

RISING GREEN SECTOR

From non-fossil energy plants to new energy cars, green industries are enjoying a boom, with financial support encouraging environmentally friendly and energy-efficient projects.

It is estimated that the energy conservation and environment protection sectors will amount for about 2 percent of this year's GDP, while the share for the added value of emerging new energy sectors might stand at 8 percent.

China plans to increase its installed capacity of wind power and solar power to 200 gigawatts (GW) and around 100 GW by 2020, about 180 times and 1,600 times that for 2005 respectively, according to the INDC plan.

Meanwhile, the Chinese government highlighted green development as a key principle in its "Made in China 2025" plan to upgrade the country's manufacturing.

China is expected to invest over 2 trillion yuan in green industries the next five years. Only about 10 to 15 percent of that capital will come from the government.

"With the INDC plan and support policies to encourage private investment, the government is sending out a clear message that a low-carbon economy is the direction for industrial development," said Gao Feng, Chinese foreign ministry's special representative for climate change negotiations.

SUSTAINABLE CONSUMERISM

Under frequently smoggy skies, the growing Chinese middle class are increasingly aware of the importance of living a green lifestyle.

In the first quarter, sales of new energy cars grew almost threefold year on year, according to the commerce ministry.

"Chinese consumers are aware that going green is not just the business of government and enterprises. They are also a key stakeholder and can do their part by adopting a green way of life — living more, not just having more," said He Jiankun, head of Tsinghua University's Low Carbon Economy Institute.

It is not just about buying energy-efficient light bulbs or fuel-efficient cars. More and more Chinese choose public transport and take part in public activities promoting low-carbon lifestyles.

The INDC plan promised China will continue to encourage green living by enhancing education and encouraging public institutions to take the lead in promotion, while it will also ensure that public transport has a 30-percent share of all motorized travel in large and medium-sized cities by 2020.

"We should develop a different vision of prosperity that balances economic growth with a clean environment. Sustainable consumption is the new fashion," He said.

1.2 CHINA UNVEILS PROPOSALS FOR FORMULATING 13TH FIVE-YEAR PLAN

http://news.xinhuanet.com/glish/2015-11/03/c_134780050.htm

The Communist Party of China (CPC) has issued the full text of proposal for China's development over the next five years.

The eight-chapter, 22,000-character-plus document, the CPC Central Committee's Proposal on Formulating the Thirteenth Five-year Plan (2016-2020) on National Economic and Social Development, was adopted at the Fifth Plenary Session of the 18th CPC Central Committee which ended on Oct. 29.

The next five-year period was described as decisive for building a moderately prosperous society by 2020 in the proposal.

China aims to double its 2010 GDP and the 2010 per capita income of both urban and rural residents by 2020.

The document analyzes the decisive stage and sets guidelines and targets for the next five years. It highlights innovation, coordination, green development, opening up and sharing.

Ensuring a "moderately prosperous society" by 2020 requires medium-high economic growth, higher living standards and a better quality environment, the proposal says.

China will continue to encourage mass entrepreneurship through major scientific and technological projects, and by building a number of national laboratories, in the hope that it will lead to new technology. The government plans better allocation of resources including labor, capital, land, technology and management.

There will be more official moves to upgrade the economy into a global manufacturing power, cultivate strategic industries and modernize the agricultural and service sectors. The government will intervene less in price formation, deregulating pricing products and services in competitive sectors.

The proposal calls for a system to control consumption of energy, water and construction land. It promises an "energy revolution" with clean, safe resources replacing fossil fuels, including wind, solar, biomass, water, geothermal and nuclear energy, as well as exploring deposits of natural, shale and coal bed gas. Energy-intense industries, such as power, steel, chemical and building materials will be subject to carbon emission control regulations.

The proposal vows to lift more people out of poverty, saying that alleviating poverty in rural areas is the most difficult aspect of building a well-off society.

The proposal promises a "healthy China" by reforming the health system, and promote the balanced development of its population through the two-child policy. The proposal calls for retaining family planning as a basic state policy, allowing all couples to have two children, while improving public services for reproductive health, maternal and child health, nurseries and kindergartens.

Families with difficulties who implement the family planning policy should be helped, the proposal says.

The document pledges to cement achievements made in the anti-corruption campaign and tightened supervision and checks over power, in addition to working out an effective mechanism to stem corruption.

1.2.1 WHAT CHINA'S "MEDIUM-HIGH" GROWTH MEANS TO THE WORLD

http://news.xinhuanet.com/english/2015-09/25/c_134660273.htm

Stressing that China's economy will keep growing at a "medium-high" pace in the coming years, President Xi Jinping has offered reassurance to global investors during his United States visit.

"China's economic fundamentals remain solid and will continue to maintain long-term steady growth," Xi told more than 30 executives from top Chinese and U.S. enterprises in Seattle in September.

He delivered similar messages on several other occasions, including a welcome dinner in Seattle and an interview with *The Wall Street Journal*.

By growing at "medium-high" speed, an annual growth rate of around 7 percent, China's economy will remain an engine for global growth.

China is capable of hitting its economic targets, supported by pro-investment policies, a vigorous service sector and progress in industrial restructuring, said Li Pumin, secretary general of the National Development and Reform Commission, the country's top economic planner.

The economy also looks set to benefit from reforms to improve resource allocation and encourage mass entrepreneurship and innovation.

"In the medium and long term, China is well-equipped and able to grow steadily and healthily," Li said.

In the first half of 2015, China's GDP expanded by 7 percent, its slowest pace in nearly a quarter of a century but still standing out from other major economies.

As long as China keeps this up, the country can realize its goal of doubling national GDP and per capita income by 2020 from their 2010 levels.

That scenario is crucial to the future of the global economy, which is still struggling on the path of recovery from the financial crisis.

Sustained growth by China's economy at around 7 percent will do a lot to boost the world economy, considering the country's economic output is about twice the scale of Japan and quadruple that of India, said Bai Ming, an economist with the Ministry of Commerce.

As the world's second-largest economy, China's development benefits not just itself but also the world. In 2014, Chinese firms investing abroad paid 19.2 billion U.S. dollars in taxes to overseas governments. They hired 135,000 employees from developed countries, an annual increase of 33,000, Bai said.

China is also the world's biggest source of outbound tourists, with overseas spending by Chinese reaching 164.8 billion U.S. dollars in 2014, four times the amount of 2008, according to China Tourism Academy.

Compared with previous double-digit expansion, medium-high growth could allow China's economy to become more sustainable and greener, contributing to the global efforts to fight climate change and environmental pollution.

China, the world's largest greenhouse gas emitter, unveiled new climate change goals in June, promising to cut carbon dioxide emissions per unit of GDP by 60 percent to 65 percent by 2030 from 2015 levels and achieve a peak in emissions around the same year.

The country's shift of focus to a more sophisticated business models will also help drive the world economy, by exploring new areas of growth, according to Bai.

Chinese economists and legislators have warned foreign investors to accept and adapt to the changes happening in China's business environment.

China can no longer afford reckless expansion as resource supply and the environment become strained and the external market is limited, Bai said, arguing that the economy will get healthier and stronger by transforming its industrial structure to make it higher-end, cleaner, more innovative and driven by domestic consumption.

"Foreign firms in China should catch up with the transition and upgrade their technologies and strategies in the country," he concluded.

1.2.2 GREEN SHOOTS OF GROWTH TO MEET CHINA'S CLIMATE-CHANGE PROMISES

http://news.xinhuanet.com/english/2015-11/04/c_134784049.htm

Rapid, breakneck and even reckless: Just a few of the words commonly used to describe China's growth in the last few decades, but for the next five years, the word on every China watchers's lips will simply be "green."

Green growth is being touted as the solution to the heavy pollution brought by industrial expansion and the best way to deliver on China's climate change commitments.

In the 13th Five-Year Plan, green growth will be one of five key development concepts, along with innovation, coordination, opening up and sharing.

Traditional manufacturing must clean up its act. From now on, low-carbon production will come through better technology. Carbon emissions are to be actively monitored and controlled, especially among the big polluters — electricity generation, steel making, construction materials and the chemical industry. All these changes will come at a cost, and to sweeten the pill, a green development fund will be established.

"Following the green path is inevitable after decades of social and economic development. It is crucial for the country in avoiding the middle-income trap and improving competitiveness," said Pan Yue, vice minister of environmental protection.

China's environmental protection industry grew by around 20 percent each year from 2011 to 2015, with more than 500 billion U.S. dollars injected into the sector during that period. During the period of 13th Five-Year Plan, the Ministry of Environmental Protection expects a further two trillion yuan (300 billion U.S. dollars) to flood in each year.

China's environmental endeavors are already showing results. In 2014, energy consumption and carbon dioxide emissions per unit GDP were down by 29.9 and 33.8 percent respectively from the 2005 level.

But climate change, especially climate change mitigation, are international issues. As China cleans the air and water, the effects will be felt around the world.

China has many climate obligations, including introduction of a national carbon cap-and-trade system before 2018; 20 billion yuan in promised aid to other developing countries to help them adapt to and combat climate change; and cutting CO_2 emissions per unit of GDP by at least 40 percent from the 2005 level by 2020, and at least 60 percent by 2030.

Rachel Kyte, World Bank Group vice president and special envoy for climate change was extremely positive when describing the announcement of China's climate aid to developing countries as "an extraordinary new development." She went on to describe China as in the leadership position in helping the global economy move to low-carbon growth, praising the plan for a national emissions trading system. "This will immediately create the largest carbon market in the world," she said, "Other carbon markets will want to link with China."

1.2.3 CHINA SHAPES GREEN ECONOMY FOR NEXT 5 YEARS: LEADING U.S. ECOLOGICAL EXPERT

http://en.xinfinance.com/html/13th_Five-year_Plan/Analysis_Comment/2015/169155.shtml

The 13th Five-Year Plan of China showed that the country is going to shape economic growth for ecological ends, Roy Morrison, a leading U.S. scholar on development of an ecological civilization, told Xinhua in an interview.

"The shape of the 13th Five-Year Plan is a reflection of China's enormous economic growth since the late 1970s, the growing maturity of the Chinese economy, and the essential need to condition future economic growth by ecological ends," Morrison said.

The 13th Five-Year Plan will be China's development blueprint for the next five years from 2016 to 2020. Early November, the Communist Party of China (CPC) issued proposals for the plan. According to the proposals, "innovation, coordination, the environment, opening up and sharing" will fulfill China's economic goals for the coming years. To improve China's environment, China will seek growth through economic transformation, optimizing industrial structure to reach the target of "maintaining medium-high growth."

"The 13th Five-Year Plan will be the first of the administration of President Xi Jinping, and as such reflects themes that have been consistently advanced. First, continued moderate economic growth with the goal of doubling per capita GDP by 2020 from 2000 levels. Second, the embrace of green goals, standards, and measures to condition this growth. Third, the embrace of innovation, coordination and sharing," Morrison added.

He said that "the 13th Five Year Plan suggests that China intends to shape economic growth for ecological ends." In his famous book *Ecological Democracy,* which was published in 1995, Morrison outlined the concept of "ecological civilization." His definition was widely accepted and has been used ever since.

In the book, which he said "is about fundamental change of the movement from an industrial to an ecological civilization, which will be as significant as the transformation from an agricultural to an industrial civilization," he predicted that in the ecological civilization future, "our concern is not to control nature and each other, but to live in harmony with nature and each other."

In another book, *Eco Civilization 2140: A Twenty-Second-Century History and Survivor's Journal,* which he wrote in 2004 he said that in 2070 to 2090, China will lead the world in sustainable development.

"China is at the point where it is moving from follower to leader on the global stage. There are many ecological challenges and hard choices facing China and the world that must be met head on," he said. "If China takes the lead, the world is likely to follow."

"China's leadership role in renewable energy, limits on coal, adoption of cap and trade programs indicates that China is ready to take a leading role at the Paris United Nations Climate Meeting in December," he added.

1.3. CHINESE LEADERS PUSH FOR "GREENIZATION"

http://news.xinhuanet.com/english/2015-03/24/c_134094125.htm

China's top leadership backed a "conservation culture" and, for the first time, adopted the idea of "greenization."

Henceforth, conservation culture should be considered in all aspects of government work—economic, political, social and cultural—in pursuit of "industrialization, urbanization, informationization, agricultural modernization and greenization," according to a meeting on March 24 of the Political Bureau of the Communist Party of China (CPC) Central Committee.

The meeting, presided over by CPC Central Committee General Secretary Xi Jinping, approved a guideline on conservation culture and highlighted "greenization" of production, the economy and lifestyles: lowering resource consumption, boosting green industries and promoting a low-carbon, thrifty lifestyle.

Leaders discussed conservation concerns in sustainable development and how to meet demands for a better environment. They stressed optimal land development, more recycling, technological innovation and adjustment to the economic structure. "Green development" can be part of national soft power and a new advantage in international competition.

The importance of a system to advance conservation culture was also discussed, with a concrete plan promised "as soon as possible." The plan will include control and use of resources, land management rights, compensation and sanctions for those who damage the environment.

Local governments should pilot conservation culture areas to gain experience that can be copied and disseminated.

The entire Party was urged to work for a conservation culture that contributes to the world's green development and global eco-safety.

1.3.1 XI'S ECO-PROTECTION FOOTPRINT

http://news.xinhuanet.com/english/2015-03/10/c_134055342.htm

Ecological protection has been a major focus for the "two sessions" in March—China's most important annual political event.

President Xi Jinping asked Chinese people to protect the environment as if they were "caring for one's own eyes and life", while reviewing the work report of the State Council together with national lawmakers from eastern Jiangxi Province.

"We are going to punish, with an iron hand, any violators who destroy ecology or environment, with no exceptions," said Xi.

LONG-TERM PROBLEM

The environment has long been a regular topic in official speeches and the public is expecting revolutionary measures to tackle the conundrum.

In this year's government work report delivered at the annual parliamentary session, pollution was called "a blight on people's quality of life" and promises were made that the world's biggest emitter of carbon dioxide will cut emissions by at least 3.1 percent this year.

Xi used the oriental culture's concept of harmony and balance to explain nature preservation.

"Mankind's pursuit of development and the limited resource supplied by Earth has been an eternal contradiction," he said during his visit to southwest China's Yunnan Province at the beginning of 2015. "The Chinese civilization has lasted more than 5,000 years. Can it last another 5,000 years and ultimately achieve sustainable development?" Xi asked.

"The ecological problem has been accumulated in history and the environment has not been damaged suddenly in a day," he said, adding it was the Communist Party of China's (CPC) responsibility to stop the environment from turning worse.

The CPC's 18th congress promised to "build a beautiful China" as part of its ecological civilization drive in November 2012. The concept was also promoted by the United Nations Environment Programme in February 2013.

Xi, general secretary of the CPC Central Committee, has stressed the concept of ecological civilization and conservation culture at political events in China and abroad more than 60 times since November 2012.

He once said that if mountains and forests are damaged, soil will be flooded by water and farmland will become barren.

SAVE FORESTS

Xi called for comprehensive measures to save the environment.

"Forests have a leading position in safeguarding homeland security and coordinating comprehensive management on environmental protection. Forests are the top level of ecosystem. To save Earth, we have to save forests first," he said.

However, forest areas have dwindled by about 50 percent globally, according to UN figures.

"(I) can't imagine what Earth and mankind will be like without forests," Xi said while planting trees with members of the public in Beijing in April 2013. He vowed severe punishment on environment destroyers.

However, there are still more than 900 million mu (about 60 million hectares) of natural forests that are not under protection, with weak ecosystems, water loss and soil erosion. Therefore, the government has expanded the scope for prohibiting commercial deforestation this year and will ultimately cease any commercial tree-cutting in the future.

Water shortage is also a headache. Xi said crude oil can be imported, or, if exhausted, replaced by new energy, "but if water is depleted, what shall we turn to?"

Official statistics show more than 200 lakes, each covering more than ten square km, have been shrinking in China. Nearly 1,000 natural lakes in the country have become extinct due to reclamation.

It is the same with air quality. Among 74 monitored major Chinese cities, only 4.1 percent reached a clean air standard.

ECOLOGY FIRST

China, over a long period in the past, stayed in a lower position on the global value chain and the environment has been damaged by highly polluting, energy-intensive industries.

"There are too many debts to pay," Xi said while visiting south China's Guangdong Province. He warned that if action is not taken immediately, more debts will lie ahead.

He told college students in Kazakhstan in September 2013 that economic development must not come at the price of the ecology.

The Chinese government has shifted from its long-time GDP-obsessed development concept to a comprehensive social and economic development evaluation system that balances GDP growth and impact on the environment.

"A sound eco-environment can benefit all members of the public," Xi said in the southern island province of Hainan in April 2013.

Xi also includes environmental preservation as part of the "Chinese dream" for the nation's revival. He told foreign dignitaries in his address at the welcoming banquet of the Asia-Pacific Economic Cooperation (APEC) meeting in Beijing last November that he hopes the sky of Bejing as well as the whole China will be clear and blue forever, and children will live in a sound eco-environment.

1.3.2 CHINA FACES UNPRECEDENTED ENVIRONMENT, DEVELOPMENT CONFLICT: MINISTER

http://news.xinhuanet.com/english/2015-03/07/c_134046757.htm

China's newly appointed environment chief said in March that the world's second largest economy is faced with the unprecedented conflict between environmental protection and development in human history.

Environmental Protection Minister Chen Jining made the remarks at a press conference on the sidelines of the ongoing annual session of the National People's Congress, China's top legislature. "China's environmental problem is still severe," he said, citing woes in poor environmental quality, grave ecological damage and high environmental risks that come with unreasonable industrial layout.

The minister said that China needs to do more to cut pollution but also stressed that environment protection is a common issue that every other country has to face.

1.4 A NEW COURSE OF GROWTH FOR CHINA

http://news.xinhuanet.com/english/2015-09/10/c_134611815.htm

As a slower Chinese economy and recent volatility on its financial markets made headlines worldwide, a new course of growth for China has been emerging.

Where the world's second largest economy goes next was the hot topic at the Summer Davos Forum in the northeastern city of Dalian, after weak performance of major economic indicators and the latest stock market rout rattled investors' nerves.

Anaemic external demand and a cooling property market have dampened exports and investment, both traditional drivers of China's growth.

However, some signals show that new drivers, including innovation, technology and consumption, are playing a bigger role.

While the shift of pattern is far from complete, those signals have charted a new course of growth for China's economy.

START-UP TIDE, HIGH-TECH BRIGHT SPOT

Speaking of these new drivers at the forum, Chinese Premier Li Keqiang pointed to mass entrepreneurship and innovation, saying an average of over 10,000 new market entities have been registered every day since last year, despite the economic slowdown.

In the first half of 2015, newly registered enterprises had a total registered capital of 12 trillion yuan (1.9 trillion U.S. dollars), up 43 percent from a year earlier.

The government has rolled out reforms to streamline business registration procedures, provided tax breaks and fee cuts and set up a 60 billion-yuan fund to support small and medium-sized enterprises.

In "maker clubs" across major cities in China, small and micro start-up companies are offered low rents and easier access to venture capital. "Almost all the young people I have met recently are thinking about starting their own business," said Huang Yiping, a Peking University professor in economics. "Some say there's a bubble, but a bubble of innovation is a good one."

The government efforts to boost innovation will play a strong role in driving China's growth in the next two or three years, said Liu Yuanchun, an economist at Renmin University.

Despite softening industrial production and investment, there has been an upturn in high-tech industries and strong growth in patented technology, Liu told Xinhua.

Output of high-tech industries expanded faster in July than the previous month, up 9.6 percent year on year, while overall industrial output growth slowed to 6 percent.

In the first seven months, investment in high-tech industries rose 16.4 percent year on year, 5.2 percentage points higher than the overall fixed-asset investment growth rate.

Though China has fewer advantages in labor costs than before as a result of an aging population, labor costs for higher-end industries have fallen as many more people have received college education, Liu explained.

College graduates made up 8.9 percent of the population in 2010, up from 3.6 percent in 2000, according to the last national census. Even if the ratio had not increased since 2010, it would still mean about 120 million people with college education in China, nearly equivalent to the whole population of Japan.

That advantage in human resources will pave the way for China's upgrade to higher-end industries, Liu said.

China already has some innovative companies of global fame, like Alibaba, Lenovo and Xiaomi, as well as other internationally competitive firms in high-tech and emerging industries, Huang noted.

"Though their total scale is not big enough to prop up overall national growth yet, it's only a matter of time until they mature and form a new pillar of the economy," he said.

CONSUMPTION SHIFT

Jeff Walters, partner and managing director of Boston Consulting Group, observed an obvious transition by China's economy from the investment-led mode to consumption-led mode.

Consumption now contributes to more than 60 percent of economic growth, while the service sector accounts for half of GDP, Premier Li said at the Dalian forum.

China's retail sales continued to grow quite strongly, increasing 10.5 percent year on year to 2.43 trillion yuan in July.

Walters attributed the strength in consumption to income growth and high employment numbers, while noting a change of consumption pattern.

"We really see shifting growth from offline to online, and also from the emerging middle class to upper-middle class," he said.

Online sales jumped 37 percent year on year in the first seven months.

In the past decade, the emergence of a middle class drove a lot of consumption growth, but now a higher-income class is driving higher-end consumption like buying cars and travelling abroad, Walters said.

China's GDP per capita exceeded 5,000 U.S. dollars in 2011 and reached 7,575 U.S. dollars last year.

China is facing an upgrading of its consumption structure, as some provinces and cities in China already saw their per capita GDP exceed 10,000 U.S. dollars, the threshold for high-income economies, said Liu.

1.4.1 BRIGHT SPOTS IN CHINA'S SLOWING ECONOMY

http://news.xinhuanet.com/english/2015-09/29/c_134671878.htm

China's economy is slowing, with downward pressure likely to persist for a while, which has spawned pessimism about the country's growth outlook.

But looking beyond headline growth numbers, positive changes have emerged and are expected to lay the foundation for sustainable long-term growth.

"China's economic fundamentals remain solid and will continue to maintain long-term steady growth," President Xi Jinping said during his U.S. visit.

The following are some highlights of the Chinese economy in 2015.

Improving industrial structure

The service industry accounted for 49.5 percent of GDP in the first half of 2015. In 2010, the share was 39.2 percent.

The bigger role the sector has played in shoring up growth has helped ease the country's reliance on resources and energy, and facilitated the economic transformation toward a more technology- and innovation-driven model.

During his U.S. visit, President Xi recognized the enormous market potential for the service industry, pledging to focus more on accelerating adjustments in the growth model and economic structure.

Consumption: fast and furious

Compared with investment and exports, consumption has been a less conspicuous growth driver for China in past decades, but it is catching up fast.

In the first half of 2015, it contributed more than 60 percent of economic growth, evidence of the success of China's restructuring.

In particular, new consumption models such as online shopping have accounted for nearly 10 percent of overall retail sales, and consumption in tourism and healthcare are expected to rise at a faster pace as society prospers.

Innovation, entrepreneurship

The Chinese government has emphasized reforms and innovation to steer the economy toward a more sustainable long-term path.

A wide range of measures for emerging businesses has been unveiled, including financial support, facility construction and administrative assistance.

There are increasing signs that innovation is being embraced as a source of competitive advantage and meaningful advances are emerging in fields ranging from mobile apps, consumer electronics and renewable energy.

A start-up boom has taken place. In the first half of 2015, newly registered enterprises had a total registered capital of 12 trillion yuan (1.9 trillion U.S. dollars), up 43 percent from a year earlier.

Government efforts to boost innovation will play a strong role in driving China's growth in the next two or three years, said Liu Yuanchun, an economist at Renmin University.

Warming property market

The housing market, a key pillar underpinning China's growth, took a downturn in 2014 due to weak demand and a surplus of unsold homes. The cooling has continued into 2015, with both sales and prices falling and investment slowing.

But as the central bank has cut benchmark interest rates four times since November and the government eased purchase restrictions, the housing market has gradually recovered.

Of the 70 large and medium-sized cities surveyed, 35 reported that new home prices climbed month on month in August, up from 31 cities in the previous month. A total of 26 cities reported month-on-month price declines, down from 29 in July.

Steady job market

Creating enough jobs and keeping the job market steady is one of the major priorities for the Chinese government.

China's registered unemployment rate in urban areas stood at 4.04 percent at the end of June, and 7.18 million new jobs were created in urban areas in the first half of the year, remaining largely stable despite economic headwinds.

Narrowing urban-rural gap

Growth of per capita net income of rural residents outpaced that for urban residents by 1.6 percentage points in the first half of the year.

Falling energy intensity

Despite the slowing economy, China has pushed harder for cleaner and greener growth. In the first half of the year, energy consumption per unit of GDP went down 5.9 percent.

The share of clean energy in total energy consumption reached 17.1 percent, up 1.6 percentage points from the same period last year.

Interest rate liberalization

After a series of reforms, China's decades-long endeavor to free up interest rates is finally reaching its last mile, giving the market a bigger say in allocating resources.

In May 2015, China began implementing the deposit insurance scheme, which is regarded as an important part of financial safety and a precondition for China to free up deposit rates.

On May 10, 2015, the central bank lifted the upper limit of the deposit rate's floating band to 1.5 times the benchmark from the previous 1.3 times, granting banks more pricing autonomy.

On June 2, 2015, the central bank allowed banks to issue certificates of deposit to both individual and institutional investors, less than two years after the issuance of certificates was rolled out among banks.

Exchange rate reform

The central bank in August adjusted the exchange rate formation system so it takes into consideration the closing rate of the inter-bank foreign exchange market on the previous day, as well as supply and demand in the market, and price movements of major currencies. The move is expected to increase currency flexibility and support China's capital account liberalization.

Wider opening-up

China is actively seeking a bigger say in international affairs by participating in and, increasingly, leading global cooperation initiatives.

The Asian Infrastructure Investment Bank and the Belt and Road initiative are among China's efforts to supplement the existing international order and overhaul global governance.

Meanwhile, China has promised to make a national "negative list" by 2018 of sectors that are not fully open to all market entities, both domestic and overseas.

"China will open its door still wider to the outside world, and the door will never be closed," President Xi said.

1.4.2 CHINA IDENTIFIES PRIORITY SECTORS FOR INDUSTRIAL UPGRADES

 http://news.xinhuanet.com/english/2015-09/29/c_134672240.htm

The consultative committee advising the government on its "Made in China 2025" plan to upgrade the country's manufacturing identified 10 industries of priority in September.

With Made in China 2025 aiming to shift the country from low-end manufacturing to more value-added production, the list includes new information technologies, numerically controlled machines and robots, aerospace devices, ocean engineering and shipping, advanced rail equipment, new energy vehicles, electrical equipment, agricultural machines, advanced materials, biological medicine and medical instruments.

The committee will update the list every two years.

The State Council, China's cabinet, unveiled the Made in China 2025 plan in May. Domestic manufacturers are expected to make technological breakthroughs in emerging industries.

1.4.3 CHINA SEES 10,000 NEW FIRMS EVERY DAY

 http://news.xinhuanet.com/english/2015-10/11/c_134702448.htm

China sees more than 10,000 firms born every day amid government support for entrepreneurship, a vice minister said in October.

Most of the firms are small enterprises. Data was collected last March through the end of August this year and about 6 million firms were registered during the period, said Xin Guobin, vice minister of Industry and Information Technology.

The government has been cutting taxes and fees, helping small firms save about 48.6 billion yuan (7.93 billion U.S. dollars) in the first half of the year, Xin said.

Lending to small firms stood at 16.2 trillion yuan at the end of June, up 14.5 percent from last year, Xin said.

However, he admitted small firms are facing challenges amid economic slowdown, slumping product prices, rising costs and production overcapacity.

1.4.4 CONSUMPTION, SERVICES PUSH CHINA TOWARD SUSTAINABLE GROWTH

http://news.xinhuanet.com/english/2015-07/16/c_134419131.htm

Zhang Kailan spends more than half of his 20,000-yuan (about 3,268 U.S. dollars) monthly salary on e-commerce sites.

The 24-year-old IT manager at a wedding planning company in the southeast China city of Fuzhou calls himself a "hand-chopping online shopper," joking that he has spent so much money online that he should chop his hands off. Though he jokes about quitting, the Chinese government is betting on tech-savvy shoppers like Zhang to bolster a slowing economy.

Due to shrinking growth and changing demographics, China must swap its traditional growth model — with its heavy reliance on exports and investment in real estate and factories — for a new one based on consumer spending and innovation.

NEW NUMBERS, NEW NORMAL

The economic transition has faced a number of problems, including a property market downturn, deflationary risk, stock market volatility, global financial turmoil, and added pressure on growth.

China set its 2015 economic growth target at "around 7 percent," the lowest in more than a decade. The GDP for the first half of the year hit the target, with growth up 7 percent from the same period last year, according to data from the National Bureau of Statistics (NBS) released in July.

Doomsayers expect the slowdown to continue, leading to an eventual collapse. But China's policymakers believe the economy is entering a new stage of slower but more resilient growth, which President Xi Jinping has called the "new normal."

The essence of the "new normal" is not fast growth, but an improved economic structure that relies more on the services industry, consumption, and innovation.

SERVICES, CONSUMPTION DRIVE GROWTH

The latest data show the services sector has become the biggest driver of economic growth, said Qu Hongbin, chief China economist at HSBC.

The sector expanded 8.4 percent in the first half and accounted for 49.5 percent of GDP.

Wang Tao, chief China economist at UBS, noted the uptick in the services sector was helped by both a strong recovery in property sales in the first half and a buoyant equity market, which sent the key Shanghai stock index to a peak in mid-June and then crashed until supportive government measures helped arrest the slide.

Consumption also played a bigger role in boosting growth, accounting for 60 percent of GDP growth in the first half, 5.7 percentage points higher than a year ago and almost double the contribution from investment.

"The demand structure is changing in line with our policy intentions, and the structure is getting better," NBS spokesman Sheng Laiyun said at a press conference.

E-COMMERCE, TECH TRANSFORM ECONOMY

Online shoppers such as Zhang are helping steer the shift toward consumption. China's e-commerce market reached 13 trillion yuan last year, and online sales surged 39.1 percent in the first half of 2015, three times faster than overall retail sales.

"The Internet has become a part of my life," Zhang said, adding that, unlike his parents, his generation lives more for the present and would rather consume than save.

Output of hi-tech industries maintained double-digit growth in the first half, nearly five percentage points higher than the overall industrial sector.

However, analysts said that the economy is still recovering and it will take time for new growth engines to fully take over, so more easing measures are needed to counter a deceleration of traditional growth drivers and sustain the recovery.

Wang expects the government to enhance funding for infrastructure investment in the second half and further lower the benchmark interest rates.

"The government cannot relax its efforts to stabilize growth," said Song Yu, Goldman Sachs/Gaohua senior China macroeconomist, adding that policymakers must continue to boost domestic demand in order to achieve the full-year growth target.

Part 2

Environmental Protection a Key Growth Driver

http://news.xinhuanet.com/english/2015-03/07/c_134046851.htm

Environmental protection is an important growth driver for China and the demand for investment would be huge in the years to come, Minister of Environmental Protection Chen Jining said in March.

Chen said at a press conference on the sidelines of the National People's Congress annual session that total investment demand for environmental protection in China will be around 8 trillion yuan (1.3 trillion U.S. dollars) to 10 trillion yuan over the next few years.

Such investment provides "good" momentum for economic growth as it has no repeated construction and yields long-term returns, Chen said.

Currently the government funds accounted for 30 to 40 percent of the total input into environmental protection, said Chen, adding that social capital does not have full access to the market.

The ministry will seek to advance price reform to build a mechanism for measuring project returns and further ease market access by means such as public private partnership, the minister said.

Financing services will be improved, and regulation and oversight will be strengthened as well, he said.

The world's most populous country, China has been seeking a "difficult balance" between economic and social development and ecological and environmental protection.

Environmental deterioration is a blight on people's quality of life and a trouble that weighs on their hearts, Premier Li Keqiang said while delivering the annual government work report.

"We must fight it with all our might," the premier said.

2.1 CHINA PROMOTES GREENER INDUSTRY

http://news.xinhuanet.com/english/2015-03/04/c_134037832.htm

China will promote clean industrial production in 2015 by encouraging green technology and more economic use of resources to protect the environment, authorities said in March.

The central government will initiate a program that aims to reduce pollution, cleanse industries and prompt sustainable development , according to a statement published by the Ministry of Industry and Information Technology (MIIT).

Companies will consume four million fewer tons of coal by the end of 2015 after the ministry helps them with technological upgrades, it said.

Coal supplies the majority of China's energy consumption, accounting for 66 percent in 2014. But its significance is falling as the country has started to encourage the use of clean energy.

Emission cuts including 70,000 tons of sulfur dioxide, 60,000 tons of nitrogen oxides, 40,000 tons of industrial fumes and 20,000 volatile organic compounds will be realized in the year, according to the MIIT.

The program is partly prompted by worsening smog in China in recent years, triggering appeals for stronger measures to clean the environment.

The authority will prioritize aid to factories in Beijing and neighboring Tianjin Municipality and Hebei Province, as well as those in the Yangtze River delta industrial zone. Those areas have been the worst effected by smog.

A mechanism to coordinate industrial resource use in Beijing, Tianjin and Hebei will be built, the statement said.

In addition, the authority promised to set up a platform to track energy use by more than 2,000 major industrial consumers nationwide.

2.1.1 CHINA FINDS NEW ENGINES AS ECONOMY SLOWS DOWN

http://news.xinhuanet.com/english/2015-10/20/c_134732475.htm

As new drivers for China's economic growth take hold, the economy is heading in the right direction.

China's GDP growth dropped to a six-year low of 6.9 percent in the third quarter, slightly lower than 7 percent for previous two quarters, the National Bureau of Statistics (NBS) announced in October.

The slowdown came along with some other disappointing figures. Industrial production was lower than expected, with September growth at a six-month low. Fixed-asset investment continued to slow and power use was also weak.

However, it is too soon to draw a pessimistic conclusion about the economy, as new sectors and new engines are playing more important roles in economic growth.

Sales of consumer goods expanded at the fastest pace so far this year in September. Final consumption contributed to 58.4 percent of GDP growth in the first three quarters amid government efforts to steer away from over-reliance on investment and export.

NBS spokesman Sheng Laiyun said the tug-of-war between economic growth and downward pressure has reached a new equilibrium.

China's economy is strongly sustained by the country's industrialization and urbanization drives, as well as a better consumption structure, according to Sheng.

As residential income rises, Chinese people hope to live better lives, so the demand for education, tourism and health care and other products will be on a constant rise, he said.

The service sector's role in the economy was also strengthened. Service output grew 8.4 percent year on year in the first three quarters, taking up 51.4 percent of the GDP, up 2.3 percentage points from the same period last year.

The positive change in China's economic structure was also reflected by different rates of power consumption. Electricity used by the service sector rose 7.3 percent in the first nine months, while that for the power-consuming industrial sector dropped 1 percent from a year earlier.

Optimizing the economic structure is going to lay a solid foundation for sustainable growth, said Wang Bao'an, head of the NBS.

"China's economic development is adjusting to the new normal and experiencing growing pains, shifting from old drivers of growth to new ones," President Xi Jinping said in a written interview with Reuters in October.

The IT, urbanization and agricultural sectors are industrializing at top speed, generating strong domestic demand and great potential for future growth, Xi said.

New impetus has also come from the government's emphasis on mass entrepreneurship and innovation.

Measures to streamline administration and simplify business registration have resulted in a surge in new businesses. In the first nine months, 3.16 million new companies were registered in China, up by 19.3 percent year on year.

In the same period, the high-tech sector reported 10.4 percent growth in value-added output, 4.2 percentage points higher than the figure for the overall industrial output.

Mass entrepreneurship and innovation are becoming a new growth engine, and the central government will continue to support such activities, Premier Li Keqiang said in October.

Innovation and entrepreneurship could generate more jobs, inspire creativity, promote structural readjustment and facilitate a medium-to-high growth of the economy, Li said.

2.1.2 CHINA TO SPEND 6.7 TRILLION USD ON LOW-CARBON INDUSTRIES BY 2030

http://news.xinhuanet.com/english/2015-09/16/c_134630365.htm

China's total investment in low-carbon industries is estimated to top 41 trillion Chinese yuan (about 6.72 trillion U.S. dollars) by 2030, China's special representative on climate change affairs told Xinhua in September.

Xie Zhenhua revealed this during the two-day China-U.S. Climate Leaders Summit.

Multiple Chinese and U.S. cities signed the Climate Leaders Declaration and nine other working agreements, such as the California-China Urban Climate Collaborative (CCUCC) and the Memorandum of Understanding between the cities of Shenzhen and Los Angeles.

Under the deals, about 10 cities and provinces in China promise to reach their peak level of greenhouse gas emissions earlier than 2030 with Beijing and Guangzhou agreeing to reach their greenhouse emissions targets by 2020, or 10 years earlier than the national schedule.

Chinese President Xi Jinping and U.S. President Barack Obama issued

China-U.S. Joint Announcement on Climate Change last November, said Xie.

"In that announcement, the goals we specified will be materialized through local governments' actions and enterprises' actions, therefore today we are holding this summit to provide an opportunity for local leaders to exchange their experience and learn from each other," Xie said.

He noted that this summit shows both China and the United States are taking concrete actions to implement the joint announcement before Xi visits the United States later this month.

The summit also shows China, the world's biggest developing country, and the United States, the world's biggest developed country, can cooperate with each other in concrete actions to address climate change and achieve win-win results to be better prepared for the Paris Climate Change Conference (COP21) scheduled to take place by the end of this year, he said.

"China aims to cut carbon dioxide emissions per unit of gross domestic product (GDP) by 60 percent to 65 percent from the 2005 level by 2030, its non-fossil energy will account for 20 percent of its primary energy consumption, and China will increase another 4.5 billion cubic meters of forest stock," Xie said.

China's whole carbon emissions will peak by around 2030, and "it shows China's utmost efforts in tackling the climate change challenge," Xie said.

"For China, we are suffering a lot from climate change," he said, adding that climate change caused more than 2,000 casualties and cost over 200 billion yuan (31.4 billion dollars) in each of the past 10 years.

"We don't take climate change as a burden; instead we take it as a good opportunity for us to transform our growth pattern, and an opportunity for economic restructuring, industrial restructuring and restructuring of our energy mix," Xie said at a press conference after the opening ceremony.

"There is a very good momentum to push forward green and low carbon development in China," he told Xinhua, adding that China's new energy industry employs around 39 million people, and the number will top 69 million in 2030.

As the first platform for mayors and governors of both countries, as well as entrepreneurs to exchange their practices and ideas on climate change, Xie hopes the summit will help promote low-carbon and green development in both countries.

"We have agreed that Beijing will host the second summit next year and we believe that this cooperation will get even better in the future," he said.

2.1.3 GREEN FINANCE BOOMING AMONG CHINESE BANKS

http://news.xinhuanet.com/english/2015-08/25/c_134554575.htm

Green finance is quickly becoming an effective credit tool in China's fight to curb pollution and develop a green economy.

At least 2 trillion yuan (around 326.8 billion U.S. dollars) of investment in industries related to environmental protection will be needed every year in the next five years, said Ma Jun, economist with the People's Bank of China, the central bank.

However, the government's financial budget can only afford 300 billion yuan of the investment, which leaves huge market opportunities worth around 8.5 trillion yuan for the banks in the coming five years, Ma said.

China introduced the green credit concept in July 2007, as part of its enforcement of eco-friendly economic policies. Communications between environmental monitors and banks saw some plants blacklisted from receiving loans because of their pollution record.

Environmental protection is a sunrise industry with huge opportunities, which means big profits for banks, said Gong Hailei, assistant to the Beijing branch president of Evergrowing Bank, a Chinese joint-stock commercial bank.

"It has only been eight months since our Beijing branch was established, but the loans we issued for green industry have already accounted for more than 20 percent of the total lending," Gong said.

In a set of green credit guidelines released in March last year, the China Banking Regulatory Commission (CBRC) urged Chinese banks to use green credit as a tool to support carbon emission cuts while achieving sustainable growth.

Banks should "pay special attention" to environmental and social impact possibly caused by their customers' projects and, based on assessment results, determine credit ratings and entry and exit terms, according to the guideline.

As of the end of 2014, China's 21 major banks had a total of 6.01 trillion yuan in outstanding loans to green-credit-related customers, 15.67 percent more than that registered in the beginning of the year, according to the CBRC.

2.1.3.1 CHINESE BANKS LEND MORE TO GREEN SECTOR

http://news.xinhuanet.com/english/2015-06/27/c_134361449.htm

Loans to low-carbon projects reached 7.59 trillion yuan (1.24 trillion U.S. dollars) at the end of 2014, China Banking Association said in June.

Of the total, lending from 21 major banks to low-carbon projects stood at 6 trillion yuan at the end of 2014, up 15.7 percent from the beginning of the year. It accounted for 9.3 percent of the total lending during the period.

Low-carbon projects are expected to save 167 million tons of coal and 934 million tons of water and cut 400 million tons of carbon dioxide annually, said a report on the banking sector's social responsibility issued by the association.

Yang Zaiping, vice head of the association, said the banking sector is actively boosting ecological progresses and helping achieve industrial restructuring through channeling more loans to the green sector.

2.1.4 CHINA ENVIRONMENT PROTECTION FIRMS ENJOY SUNNY OUTLOOK

http://news.xinhuanet.com/english/2015-05/20/c_134255270.htm

With stocks for Chinese listed environmental protection companies booming in recent months, the industry's future prospects look bright, analysts said.

Beijing Originwater Technology (BOW), a premier listed water treatment firm, witnessed its share price surging 74 percent from the start of this year to close at 59.15 yuan (9.7 U.S. dollars) on May 19, beating the upswing of 31.9 percent posted by the benchmark Shanghai Composite Index in the period.

BOW's performance pointed to investors' confidence in strong growth momentum of listed domestic air pollution, water and solid waste treatment companies, as big cities like Beijing face environmental pressure due to population and city expansions, said Sun Xiwei, a senior analyst with CITIC Securities.

Investors' enthusiasm has fueled rocketing valuations for many energy saving and environmental protection-related firms, with the average share price of 173 companies in this sector surging 63.9 percent as of May from the beginning of this year, Sun said.

Aquatic ecosystems and air quality have been severely damaged in many regions after decades of fast economic growth, threatening public health and sustainable economic development.

China has responded by releasing of a list of policies beneficial to environmental protection firms in hopes of spurring industry growth.

A four to five trillion yuan joint-investment from the government and the private sector is expected to be rolled out to fulfil goals outlined in a national plan to tackle water pollution, said Zheng Binghui, deputy director of Chinese Research Academy of Environmental Sciences.

The State Council, China's cabinet, in mid-April unveiled a detailed action plan to fight water pollution, saying more than 70 percent of the water in the seven major river valleys, including the Yangtze and Yellow rivers, should be in good condition by 2020.

"Such an action plan calls for efforts to ramp up investment, and will inject strong growth impetus to companies focusing on water treatment equipment, damaged ecosystem recovery and environmental protection facility surveillance, with some sectors being newly emerging ones," said Zheng.

BOW raked in 19.5 million yuan net profits in the quarter through March, up 13.9 percent from a year earlier, attributing it to technology innovation, strong market demand and supportive industry policies. It projected huge water treatment business opportunities at several trillion yuan in the near term.

"China is at the crossroads of environmental protection and it brings unprecedented opportunities to companies. When environmental protection companies become more professional, the ecosystem recovery can become more professional thereafter," said Chang Jiwen, an expert with Development Research Center of the State Council, a government think tank.

However, environmental protection projects are time-consuming and highly reliant on investment, as a single water pollution plant might take hundreds of millions yuan to build. Against the backdrop of waning government tax revenues, effective ways have to be found to tap market resources in tackling the funding bottlenecks, experts said.

China's Ministry of Finance and the Ministry of Environmental Protection earlier this month jointly released the implementation opinions regulating the public-private-partnership (PPP) mode for water pollution prevention and control to encourage private investment in big projects.

The investment threshold for the private sector should be further lowered, while banks and other financial institutions should be encouraged to create innovative financial products to expand financing channels for companies, Chang suggested.

Professional companies' participation in those projects can not only reduce the government's financing burden, but also improve efficiency of environmental protection facilities with the shift of governments' role from a public service provider to a supervisor, analysts believed.

2.1.5 CHINA'S NATIONAL EMISSIONS TRADING SYSTEM PLAN IS "A VERY IMPORTANT SIGNAL": WB VP

http://news.xinhuanet.com/english/2015-09/30/c_134672812.htm

The recent announcement by China to start its national emissions trading system in 2017 is a clear signal of China's commitment to a low carbon future, said Rachel Kyte, World Bank Group Vice President and special envoy for climate change.

In an exclusive interview with Xinhua in Septermber, she said that "the announcement over moving to a national carbon market sends a very important signal that after the pilots that have been operating in China, the government stands behind its decision to go national."

"The announcement of the generosity in China in providing climate finance to developing countries is an extraordinary new development, (and is) very positively received," she said.

The joint statement of China and the United States was issued during Chinese President Xi Jinping's state visit to the United States, where the two sides reaffirmed their commitment to reach an ambitious agreement in 2015 that reflects the principle of common but differentiated responsibilities and respective capabilities.

In the statement, China vows to start its national emissions trading system in 2017, a system that will cover key industry sectors such as iron and steel, power generation, chemicals, building materials, paper-making, and nonferrous metals.

"The announcement reaffirms the cooperation between the two largest economies. It sends a very clear signal from the president of the People's Republic of China that he is personally driving this pathway to lower carbon growth," said Kyte.

Kyte has been working closely with China in providing technical support.

"As China began to pilot through different ways of creating emissions trading systems or emissions reductions systems, we have, through, what is called, a partnership for market readiness, provided a mutual platform for techno-crafts from different economies in the world to share their experiences of introducing emissions trading systems so that we can all learn from each other," she said.

"An emissions trading system has existed in Europe for some time. Now we have an auction in California. We have pilots in China. We have a trading system in Korea. Some countries are putting carbon taxes in place," she said. "We provide a mutual technical platform to let these experiences be exchanged."

"We have been very pleased to help other economies to learn from China's experiences as well as to support China," she said.

Recognizing that China's plan for a national market shows "China is ready to learn from those pilots (projects) and move to a national system," Kyte said that "And this will immediately create the largest carbon market in the world. Other carbon markets in the world will want to link with China. This does put China in a leadership position in helping the global economy move to low carbon growth."

Kyte also highlighted the importance of setting the right prices in the success of a trading system.

"The prices must be set in such a way that the prices reflect the ambition, that the emissions are reduced, that the poor people are treated fairly, that they are transparent and that they can be understood by the consumer," she said.

Speaking on the "common but differentiated responsibilities", Kyte said that the principle is reflected in the fact that the journey towards a low carbon future means different things in different economies.

"It might mean a revolution in energy efficiency for some economies, for other economies it might mean managing the landscape in a very different way. So we have to help each economy move in the direction of low carbon and we must provide the financial resources to help economies do that, especially the poorest," she said.

"The secretary-general has said that we are the first generation that have the chance to end poverty, and we are the last generation that have the chance to stop climate change," she said.

"And now, in Paris, we have the first opportunity to show we are serious when we say what we have said this weekend. And we are actually moving in that direction," she said.

2.1.6 CHINA'S GREEN ECONOMY COULD CREATE ENORMOUS BUSINESS OPPORTUNITIES

 http://news.xinhuanet.com/english/2015-10/05/c_134685904.htm

China's march toward a low-carbon economy and establishing a global energy network will bring more opportunities than risks, experts said.

The State Council, China's cabinet, released an integrated reform plan on the environment on Sept. 21, outlining the efficient use of resources, and ensuring that modernization is in harmony with nature.

Also in September, President Xi Jinping told the UN Sustainable Development Summit that China wants discussion on establishing a global energy network to meet the global power demand with clean and green alternatives.

"The green economy is unprecedentedly stressed in China, indicating both large investment requirements and huge business opportunities," said Mu Lingling, general manager of Tianjin Green Supply Chain Center.

China is promoting green, low-carbon, climate resilient and sustainable development through institutional innovation, policy and action, according to China-U.S. Joint Presidential Statement on Climate Change signed on Sept. 25 Xi's trip stateside.

"China plans to further develop its green financial system by encouraging financial institutions to issue more green credit (credit which takes the environmental credentials of companies into account), and develop more green investment products which are able to use capital market institutions such as green stock indices," said a HSBC report in October.

The government will also encourage banks and enterprises to issue more green bonds, to establish green development funds that support environmental management and protection, the report said.

China regards the battle against climate change as a major opportunity to accelerate its economic restructuring and achieve sustainable development, the National Development and Reform Commission (NDRC), China's economic planner, has said.

The government will put more emphasis on the green economy, improve industrial structure, support low-carbon energy consumption and encourage carbon-emissions permit trading, the NDRC said.

China will lower carbon dioxide emissions per unit of GDP by 60-65 percent from the 2005 level by 2030 and establish a 20 billion yuan (3 billion U.S. dollar) fund to help other developing countries combat climate change, according to the joint presidential statement.

In 2017, China will launch a national emissions trading system (ETS) covering power generation, steel, cement, and other high-emitting sectors. China has ETS pilot programs in Beijing, Tianjin, Shanghai, Chongqing and Shenzhen, and Guangdong and Hubei provinces.

Although the ETS pilot programs are not universally successful yet, Jennifer Turner, director of the China Environment Forum at the Woodrow Wilson International Center for Scholars, sees them as a useful experiment of what could be expanded nationally.

By committing at the highest level to such a program, China is making its intentions clear to businesses and investors about its shift to a low-carbon economy.

2.1.6.1 WATER POLLUTION TREATMENT OPEN FOR TRILLIONS YUAN OF PRIVATE INVESTMENT

http://news.xinhuanet.com/english/2015-05/07/c_134218315.htm

China is expected to roll out a string of supportive policies to encourage private investment for developing projects worth of millions of dollars, according to sources from the state environment watchdog.

China's Ministry of Finance (MOF) and the Ministry of Environmental Protection (MOEP) are considering polices to promote public-private-partnership (PPP) in addressing water pollution, the sources told Xinhua after they jointly released the implementation opinions regulating the PPP mode for water pollution prevention and control in May.

The opinions encourage PPP mode's participation in water pollution prevention and control areas; and require clarifying boundaries for projects, improving return mechanisms, and standardizing operating procedures.

"The government will offer more preferential financial policies to support project operation and reward outstanding performers," said Zhao Hualin, a senior financial official with MOEP.

Meanwhile, more innovative financial products and services such as pollution rights purchasing will be introduced to support private investment in water pollution control, Zhao added.

The aquatic ecosystem has been severely damaged in many parts of China, threatening public health and economic development.

The State Council unveiled a detailed action plan to fight water pollution in mid-April. It said more than 70 percent of the water in the seven major river valleys, including the Yangtze and Yellow rivers, should be in good condition by 2020.

However, water pollution projects are always time-consuming and highly reliant on investment.

A single water pollution plant might take thousands of millions yuan to build and some analysts expect total investment would reach four to five trillion yuan if the outlined targets are to be met in 2020.

Meanwhile, most water pollution projects only offer returns of eight to nine percent while the financing cost for private firms from the banks could reach more than seven percent.

"High cost and low return in water pollution control projects have turned many private investors away and the whole mechanism is more administration-controlled than market-driven," said Chang Jiwen, an environmental policy expert with a state think tank of the State Council.

Chang suggested the government lower the investment cost and threshold for social capital to make water pollution control an affordable and profitable business.

"Banks and other financial institutions can roll out innovative environment-related financial products such as stocks or bonds to expand financing channels," Chang said.

2.1.6.2 CHINA LENDS HUGE FUND TO BATTLE HEAVY METAL POLLUTION

http://news.xinhuanet.com/english/2015-07/02/c_134376875.htm

The central government has earmarked some 2.8 billion yuan (451 million U.S. dollars) to help 30 cities tackle heavy metal pollution for the next three years, according to the Ministry of Environmental Protection.

The beneficiaries, 11 of which are in central China's Hunan Province, were selected based on applications by governments of polluted areas, a more competitive approach than the routine mode wherein local areas wait passively for central authorities' financial push.

Funding criteria set by the ministries of finance and environmental protection included polluted conditions, feasibility of prevention and control projects, anti-pollution infrastructure resources, among others.

Financial support for cities with unsatisfactory pollution control results in 2014 will be reduced, the ministry said.

Officially, 16 percent of China's soil and nearly 20 percent of farmland is polluted, but this may just be the tip of the iceberg.

Last year, police arrested 23 staff at a company that poured 300,000 tons of toxic sludge from a leather works into a waterway in east China's Zhejiang Province.

Central and local governments spent 41.6 billion yuan between 2012 and 2014 on heavy metal pollution, and the emission of pollutants was "greatly reduced," the environmental ministry said in Sept. last year.

Finance and environmental protection departments at the province level were asked to spell out specific goals, timetables and the liabilities of those involved.

2.2 CHINA'S ECONOMIC DOWNTURN "VASTLY OVERSTATED": REPORT

http://news.xinhuanet.com/english/2015-10/21/c_134737116.htm

China's recent economic downturn is less a sign of catastrophe than of the long-awaited shift to a market economy model that is service-based and consumption-driven, a new report from international think tank European Council on Foreign Relations (ECFR) said.

"Doom-mongering predictions about the decline of the Chinese economy are vastly overstated," Francois Godement, head of ECFR's Asia and China program, said in his report "China's economic downturn: The facts behind the myth."

"After years in which China's economic hyper-growth was taken for granted, there has been a dramatic reversal of international sentiment. The Chinese economy is now widely believed to be faltering. This is an exaggeration," Godement said.

Godement asserted that recent economic issues in China should be seen as part of China's transition to a service-driven economy, rather than a deep-rooted economic downturn.

The report highlights variances between different economic sectors within China, where the service sector continues to expand strongly—particularly in e-commerce, with web retail sales growing 36 percent in the first three quarters of 2015.

Meanwhile, declines in sectors such as steel and housing are desirable due to overproduction, and their environmental impact, the report said.

Godement said these patterns reflected China's economic structural changes. Godement also asserted that ideas of China's impact on the global economy were exaggerated, claiming that these ideas were essentially "psychological."

He cited limited non-Chinese exposure to the Chinese stock market and its positive current account and trade balances as factors limiting any real contagion to the global economy.

Nevertheless, he highlighted some possible effects of China's economic changes on parts of the world economy, which do impact Europe.

Worst hit by the transition will be big exporters to China, including commodity providers like Brazil and Venezuela.

For consumer markets such as Europe, which are neither producers of primary material nor large exporters to China, the benefits from a Chinese slowdown are twofold: the downward trend in primary material prices benefits all importers; and the reduced price of Chinese exports is a boon to living standards, the report said.

However, for various European countries, the impacts of China's economic transition would be mixed.

For Eastern Europe, it would be mostly positive, due to lower primary prices and cheaper consumer products from China.

The effects for Germany may turn out to be negative as the country relies on China as an export market.

As for southern European economies, including France, the price deflation may well increase their relative debt burden.

"There will be losses but they will, in the main, be limited in scope, although exporters to China or those with high public or private debt levels may feel the effects very sharply indeed," Godement said.

Instead of a crisis, the expert said China's economic transition would be an "opportunity" for European counties.

The expert said some more liberal economies — chiefly, Britain and Sweden — and Eastern European economies were right to seek China as a main funder of infrastructure projects, albeit with Chinese suppliers.

"The terms for long-term financing have never been so good; China's supply prices, thanks to deflation and excess capacities, are becoming almost unbeatable; and the quality gap with Western supply has decreased in all but the very top technologies," the report said.

The report also said the turn in China's economy towards services and the changing trends in consumption would facilitate investment or free-trade negotiations between China and the European Union.

"A deal whereby Europe would participate more in China's new economy while opening itself to the older Chinese sectors seems like a win-win proposition," the expert advised.

2.2.1 CHINA 2014 GROWTH REVISED DOWN TO 7.3%

http://news.xinhuanet.com/english/2015-09/07/c_134597747.htm

China's statistics authority in September lowered the country's growth rate for 2014 to 7.3 percent based on its preliminary verification.

The revised gross domestic product (GDP) for 2014 came in at 63.61 trillion yuan (10 trillion U.S. dollars), down 32.4 billion yuan from the preliminary calculation figure that put the annual rate at 7.4 percent, the National Bureau of Statistics (NBS) said in a statement.

Primary industries accounted for 9.2 percent of the GDP structure, unchanged from the preliminary calculation. The secondary sector accounted for 42.7 percent of GDP, up 0.1 percentage points from the preliminary calculation, while the tertiary sector accounted for 48.1 percent, down 0.1 percentage point from the earlier statistics.

NBS calculates each year's GDP three times — the preliminary calculation, followed by the preliminary verification and then the final verification, which is released several months later.

Last year marked the weakest annual expansion for China in 24 years due to a housing slowdown, softening domestic demand and unsteady exports, and growth further slowed to 7 percent in the first half of 2015 as the country braces for a "new normal" period of slower growth but higher quality.

In an assuring message to the market, China's top economic planner said the world's second largest economy is stabilizing and turning for the better, citing stabilizing rail freight and a warming property market as proof for the improvement.

Since August, economic indicators such as power use, rail freight, home prices and transactions have all taken a favorable turn, showing economic operations stabilizing amid fluctuations, according to a statement on the website of the National Development and Reform Commission.

A recent report by Fitch Ratings' on China's new normal said that "pessimism over China's short-term outlook is overdone and a growth pick-up in the second half is already in the pipeline." Fitch, however, also expects more volatility around the new normal of slower growth, both in real economic activity and in financial markets.

2.2.2 POWER CONSUMPTION REVEALS CHINA'S ECONOMIC TRANSITION

http://news.xinhuanet.com/english/2015-04/17/c_134159989.htm

A deep look into China's most recent power consumption data may stir concerns over a slowing economy, but the shrinking figures could also indicate a transition taking place in economic structure, analysts say.

Official data showed electricity consumption, an important indicator of economic activity, grew only 0.8 percent year on year to 1.29 trillion kilowatt hours in the first quarter, down 4.6 percentage points from the same period last year.

The weakness accompanied other key economic indicators, including investment and industrial output, which both fell below market expectations. The economy grew at the lowest quarterly growth since 2009, expanding 7 percent in the first quarter.

However, a detailed analysis of the power data reveals some encouraging trends in the economy such as a growing tertiary industry and energy conservation efforts making progress.

The service sector consumed 7 percent more power from a year ago in the first quarter and power use for residential purposes gained 2.6 percent.

The service sector, which grew much faster than the industrial sector and the economy as a whole, accounted for 51.6 percent of GDP in Q1, up from 48.2 percent in 2014 and 46.9 percent in 2013, according to data from the National Bureau of Statistics (NBS).

The slowdown in power consumption was also due to the nation's energy conservation efforts, NBS spokesman Sheng Laiyun said this week. The NBS data showed energy consumption per unit of GDP continued to fall, marking a drop of 5.6 percent in the first quarter after last year's 4.8-percent decline.

According to analysts, the decelerating power consumption growth was mainly the result of declines in the secondary industry, which saw power consumption fall 0.7 percent in Q1 and dive 4.1 percent in March.

"The slowed increase of power consumption in Q1 suggested rising downward pressure of the industrial economy," said Ouyang Changyu, deputy secretary-general of the China Electricity Council (CEC).

Major energy-intensive industries account for 30 percent of China's general industrial output, however, they use more than 60 percent of electricity for industrial production, according to NBS data.

When the economy slows, the slowdown in heavy industries will result in a strong negative impact on power consumption, Sheng said.

Power consumption in the ferrous metal industry, for instance, edged down 5.6 percent year on year during the Jan.-Feb. period, along with decreases in other high energy-consuming sectors including chemical, non-ferrous metal and building materials, according to the CEC.

The divergence in power use among different industries was evidence of the transformation in the Chinese economy, said Shan Baoguo, a researcher at the Energy Institute with SGCC (State Grid Corp. of China), China's largest power distributor.

Shan said it suggested traditional sectors, with heavy reliance on power use, are slowing, whereas high-end equipment manufacturing is becoming a new engine of growth.

While the nation's industrial output grew 6.4 percent year on year in the January-March period, the industrial structure continued to improve. The industrial value added of the high-tech sector and equipment manufacturing jumped by 11.4 percent and 7.7 percent respectively in the first quarter, outpacing overall growth.

In the long term, national power consumption will shift from the double-digit growth to a medium growth of 4 percent to 6 percent as a result of the change from high-speed growth to medium-high growth of Chinese economy, Ouyang predicted.

2.2.3 IMF CONFIDENT ABOUT CHINA'S GDP GROWTH EXPECTATIONS AT 6.5-7.5 PERCENT THIS YEAR

http://news.xinhuanet.com/english/2015-10/07/c_134688062.htm

The International Monetary Fund (IMF) is confident about its GDP growth expectations for China in the range of 6.5 percent to 7.5 percent in 2015, according to the organization's latest World Economic Outlook released in October.

According to the report, there are two main reasons for the economic growth this year: China having unrolled fiscal measures and the country's infrastructure investments.

China's economic transformation, the fall in commodity prices and the approaching normalization of U.S. monetary policy are the three main forces currently impact the global economy, leading global growth to hit only 3.1 percent in 2015, said Maurice Obstfeld, the IMF economic counselor.

"China's rebalancing from exports and public investment to consumption, from manufacturing to services. This is healthy and necessary in the long-term . . . but there will be repercussions for the world, especially developing countries," added Obstfeld.

The IMF's support for Beijing's decision is seen as crucial, since it could impact the international financial organization's decision to include the Chinese currency, the yuan, in its basket of Special Drawing Rights currencies in November.

2.2.4 CHINA TRANSITIONS TO SLOWER BUT BETTER GROWTH — IMF

http://news.xinhuanet.com/english/2015-08/15/c_134520759.htm

China is transitioning to a slower yet safer and more sustainable growth, which involves giving the market a more decisive role in the economy, the International Monetary Fund (IMF) said in August.

The IMF expected the growth to slow to 6.8 percent this year, reflecting progress in addressing vulnerabilities, especially a needed moderation in real estate investment. It expected the growth to further slow to 6.3 percent in 2016, as the country continues to rein in vulnerabilities.

ECONOMY ON SUSTAINABLE PATH BUT CHALLENGES STILL AHEAD

"The labor market has remained resilient despite slower growth, as the economy pivots toward the more labor-intensive service sector. This, in turn, has supported household consumption," the IMF said in its annual Article IV Consultation Staff Report for China.

The Washington-based institution further said in the report that China has made progress in reducing vulnerabilities, for example by slowing down credit growth, moderating investment, and passing a new budget law aimed at safeguarding fiscal sustainability.

Despite the data on slowing industrial growth, China's service sector is holding up well, IMF China Division chief Steve Barnett said at a conference call in August. Now China's industrial sector has a smaller share of economy than before, while the service sector is taking up a larger share, Barnett said.

The trend of a continued slowdown in the manufacturing sector and continued resilience in the service sector will continue, he said.

According to the report, a key challenge facing China now is to ensure sufficient progress in reducing vulnerabilities while preventing growth from slowing too much.

In regard to managing the slowdown, the IMF suggested China should calibrate its macroeconomic policies to achieve an orderly adjustment by aiming for GDP growth of 6 to 6.5 percent next year.

"Going too slow will lead to a continued rise in vulnerabilities, while going too fast risks a disorderly adjustment," IMF mission chief for China Markus Rodlauer said in a press release. "The key to managing this trade-off is structural reforms to boost potential growth."

The IMF urged China to undertake "bold" structural reforms, such as moving to a more market-based financial system, improving the management of government finances, and leveling the playing field between state-owned enterprises and the private sector.

RMB NO LONGER UNDERVALUED

In the report, the IMF said that the substantial appreciation of the Chinese currency, the renminbi (RMB), in real effective terms this year has brought the exchange rate to a level that is "no longer undervalued."

The IMF considers China's recent move to improve its exchange rate formation system as "a welcome step" to allow market forces to play a greater role in determining the exchange rate. It reiterated that China can, and should, aim for an effectively floating exchange rate regime within two or three years.

In the conference call, Rodlauer said that China's move to link the RMB's value to market forces is an encouraging step towards a flexible floating exchange rate system.

The official said as China is quickly moving towards an open capital account and integrating more and more into the global economy, it's increasingly important for China to have a flexible floating exchange rate, as the exchange rate can act as a shock absorber to capital flows that cannot be absorbed alone by other macroeconomic tools.

He believed China's move to improve the central parity formation system is just the first step towards a floating exchange rate system, and he expected China to further widen its exchange rate trading band in the future.

Following China's decision to adopt a more market-determined exchange rate, the Chinese yuan's central parity rate against the greenback has fallen 4.6 percent over the last four days.

"What has happened now over the past few days does not change our assessment (that the RMB is no longer undervalued)," Rodlauer said.

2.3 CHINA MOVES FORWARD IN DEVELOPING CIRCULAR ECONOMY

http://news.xinhuanet.com/english/2015-03/19/c_134081587.htm

China has seen notable achievements in developing a circular economy, with its key measurement index increasing to 137.6 between 2005 to 2013.

The National Bureau of Statics (NBS) announced in March that it has set up a comprehensive evaluation index system to measure the development of China's circular economy, and calculated an average rise of 4 points per year from 2005 to 2013.

The amount of resource consumption declined steadily, with four out of five indicators in 2013 registering obvious drop compared to 2005. Water consumption per unit of GDP fell by 26.4 percent, and the indexes for biological resources, energy and nonmetallic materials all decreased by varying degrees.

Considerable advancements are also achieved in reducing waste emissions and improving the ability of disposing pollutants.

Emission per unit of GDP for industrial Sulphur Dioxide (SO) dropped

62.8 percent in 2013 compared to 2005, and that for waste water fell by 38.5 percent.

A rather slower progress was seen in waste recycling, with the smallest rate rise in the four major sub-indexes.

China urged a comprehensive system to protect the environment, according to the communique issued after the 18th Central Committee of the Communist Party of China (CPC) held in Beijing 2013.

2.3.1 MULTI-BILLION DOLLAR RECYCLING PROJECT TARGETS INDUSTRIAL WASTE AROUND BEIJING

http://news.xinhuanet.com/english/2015-07/26/c_134448222.htm

Six provincial regions have jointly launched a resource recycling project to handle industrial waste in areas surrounding the Chinese capital.

By 2017, 400 million tons of industrial solid waste will be disposed of annually after the implementation of the project. The project was initiated by Beijing and its surrounding municipalities and provinces, including Tianjin, Hebei, Shanxi and Shandong, as well as the Inner Mongolian Autonomous Region.

Under the project, planners aim to develop an industry able to recycle 20 million tons of resources each year and with its output value reaching 220 billion yuan (35.4 billion U.S. dollars) by 2017.

The project will help foster new economic growth, alleviate environmental and resource restrictions and promote regional coordinated development, said Mao Weiming, deputy head of the Ministry of Industry and Information Technology (MIIT).

The move is also part of an interprovincial program for integrated development between Beijing and the nearby Tianjin Municipality and Hebei Province. Environmental protection is a priority of the program.

As an economic hub in north China, Beijing and its surrounding areas produce a large chunk of the country's industrial solid waste, such as gravel, slag, plastics and coal ash.

That has put increasing pressure on the environment, especially with a growing threat to water quality in those regions.

In 2014, 2.37 billion tons of bulky industrial solid waste was produced in Beijing and the five provincial regions surrounding it, taking up more than 70 percent of the country's total.

To meet the construction demand in these areas, pollutants from explosives used in quarrying each year exceed the annual emissions of all motor vehicles in Beijing.

Resource recycling is a fundamental solution to the industrial waste threat, but the development of the industry faces several problems, including technological difficulties and lack of integration, said Bi Junsheng, an official with the MIIT.

2.3.2 CHINESE RESEARCHERS HELP PAPER PLANT REALIZE ZERO WASTE DISCHARGE

http://news.xinhuanet.com/english/2015-05/19/c_134252779.htm

Chinese researchers have achieved the breakthroughs necessary for zero waste paper plants, significant for environmental protection.

Xu Nanping of the Chinese Academy of Engineering, told Xinhua that treatment film filtering technology has turned the 32,000-tons of waste water discharged by Jiangsu Oji Paper Co., Ltd each day into clean water, industrial salt and dried mud.

It took Xu and his team from Nanjing Technological University nine months to design the equipment. Xu is also deputy governor of east China's Jiangsu Province and head of the provincial department of science and technology.

The project is managed by a local water treatment firm and has been running successfully since January 2014.

"Zero discharge of pulping waste water is unprecedented," said Oshima Tadashi, deputy general manager of Jiangsu Oji, a Japanese company with an investment of nearly two billion U.S. dollars.

Paper plants are major polluters worldwide and it is common practice to discharge waste into rivers or the sea after treatment. The Oji plant once planned to discharge waste water into the Yellow Sea via a pipeline but the project was canceled due to protests by people living along the coast. The recycling project cost half as much as the pipeline was expected to and its operation costs are 30 percent lower.

Currently, Oji Paper buys back 12,000 tons of reclaimed water from the treatment company every day. The recycled water is also bought by other companies. The quality of the water is better than that taken directly from the Yangtze or even tap water in terms of major quality indices, said Wang Chaohui, director of the area's environmental protection bureau.

"The reuse of reclaimed water is of great value, especially for the Yangtze basin and regions short of water," said Xu.

His success has made Xu confident that he can solve treatment issues for all industrial waste water. With analysis of waste components and use of membranes, zero discharge and maximum reuse is possible. The technology could play a vital role in water resource conservation around the world, said Xu.

2.4 HIGH-SPEED TRAINS MAKE CHINA SMALLER, GIVE TOURISTS BETTER MOBILITY

http://news.xinhuanet.com/english/2015-10/06/c_134686679.htm

With an high-speed rail (HSR) network crossing 28 of China's 31 provincial regions, China is getting smaller despite its geographical vastness. People are no longer discouraged by the distance of faraway destinations.

On the first day of a week of national holidays in early October, a record number of 12.5 million trips were made by train, up 6.9 percent from last year. The number is expected to exceed 100 million for the whole holiday and is largely due to HSR.

"High-speed trains operate like intercity shuttles and have changed people's perceptions of time and space. Their willingness to travel has grown remarkably," said professor Sun Zhang of Tongji University.

"Now, I can go back to my hometown in Guizhou Province many times a year to see my family," said Pan Jinkui, a migrant worker in Foshan City's Sanshui District, in the southern province of Guangdong.

The railway Pan uses opened at the end of last year and connects Guiyang with Guangzhou, the capitals of Guizhou and Guangdong provinces. At a speed of 300 km/h, travel between the two cities has been cut to four hours from more than 20 hours before.

The Beijing-Guangzhou HSR, which extends for more than 2,000 km and is the longest of its kind in the world, cuts travel time between the two cities to only eight hours.

Bullet trains have made the experience of traveling on Chinese railways—once cramped with pungent odors and long queues for the lavatory—a distant memory.

Bullet trains not only take the tourists to areas of natural beauty but also places with famed delicacies. The Chengdu-Mianyang-Leshan line has given food aficionados great opportunities to taste snacks in cities along the line.

As a vast country, China needed to prioritize railway construction to accommodate the huge mobility needs of tourists, migrant workers and students, said transportation expert Gu Zhongyuan, as "the old, creaking railway system was a bottleneck for economic development."

While HSR expansion shows no signs of slowing, it has made China smaller and will surely make the country a bigger attraction to for foreign tourists.

2.4.1 "HIGH-SPEED TRAIN TRIBE" GROWS WITH CHINA'S EXPANDING RAIL NETWORK

http://news.xinhuanet.com/english/china/2015-01/12/c_133913112.htm

China's expanding high-speed train network and soaring property prices in big cities have seen the birth of the "high-speed train tribe," a new set of commuters who travel to and from work by bullet train.

Starting in January, Beijing will be connected to Yanjiao Town in neighboring Hebei Province via three bullet trains during morning and evening rush hours. The new trains are a high-speed alternative for white-collar workers in the town who are used to suffering on slow, cramped buses on their way to the capital city.

The trains, coded D9022, D9023 and D9024, will help Yanjiao commuters reach Beijing in only half an hour, much shorter than buses, which typically take an hour.

Yanjiao, only 30 kilometers away, has been dubbed the "town of sleep" because its residents often work in Beijing and return to sleep there at night. The town has 600,000 residents, a majority of whom work in Beijing.

The new rail routes came as welcome news to commuters in Yanjiao, many of whom said they will finally be spared the trouble of being crammed on overloaded buses.

In recent years, more residents living in the outskirts of big cities have opted to take high-speed trains to work. Chinese rail operators have launched multiple routes catering to the needs of the "train tribe." In November, Beijing was connected by rail to Hebei's Langfang City, also 30 kilometers away.

With high-speed train construction in metropolises like Tianjin,

Shanghai and Chengdu, more office workers are likely to jump on the rail commuting bandwagon.

"I hope that there will be more routes in the future so that our commuting days will be easier," a netizen said on Weibo.

Part 3

China Carbon Emissions Expected to Peak Well Ahead of 2030: NGO

http://news.xinhuanet.com/english/2015-09/08/c_134603306.htm

A survey of China-based experts and businesses has shown strong confidence that carbon price levels in China will rise over time, and that carbon pricing will increasingly affect investment decisions.

Over 80 percent of the survey respondents expect that China will meet its target of peak emissions by 2030, and many expect that the peak will be reached significantly sooner.

The 2015 China Carbon Pricing Survey was conducted by China Carbon Forum (CCF), an independent Beijing-based non-profit organization, and climate change consultancy ICF International. It collected over 300 responses from stakeholders in China's emerging carbon market.

The Chinese government has announced that a national emissions trading scheme (ETS) will be established in early 2017, although many of the survey respondents expect that it could take until 2020 or so before the national ETS will be fully functional across mainland China.

Prices in the national ETS are expected to steadily rise from about 40 yuan (6.29 U.S. dollars) per ton of CO_2 emitted in 2017, to about 70 yuan per ton in 2025.

China is quickly gaining experience with carbon trading through the seven ETS pilots, and is making every effort to establish a national ETS by 2017, said Wang Shu of the National Development and Reform Commission's Climate Change Department.

According to the survey by China Carbon Forum, it is expected that the cost of emitting carbon will rise over time. "The policy framework of China's carbon market should factor in this rising carbon price, and establish appropriate market regulation mechanisms, while actively enhancing the capacity of market participants based on their actual needs, to maintain a healthy and stable carbon market," Wang said.

Zou Ji, deputy director of the National Center for Climate Change Strategy and International Cooperation, a government-affiliated think tank, said that the government is moving towards market-based methods for environmental protection to mitigate climate change.

"This survey is enlightening as it quantifies the positions and expectations of market participants," Zou said.

Dimitri de Boer, vice chairman of China Carbon Forum and a co-author of the study, believes its results will bolster confidence in China's action on climate change.

"As governments around the world are preparing for the climate conference in Paris in November, they are carefully looking at China and its efforts to mitigate greenhouse gas emissions."

China currently has seven pilot emission trading schemes, but prices have been depressed in recent months due to over-allocation of allowances. It is expected that prices will quickly rebound, reaching 33 to 55 yuan by the end of 2016.

The survey suggests that until 2025, China's mix of policy instruments to control carbon emissions will markedly shift towards carbon trading, tax, and information disclosure, although most respondents expect that a carbon tax will eventually be introduced, there remains much uncertainty over its timing.

3.1 CHINA'S CARBON GROWTH RATE IN DECLINE: REPORT

http://news.xinhuanet.com/english/2015-07/14/c_134409024.htm

Despite the continued increase in global carbon emissions in China, the growth rate of carbon emissions has been "in a steady decrease" since 2005, and was near zero in 2014, according to a new climate report released in July.

The report, commissioned by Britain's Foreign Office, was written by experts from Britain, China, the U. S. and India. It gives a detailed assessment of the progress made in reducing carbon emissions, and various threats posed by global warming.

Several factors have played key roles in bringing down the carbon growth rate in China, including better energy efficiency in major sectors, development of renewable energy, and concern for air pollution, the report said.

By the end of 2014, China's energy intensity had decreased by about 30 percent from the 2005 level, and "the national average efficiency of all power plants is now rising to among the best in the world," according to the report.

Meanwhile, China is now leading the world in investing in renewable energy, contributing a quarter of the world total, the report also said. Taking solar power as an example, experts predicted that China is likely to overtake Germany to become the largest developer of solar power in the world by the end of 2015.

Another noticeable factor is that China's concern for air pollution has helped to "set a cap for coal consumption in key regions, which will eventually extend to the whole country," according to the report.

The Chinese government is fully aware of the challenges, and is very keen to have a detailed analysis of the impact of climate change, said Prof. David King, the leading author of the report and Britain's climate change envoy.

China has recently announced its plans to cut carbon dioxide emission per unit of GDP by 60 to 65 percent from the 2005 level by 2030.

Last year, China signed a bilateral agreement on climate change and clean energy cooperation with the U. S., promising to achieve the peaking of carbon emissions around 2030, make best efforts to peak early, and increase the share of non-fossil fuels in primary energy consumption to around 20 percent by 2030.

If these goals are achieved, it opens the possibility that economies of scale will bring down the cost of non-fossil technologies, enabling them to become more widely used in the rest of the developing world, the report said.

3.1.1 CHINA'S ENERGY USE SLOWS IN 2014

http://news.xinhuanet.com/english/2015-08/14/c_134513735.htm

Energy consumption for every 10,000 yuan (1,563 U.S. dollars) of China's GDP fell 4.8 percent year on year in 2014, the biggest in the past five years, data showed.

Shanghai Municipality and Hebei and Jilin provinces posted the greatest year on year decline, dropping energy use by 8.71 percent, 7.19 percent and 7.05 percent, respectively, according to the figures released by the National Development and Reform Commission, the National Bureau of Statistics, and the National Energy Administration.

The government also evaluated energy use for every 10,000 yuan of industrial value-added output in 2014. Guizhou Province topped the list with a decline of 13.39 percent from the previous year. Xinjiang Uygur Autonomous Region ranked last, with a 2.31-percent increase in power usage per 10,000 yuan of industrial value-added output.

China aims to cut energy use by 16 percent by the end of this year from the 2011 level, which was 0.793 tons of standard coal per 10,000 yuan of GDP. It also aims to bring the share of non-fossil energy to 15 percent by 2020 and 20 percent by 2030.

In the first half of 2015, China's power use rose only 1.3 percent, while economic growth held steady at 7 percent, the lowest quarterly growth rate since 2009.

3.1.2 CHINA ON BOLD MOVE TO BUILD LOW-CARBON ENERGY SYSTEM

http://news.xinhuanet.com/english/2015-06/30/c_134369817.htm

China is making concrete efforts to battle climate change by building a low-carbon energy system, according to the country's national pledge plan submitted to the United Nations on June 30.

China planned to increase its installed capacity of wind power and solar power to 200 gigawatts (GW) and around 100 GW by 2020, respectively, according to the plan titled "Intended Nationally Determined Contributions (INDC)".

By 2014, China's installed capacity of grid-connected wind power reached 95.81 GW, 90 times of that for 2005, while installed solar power capacity was 28.05 GW, 400 times of that for 2005.

The country pledged to increase the use of natural gas, which is expected to make up more than 10 percent of its primary energy consumption by 2020, and lower coal consumption by improving efficiency of new-ly-built coal-fired power plants, according to the plan.

China has been aggressively investing in low-carbon energy development as the world's largest greenhouse emitter tried to switch its power grid to cleaner energy sources.8 As a result, installation of new hydropower, wind and solar electricity generation capacity boomed, though coal remained China's main power source.

Coal consumption accounts for about 66 percent of China's primary energy consumption, 35 percentage points higher than the world average.

China vowed to raise the share of non-fossil fuels in its primary energy consumption to around 20 percent by 2030, according to the plan. The ratio was 11.2 percent in 2014.

To help cut carbon emissions, the country will further increase financial support and expand a carbon emission trading system nationwide from a pilot scheme that ran in seven cities, including Beijing, Shanghai and Shenzhen.

3.1.3 CHINA'S SUSTAINABLE ENERGY COMPETITIVENESS TOPS GLOBAL RANKING

http://news.xinhuanet.com/english/2015-06/29/c_134365302.htm

China's sustainable energy competitiveness was ranked first among 21 major countries, overtaking the United States and European countries, said a report published in June.

The report, issued by Zhejiang University Environment and Energy Policy Center and published at the Eco Forum Global in Guiyang, Guizhou Province, southwest China, evaluated 19 of the G20 members, excluding the European Union, as well as Denmark and Spain, which are leading players in sustainable energy.

China scored high in sustainable energy resources, investment, labor force, market size, policy support, industrial development and competitiveness of its firms. However, it has a notable weakness in technological development and less incentive than developed countries to replace fossil fuels with sustainable energy, according to the report.

Sustainable energy refers to wind power, solar power, hydropower, biological and geothermal power. It does not include nuclear power that is not sustainable and tidal energy that is not commercialized on a large scale.

According to the report, assessed by ten indicators, China scored slightly higher than the United States while Germany was ranked third. Indonesia was last.

Guo Sujian, director of the center and leading scientist of the research program, told Xinhua that China had obvious advantages in market size, government support, investment and the number of competitive companies.

In terms of sustainable energy resources, China was among the most resourceful countries together with the U.S., Canada, Australia, Brazil and Russia, while smaller nations, such as Denmark and Japan did not score high in this regard.

In terms of investment, China invested 219.2 billion U.S. dollars in the sector from 2010 to 2013, much higher than 64.9 billion dollars by the U.S.

There are 2.6 million people working in the sustainable energy sector in China, more than a third of the world total.

In terms of market size, China's installed capacity of sustainable energy is about 1,200 gigawatts (GW) while the U.S., the second, has 111 GW less.

The country also had 163 companies listed in the world's top 500 new energy firms, much more than the U.S., which has between 80 and 90.

However, technological development of sustainable energy in China is not as advanced as other nations, Guo said.

The report cited the Global Cleantech Innovation Index provided by Cleantech Group, which put the U.S. in first place and China in ninth.

Despite a large number of Chinese companies in the top 500 list, they reported much lower revenue and returns than U.S., German and Japanese firms, Guo said.

Also, compared with European countries, China is less motivated since its per capita carbon emissions are low, the report said.

To further sharpen competitiveness in this sector, the report suggested that the government shift the focus of policy support, from investment to consumption of sustainable energy.

The installed capacity of wind power accounted for 7 percent of China's power generation but these facilities only produced 2.8 percent of the total electricity.

"Preferential policies of financing, tax and pricing should go to power grid firms and consumers who buy sustainable energy," Guo said.

To tackle the technological weakness, investment and policy support should go to research and development, especially creative private companies, he said.

3.1.3.1 RENEWABLE ENERGY TO LEAD WORLD POWER MARKET GROWTH: IEA REPORT

http://news.xinhuanet.com/english/2015-10/02/c_134680597.htm

Renewable energy will become the largest single source of electricity over the next five years, the International Energy Agency (IEA) said in a report released in October.

The report stated that the renewables are increasingly becoming affordable, enhancing the energy security and mitigating climate change, and set to dominate the growing systems of the world.

The IEA's annual Medium-Term Renewable Energy Market Report came as the Group 20 (G20) energy and natural resources ministers were wrapping up a two-day meeting, the first of its kind for the group of 20 major economies.

Meanwhile, IEA Executive Director Fatih Birol urged the Chinese government to take over the renewable energy issue next year when Beijing assumes the G20 presidency.

Birol noted that China is taking major moves over renewable energy and the world needs its experience and investment.

According to the IEA report, 40 percent of the new renewable power plants in the world comes from China, producing hydropower, solar and wind energies.

"In 2014 the renewable energy investment in China was bigger than the investments in the United States plus all European countries all put together," Birol said at a press conference.

He urged China to make more investment in energy-hungry Africa and beyond Asia.

China has a huge experience to share with Africa and Asia as the country has brought electricity to half billion of people in a period of 10 years, he said. "It is the biggest achievement in the history of energy," he stressed.

IEA officials also called for world governments to reduce policy uncertainties on renewable energy, saying they are acting like brakes on greater deployment.

"Governments must remove the question marks over renewables if these technologies are to achieve their full potential and put our energy system on a more secure, sustainable path," Birol said.

3.1.3.2 UNEP HAILS CHINA'S LEADERSHIP IN RENEWABLE ENERGY INVESTMENT

http://news.xinhuanet.com/english/2015-04/18/c_134162236.htm

China is showing global environmental leadership in the adaptation of renewable energy strategies and investments, which will help other developing countries to embrace sustainable development at a lower cost, Executive Director of the United Nations Environment Programme (UNEP) Achim Steiner said on in April.

Steiner said a new report compiled by the Nairobi-based UN body showed remarkable worldwide investments in renewable energy.

"Renewable energy is becoming part of the energy infrastructure around the globe, especially in the developing world," Steiner told Xinhua ahead of a Summit of environment Ministers from Brazil, Russia, China, India and South Africa (BRICS) to discuss sustainable development.

"China is investing in renewable energy. They have reduced the price of renewable energy technologies. India has also announced plans for 10,000 megawatts of renewable energy. This shows renewable energy will become a central player in economic transformation within the BRICS economies," Steiner explained in an exclusive interview.

The environment ministers from the BRICS economies are set to meet from April 22 in Russia to discuss how the world's fastest developing countries could transform their economies.

These countries are using "green energy initiatives" to avoid pollution caused by industrial growth driven by growing consumer demand.

Statistics show that the developing countries' investment into green energy in 2014 jumped to 131.3 billion U.S. dollars with China taking the lead.

Steiner said the UNEP, created in 1972 to provide the "best possible scientific analysis" on how to "use science for effective policy-making," was now more focused on the future of the global economy and how it could avoid worsening the risks caused by faster industrial development.

"UNEP is talking about opportunities for the use of science to solve emerging challenges. There are opportunities. We know, for example, that 700 million people in Africa still need electricity. We know that global demand for energy will affect the global energy markets," Steiner said.

He said the ministerial meeting in Russia would focus on how effective policies could be arrived at to ensure that economic development helps to reduce poverty.

"UNEP considers BRICS as the key to innovation," Steiner said, referring to the need for innovative financing mechanisms to address the energy challenges facing cities.

The BRICS ministerial meeting is expected to lay the foundation for further discussions on the Chinese-backed Asian Infrastructure Investment Bank, which UNEP said would provide the first ever reliable means to finance initiatives to address sustainable financing for economic growth.

"We need more green finance and the Asian Bank plans to mobilize finance from China. We hope this will provide the funding for Climate change," Steiner said.

3.2. CHINA TOPS GLOBAL LIST OF CLEAN ENERGY INVESTMENT

http://news.xinhuanet.com/english/2015-11/23/c_134846679.htm

China invested 89 billion U.S. dollars in clean energy in 2014, the largest among 55 nations surveyed in a global report, representing the country's commitment to a low-carbon future.

China scored the highest at 2.29 on a 0-5 scale on the list of clean energy investment and deployment after topping the list last year with a score of 2.23, according to Climatescope 2015, an independent industry report.

The annual report, sponsored by Britain's Department for International Development and the U.S. Agency for International Development, surveyed 55 of the world's most important developing nations on their performance with clean energy investment and deployment.

In addition, China added 35 GW of new renewable power capacity on its own last year, more than the entire operating capacity in sub-Saharan Africa's 49 nations combined, excluding South Africa and Nigeria, said the report.

"China continues to play a critical role in clean energy's evolution, not just in emerging markets but in all countries," said the report.

Besides China, Brazil, Chile, South Africa and India rounded out the top five of the list.

3.2.1 CHINA'S INSTALLED WIND POWER CAPACITY HIT RECORD HIGH IN 2014

http://news.xinhuanet.com/english/china/2015-02/12/c_133990866.htm

China's newly installed wind power capacity jumped to a record high of 19.81 million kilowatts in 2014, according to an industry briefing by the National Energy Bureau (NEB) in February.

Wind power generated 153.4 billion kilowatt hours of on-grid electric power in 2014, contributing to 2.78 percent of the country's total generated electricity, said Shi Lishan, deputy director of the NEB's new and renewable energy department.

The year saw more wind power construction and development, with newly-approved wind power capacity reaching 36 million kilowatts, a year on year increase of 6 million, Shi said.

The average usage of wind power in 2014, however, slumped to 1,893 hours from 2,074 hours in the previous year, partly due to weak wind conditions throughout the year, Shi added.

The wind power sector generated 134.9 billion kilowatt hours of electricity in China in 2013, making it the country's third-largest source of electricity, after thermal power and hydro power.

3.2.1.1 WIND POWER HELPS CLEAN CHINA'S AIR

http://news.xinhuanet.com/english/2015-10/07/c_134688843.htm

Beijing's notorious smog has eased slightly this year. Azure blue skies with cotton-white clouds prompted locals to take out their mobile phones and cameras to record scenes they feared would soon vanish into history again.

The atmosphere is described as both "APEC blue" and "parade blue." Beijingers witnessed similar clear skies when the Asia-Pacific Economic Cooperation meetings convened in their city in November 2014 and a military parade marking the 70th anniversary of the victory of Chinese People's War of Resistance against Japanese Aggression and the world's anti-Fascist war was held in September 2015.

Back then, the fresh air was achieved with stern government decrees to curb the operations of polluting enterprises and to reduce the number of motor vehicles on roads before and during the events. The wind did the rest. But such provisional measures are unsustainable.

This year saw stronger winds to blow the smog away, but the winds were also harnessed to generate an alternative clean source of electricity, replacing and reducing the use of fossil fuels.

The use of fossil-fuelled energies is the major culprit in smog. Research by the Chinese Academy of Sciences found fossil fuels contribute almost 70 percent of the pollutants that cause the extraordinarily high ratio of PM2.5 (particulate matter that is two and a half microns or less in width) in the air, which becomes smog.

PM2.5 is a health hazard. In the last three decades, the number of lung cancer cases in China has quadrupled. "This might be to do with the increase in smoggy days, as the country's smoking rate declined in the same period," Dr. Zhong Nanshan, an academician with the Chinese Academy of Engineering and a national hero in the battle against the 2003 SARS epidemic, said at a public forum.

Wind power is a clean renewable energy. But its large-scale exploitation was only made possible in the last century. The installation of three Denmark-made 55-kw wind turbines in Rongcheng, Shandong Province,in 1986 inaugurated the era of grid-connected wind power generation in China. However, progress was slow in the following two decades.

Wind power developments accelerated in an astonishing manner in the new millennium. From 2006 to 2010, China's new wind installations doubled almost every year. Statistics from the Chinese Wind Energy Association show the country ranked top globally in new installations in 2009. The next year, China ranked first in total installed wind capacity, a position it still retains.

According to the Global Wind Energy Council, China built 23.2 gw of new wind capacity in 2014, accounting for about 45 percent of the world total that year. China's total wind installations reached 114.61 gw. The United States followed with 65.88 gw; Germany with 39.17 gw; Spain with 22.99 gw and India with 22.47 gw.

Wind power is expected to play a bigger role as an alternative source of energy. Wind power generation has no greenhouse gas emissions. It is a major contributor to China's response to global climate change.

In the national Energy Development Strategic Action Plan (2014-2020) published in June 2014, the central government pledged to raise the proportion of non-fossil-fueled power in total primary energy consumption from less than 11.4 percent then to 15 percent by 2020. The ratio will rise to 20 percent by 2030. The ratio of wind power in total electricity production will rise from 2.78 percent at the end of 2014 to 5 percent by 2020.

China's goal of installing 100 gw of wind capacity by 2015 was reached ahead of time. The longer term goals are 200 gw by 2020, 400 gw by 2030 and 1,000 gw by 2050. In the final year of this grand plan, wind power is to meet 17 percent of domestic electricity demand. And it will avert emissions of 1.5 billion tons of carbon dioxide that year.

Last year when the smog lingered, some people blamed the multitude of wind turbines erected in areas north of Beijing for obstructing the wind. This frustrated many wind power insiders and was dismissed by experts as unfounded. The experts proved right this year when the same amount or more of wind installations did not prevent the strong winds.

If wind blows smog away, the dirty air with a high degree of PM2.5 is dispersed or simply driven to other places. Through reducing emissions of pollutants, wind power is a more fundamental way of cleaning the air.

But it is too early to say the battle against air pollution is succeeding. More work needs to be done in developing alternative energy before we can have a better chance of seeing azure blue skies with cotton-white clouds in future.

3.2.1.2 N CHINA LOOKS TO WIND POWER FOR WINTER HEATING

http://news.xinhuanet.com/english/2015-06/15/c_134328708.htm

China is promoting the use of wind-generated electricity for winter heating in northern regions as part of its effort to alleviate air pollution.

The National Energy Administration (NEA) in June demanded the provinces of Liaoning, Jilin, Heilongjiang, Hebei and Shanxi, as well as Xinjiang Uyghur Autonomous Region and Inner Mongolia Autonomous Region come up with plans to include wind power into their heating system before next winter.

The goal is allow wind-powered heating to replace coal and make it accessible to places with no natural gas pipelines, the NEA said.

The NEA said the standard is 10,000 kilowatt of wind power capacity for the heating of every 20,000 square meters.

The latest move also aims to combat the issue of wind power waste, a headache for China thanks to imbalanced distribution of wind resources and imperfect grid system. Wind-rich provinces are mainly in the less developed north and northwest regions where electricity supply exceeds demand.

An average of eight percent of wind electricity was abandoned last year. The rate climbed to 18.6 percent in the first three months of the year.

3.2.2 CHINA'S PV POWER CAPACITY TO HIT 150 GIGAWATTS BY 2020

http://news.xinhuanet.com/english/2015-10/13/c_134710495.htm

China's photovoltaic (PV) power capacity will hit 150 gigawatts by 2020, said a senior official in October.

Dong Xiufen, director of the new energy office with National Energy Administration (NEA), said that the country will continue expanding PV power generation in the next five years.

According to the NEA's data, the country's total PV power capacity stood at 35.8 gigawatts by the end of June this year.

Dong stressed that future work will focus on distributing PV in central and east China as well as PV stations in west China, to increase PV capacity by 20 gigawatts annually from 2016 to 2020.

Lower cost, technological innovation and better PV services are also expected, Dong added.

Huai Jinpeng, deputy head of the Ministry of Industry and Information Technology (MIIT), said the MIIT will continue to advance mergers and acquisitions among domestic solar PV companies and push forward technology upgrades.

He said further efforts are needed in technology research and development and company financing, and more policies are expected for PV power grid connection and subsidies.

3.2.2.1 CHINA'S LARGEST SOLAR POWER TOWER PLANT STARTS CONSTRUCTION

http://news.xinhuanet.com/english/2015-07/22/c_134435855.htm

Construction has begun on China's largest solar power tower plant in the northwestern province of Qinghai.

Occupying 2,550 hectares of the Gobi Desert in Golmud City, the plant will have an installed capacity of 200 megawatts, and be capable of supplying electricity to 1 million households, according to Qinghai Solar-Thermal Power Group.

"It's designed heat storage is 15 hours, thus, it can guarantee stable, continual power generation," said group board chair Wu Longyi.

Once operational, the plant will slash standard coal use by 4.26 million tons every year, reducing emissions of carbon dioxide and sulfur dioxide by 896,000 tons and 8,080 tons, respectively.

Using heliostats to transfer sunlight into power, the system is more efficient and boasts better energy storage than the more commonly used system.

Located 2,870 meters above sea level on the Qinghai-Tibetan Plateau, Golmud has particularly favorable conditions for the developing new energy industry, said Wu Tianxiao, Communist Party of China Golmud deputy secretary.

The plant will also be China's first large-scale solar power plant under commercial operation, said Yu Mingzhen, vice director of Qinghai development and reform commission, heralding the project a landmark in China's solar energy development.

China has been focusing on increasing its proportion of clean energy. By 2014, the country's solar power capacity was 28.05 gigawatts, 400 times more than 2005, and there are plans to increase this to around 100 gigawatts by 2020.

3.2.2.2 CHINA BUILDS PV POWER BASE IN DESERT

http://news.xinhuanet.com/english/2015-03/02/c_134030646.htm

China is building a huge photovoltaic (PV) power generation base in the Ulan Buh Desert, the country's eighth largest desert, to boost new energy development, the local authority said in March.

The base is located in Dengkou County in north China's Inner Mongolia Autonomous Region.

A number of energy companies are expected to invest 4.9 billion yuan (797 million U.S. dollars) within three years in PV power projects with a combined installation capacity of 500 megawatts (mw), said Yuan Haiwen, deputy head of the county's industrial park administration committee.

Investors include state-owned China Power Investment Corp. (CPIC), China Guodian Corp., Shenhua Guohua Power Co. Ltd. and the local Menghua Group.

A CPIC 50 mw PV power program began operation at the end of 2014.

Ecological rehabilitation will also be integrated in the base. An eight-meter gap between PV panels will provide space for sand grass, said Yuan.

China is the world's largest energy consumer and it is concerned with environmental pollution and energy security.

Installed capacity of hydro, wind and solar power is expected to stand at 350 gigawatts (gw), 200 gw and 100 gw by 2020, respectively, according to the Energy Development Strategy Action Plan (2014-2020) published in November.

3.2.2.3 600,000 TIBETANS HAVE ACCESS TO SOLAR POWER

http://news.xinhuanet.com/english/2015-07/21/c_134432826.htm

With solar power plants aplenty and household solar facilities a commonplace, over 600,000 people in Tibet Autonomous Region use solar electricity, the local government said.

China has spent over 4 billion yuan (644 million U.S. dollars) to increase solar power capacity to 200 megawatts in the southwestern region, with the sunniest skies in China, according to Tibet science and technology department.

The Xigaze sand Yangbajain photovoltaic plants have gone online in the last five years, with solar water heaters and 400,000 solar cookers given to Tibetan families.

"The solar cookers have saved the trouble of burning yak dung, and now we can use electric blenders to make buttered tea," said Ngawang Quco, whose village in Comai County in Lhoka installed photovoltaic facilities last year.

The region also has many solar-powered phone base stations run by China Mobile. About 79 percent of the company's 1,000 base stations in Tibet are driven by solar energy. Even the mobile signal and network coverage along the climbing routes on the north face of Mount Qomolangma come through solar power.

China has been raising the proportion of clean energy in its energy structure. By 2014, solar power capacity reached 28.05 gigawatts, 400 times of that of 2005, and there are plans to increase the amount to around 100 gigawatts by 2020.

During an interview with the BBC in June, Maria van der Hoeven, executive director of the International Energy Agency (IEA), said China should be given more credit for its clean electricity.

IEA says China spent more than 80 billion U.S. dollars on new renewable generating capacity in 2014, as much as the EU (46 bln dollars) and the U.S. (34 bln dollars) combined.

3.2.2.4 APPLE TO BUILD FIRST INT'L SOLAR PROJECT IN SW CHINA

http://news.xinhuanet.com/english/2015-04/16/c_134157878.htm

Apple is helping to build a 40-megawatt solar power project in China's southwestern plateau in order to work toward its environmental and climate commitments, according to a company senior executive.

The project, which will be able to power 61,000 homes a year, will add 80 million kilowatt hours of clean energy to the grid annually, said Lisa Jackson, vice president for environmental initiatives at Apple.

"We are excited about the amount because it will generate far more energy than is being used by all of our offices and retail stores in China," Jackson told Xinhua through a telephone interview in April.

Currently, Apple has 19 corporate offices in China, including 17 in the mainland and two in Hong Kong, as well as 21 retail stores in the country.

The project will contain two arrays of solar panels, which will be installed 85 miles apart in Hongyuan County and Zoige County of Ngawa Tibetan and Qiang Autonomous Prefecture, Sichuan Province, Jackson said.

"We will put the clean energy onto the local grid in Sichuan and buy the power wherever the stores and offices are," she said. In the United States, solar farms are often built near Apple's facilities.

The project, the first of its kind Apple has launched outside the United States, will add China to the list of countries that power Apple's facilities entirely with renewable energy.

Those already on the list include the United States, Germany, the UK, Australia, Spain and Italy.

To develop the new project, Apple has worked closely with both its old and new partners, including SunPower, a U.S.-based company that Apple has cooperated with regularly, and four Chinese companies, Jackson said.

According to Jackson, two of the four Chinese companies are based in Tianjin, a port city in north China. They are Tianjin Zhonghuan

Semiconductor Co., Ltd. and Tianjin Jinlian Investment Holding Co., Ltd. Another two are based in Sichuan Province, namely Sichuan Development Holding Co., Ltd. and Leshan Electric Power Company.

Tianjin Zhonghuan Semiconductor Co., Ltd. and Leshan Electric Power Company are publicly listed companies.

Apple will work collectively with all five partners on the two construction sites, and two joint ventures, Ngawa Hongyuan Huanju Eco-Energy Ltd. and Zoige Huanju Ecological Energy Co., Ltd., have been established to manage the project in the two locations, according to Apple.

A press release from SunPower revealed that each of the two arrays will have a capacity of 20 megawatts. The Hongyuan array has already had two megawatts built and connected to the grid as a pilot. The project is expected to be completed in the fourth quarter of this year.

In this project, SunPower combines single-axis tracking technology with rows of parabolic mirrors, making its solar cells highly efficient, said the press release.

When complete, the project will be co-owned by Sichuan Shengtian New Energy Development Co., Ltd., SunPower's project development joint venture, and Apple, it said.

Noting that the project is built in an environmentally sensitive area, Jackson said it is a beautiful plateau with wonderful sunlight, which is great for solar projects, and an indigenous yak population, which local people raise for a living.

"We will not use cement to install solar panels or dig into the ground to lay cables in order to minimize the project's impact on local ecology and to ensure the pastures flourish," according to Apple.

"We are very proud that we come up with technologies that actually complement the natural environment and preserve the grassland, so that the area can still be used for grazing even as it is producing such a huge amount of clean energy," Jackson said.

Liu Zuoming, Ngawa's Party chief, said the new energy project will not only help protect the environment, but also bring social and ecological benefits to local people.

"We hope that it can be copied and spread to other parts of the prefecture and the province," Liu said.

Jackson said she hopes that this project will set a model for Apple' s suppliers in China to follow. The company has a total of 334 suppliers in China.

"Although they are not our facilities, we believe we should work together to remove their pollution and share climate responsibilities, since they are making Apple equipment," Jackson said. "When the project generates power onto the grid, we will learn a lot about how to do this in China and we are happy to share the information with our suppliers."

Apple has been striving to power all of its facilities worldwide with 100 percent renewable energy, and it has achieved a level of 87 percent so far.

The company increasingly relies on solar power. In February, it announced an ambitious deal to pay 848 million U.S. dollars over 25 years to buy electricity from a large solar power plant to be built in Monterey County, California, by First Solar.

Apple also has solar farms built near its data centers in Maiden, North Carolina and Reno, Nevada.

3.2.3 CHINA TO LOWER ON-GRID PRICE OF WIND POWER, PV POWER

http://news.xinhuanet.com/english/2015-12/24/c_134948304.htm

China will reduce benchmark on-grid price of onshore wind power and photovoltaic (PV) power generated electricity to promote a sound environment for the green energy industry, the country's top economic planner said in December.

The benchmark price of onshore wind power in the first, second and third grade resource areas will be reduced by 0.02 yuan (less than one cent) in 2016 and 0.03 yuan in 2018, the National Development and Reform Commission (NDRC) said in an online statement.

The price in a fourth grade resource areas will be cut by 0.01 yuan and 0.02 yuan in 2016 and 2018, respectively, said the NDRC.

Resource area grades identify the amount of a certain resource produced in a region and help determine the price for such products. A first grade resource area would produce the most and hence generally have cheaper prices. Wind power grades range from first to fourth, while PV power ranges from first to third.

The benchmark price of PV power in the first grade resource area will be reduced by 0.1 yuan in 2016. The second and third grade resource areas will be reduced by 0.07 yuan and 0.02 yuan respectively.

The move is aimed to promote effective new energy investment and a sustainable and sound development of renewable energy industry, according to the NDRC.

The State Council released an action plan on energy development for 2014-2020 in November, promising more efficient, self-sufficient, green and innovative energy production and consumption.

By the end of 2020, China aims to increase non-fossil energy to 15 percent of total primary energy consumption and raise the share of renewable energy in production.

3.2.4 CHINA EYES HUGE SOLAR-THERMAL POWER PROJECT

http://news.xinhuanet.com/english/2015-09/30/c_134675810.htm

China is planning a series of solar-thermal power pilot projects to help develop the technology.

The industrial scale of solar thermal power needs to be expanded, and an industrial chain on thermal equipment manufacturing and processing should be established, according to an announcement by the National Energy Administration (NEA).

To achieve that, the statement demanded, the pilot projects must be large enough to be used commercially, with capacity being no less than 50,000 kilowatts per unit.

Industry experts will review the technical proposals and equipment, and all preliminary work for the project.

China is promoting clean energy, including hydropower, wind power, solar power and nuclear power. By 2014, solar power capacity was 28.05 gigawatts in China in 2014, 400 times more than 2005, and there are plans to increase this to around 100 gigawatts by 2020.

3.2.5 CHINA'S FIRST BIOMASS-SOLAR POWER PLANT BEGINS INITIAL OPERATION

http://news.xinhuanet.com/english/2015-04/02/c_134119837.htm

China's first power plant producing electricity both from biomass power generation and photovoltaic power generation started its first phase operation in April.

The Zhejiang Longquan Biomass Power Plant in east China's Zhejiang Province began operating its two biomass power generators, which boast a total installed capacity of producing 162 million kilowatt-hours of electricity a year.

To reach the capacity, the generators need to consume 250,000 tons of biomass fuel, which is processed from rural waste.

The plant will see the installation of its 1.44-megawatt photovoltaic power generation system later this month. It is expected to go into operation 4 months later. The solar power generation is able to add 1.3 million kilowatt-hours of electricity a year to the power grid, which is equivalent to the thermal power generation of burning 430 tons of coal.

In April, Ji Maoqing, a farmer from Longquan City, Zhejiang, sent a truck of saw dust to the power plant. After going under scalage, the waste earn him 1,500 yuan (242 U.S. dollars).

Saw dust, along with straw and other agricultural waste, is the main raw material that the plant purchases from farmers to fuel the biomass power generation.

If recycled, rural waste has the potential to produce the biomass energy equivalent to thermal power generation from 656 million tons of coal a year, or half of the country's annual coal output.

3.3 CHINA UNVEILS NEW ENERGY MICRO-POWER GRID GUIDELINES

http://news.xinhuanet.com/english/2015-07/22/c_134436848.htm

China will develop a renewable energy micro-power grid, to further promote the sustainable development of energy resources, according to the National Energy Administration in July.

Micro-power, the opposite of large power stations, refers to electricity sources that are small, mass producible, quick to deploy, cost competitive and rapidly scalable.

The micro-power grid is an innovative approach to energy saving and emission reduction, according to guidelines released by the National Energy Administration.

The guidelines listed specific requirements on the technological and operational management of micro power.

New energy micro-power grid should make use of a mix of various renewable sources such as wind, solar, natural gas and geothermal sources.

The guidelines acknowledged recent developments in research on technology and application of new energy micro-power grid, adding that this gave them the ability to build test projects.

Micro-power operation releases little carbon, and allows all kinds of groups including individuals to generate power, which could encourage competition in power generating industry.

3.4 CHINA GIVES FRESH SUPPORT FOR NEW-ENERGY CARS

http://news.xinhuanet.com/english/2015-09/30/c_134675091.htm

China's new energy vehicles (NEVs) are shifting into high gear fueled by a string of favorable policies, with strong sales despite a lackluster automobile market.

The State Council, China's cabinet, asked local authorities in September to lift purchase restrictions and remove traffic controls for NEVs, while retaining curbs for cars running on fossil fuels, to stimulate sales and development of eco-friendly vehicles.

Buyers of electric cars will be able to obtain license plates without applying through the usual lottery systems in place in some major cities. In Beijing, 40 percent of applicants obtained permits to buy NEV cars in August, while the acceptance rate for traditional car buyers was only 0.5 percent.

China will encourage local governments, public institutions and bus companies to use more NEVs, according to a statement released after a State Council executive meeting chaired by Premier Li Keqiang.

"These measures are aimed at relieving China's energy and environmental pressure, boosting green vehicle production and consumption, and fostering new growth areas," the statement said.

The move marked the second straight week for China's policymakers to discuss perks for greener vehicles at a top-level government meeting.

On Sept. 23, the government promised to build more charging stations in urban areas and fast-charge facilities between cities. New residential complexes should build chargers or save space for them, while no less than 10 percent of public parking lots should have charging facilities.

At the meeting, it was also decided that authorities will provide tax and land support and welcome private investment in the charger-building project.

China has been promoting the use of NEVs with subsidies and tax cuts in a bid to cut emissions and save energy, and the sector saw explosive growth in the past two years.

In the first eight months of 2015, NEV sales surged 270 percent to 108,654, according to the China Association of Automobile Manufacturers (CAAM).

Li Jin, chief researcher with the China Enterprise Research Institute, expects the new measures to further push NEV development, ease pressure on the environment and facilitate the upgrade of automobile manufacturing.

Despite years of support, NEVs are still a reluctant choice for car buyers due to exorbitant prices and inconvenient charging. As for car makers, production costs remain high and technologies are not yet mature.

Dong Yang, vice president of CAAM, advised authorities to expand favorable measures to benefit more buyers, such as including plugged-in hybrid cars on the list and promoting lower-emission cars for air pollution control.

In addition, experts believe a robust NEV sector is possible to shore up the gloomy automobile market. China's automobile production and sales continued year-on-year drops for a fourth month in August, down 8.4 percent and 3 percent in August respectively.

3.4.1 CHINA SLASHES TAX TO PROMOTE GREEN VEHICLES, SHIPS

http://news.xinhuanet.com/english/2015-05/18/c_134249683.htm

China announced in May that new energy cars and ships will be exempted from vehicle and vessel tax in a bid to save energy and combat pollution.

Cars exempted include pure electric commercial cars, plug-in hybrid vehicles and fuel-cell commercial cars, according to a joint statement by the Ministry of Finance, State Administration of Taxation and the Ministry of Industry and Information Technology.

In addition, vehicle and vessel tax will be halved for users of energy-saving cars and ships, said the statement.

China's new energy vehicle production jumped threefold year on year to 25,400 in the first quarter of 2015 thanks to intense government promotion and support.

In March, the Ministry of Transport set a target of 300,000 new energy vehicles on China's roads by 2020: 200,000 new energy buses and 100,000 new energy taxis and delivery vehicles.

The Ministry of Commerce also announced earlier this year that China will continue to encourage the construction of charging facilities in cities and implement tax exemptions and subsidies for car purchases.

3.4.1.1 NEW PERKS FOR GREEN CAR BUYERS

http://news.xinhuanet.com/english/2015-09/29/c_134672388.htm

Buyers of new energy vehicles (NEVs) will get license plates without having to apply through the usual lottery system, under plans announced by the State Council in September to promote greener cars.

China will also encourage local governments, public institutions and bus companies to use more NEVs, according to a statement released after a State Council executive meeting chaired by Premier Li Keqiang.

Purchase tax on passenger vehicles with a displacement of less than 1.6 liters will be halved from Oct. 1, 2015 to Dec. 31, 2016, and the government vowed to quicken the phasing out of old and highly polluting vehicles. All such vehicles will be taken off the road by 2017, according to the statement.

"These measures are aimed at relieving China's energy and environmental pressure, boosting green vehicle production and consumption, and fostering new growth areas," it said.

3.4.1.2 BEIJING RESIDENTS TO BUY FOREIGN NEW ENERGY VEHICLES MORE EASILY

http://news.xinhuanet.com/english/2015-09/30/c_134676073.htm

Beijing residents will be able to buy Tesla and BMW new energy vehicles (NEVs) more easily thanks to a less-competitive lottery system.

To buy a car running on fossil fuels in Beijing, drivers must join a lottery to obtain a license plate first. Those who want certain new energy car can participate another lottery system, if the model is on an official list.

According to the Beijing Municipal Commission of Economy and Information Technology, six Tesla models and one BMW are included in a catalogue for the lottery system exclusive to new energy cars.

It is the first time foreign brands have been included in the list, previously exclusively for domestic auto makers and joint ventures.

Those who want to buy new energy models not included in the catalogue must compete in the gasoline lottery.

In August, 38 percent of Beijingers who applied via the NEV lottery system obtained permits, while the acceptance rate for buyers of cars running on fossil fuels was only 0.5 percent.

The State Council in September asked local authorities to lift purchase restrictions and remove traffic controls for NEVs, while retaining curbs for cars running on fossil fuels, to stimulate sales and development of eco-friendly vehicles.

3.4.2 CHINA'S NEW ENERGY VEHICLE OUTPUT SURGES

http://news.xinhuanet.com/english/2015-12/14/c_134916477.htm

China's production of new energy vehicles surged by 600 percent year on year in November thanks to government support.

Total production in November stood at 72,300 units, the Ministry of Industry and Information Technology said Monday in a statement.

During the month, output of pure electric passenger vehicles soared 700 percent from a year earlier to 30,000 units and that for plug-in hybrid passenger vehicles tripled to 7,509.

Pure electric and plug-in hybrid commercial vehicles skyrocketed by 18 times and 97 percent, the statement said.

China rolled out a raft of measures to promote new energy vehicles in a bid to save energy and combat pollution, including tax exemptions, subsidies for car purchases and a requirement for government departments to buy more new energy cars.

Official data showed that 95 percent of new energy vehicles produced in November would benefit from the favorable taxation policies.

In the first 11 months, China produced 279,200 new energy vehicles, up by four times from the same period in 2014.

3.4.2.1 CHINA'S ELECTRIC CAR PRODUCTION GROWS IN 2014

http://news.xinhuanet.com/english/business/2015-01/09/ c_133908938.htm

China's electric car production jumped fourfold to 83,900 vehicles in 2014,, the Ministry of Industry and Information Technology said in January.

In 2014, output of pure electric passenger cars rose 300 percent from a year earlier to 37,800, with plug-in hybrid passenger cars rising to 16,700 units.

Output of pure electric and plug-in hybrid commercial vehicles went up by 400 percent and 200 percent, respectively.

In December 2014, Chinese carmakers produced 27,200 new energy vehicles, four times as many as they did in December 2013.

Intense promotion by the government has brought more and more new energy vehicles onto China's roads, saving energy and combating pollution.

Measures including tax exemptions, price subsidies and requirements for government bodies to buy green cars are in place, however, new energy cars still account for only a tiny proportion of total output. In the first 11 months of 2014, the automotive industry produced 21.1 million vehicles.

3.4.2.2 ELECTRIC CAR SALES ACCELERATE IN BEIJING

http://news.xinhuanet.com/english/2015-07/27/c_134451936.htm

A growing number of electric cars are running on the streets of Beijing as the Chinese capital battles air pollution that is partly caused by vehicle emissions.

BAIC BJEV, which has a 66-percent of the electric vehicle market in Beijing, sold 6,223 electric cars in the first half of 2015. The company shifted 5,510 electric cars in the whole of last year.

The government has made electric cars more appealing by offering subsidies. In the lotteries through which many Chinese cities allocate number plates, drivers also have a far better chance of getting a plate for an electric car than for a regular vehicle.

One major electric vehicle store said customers need to wait a month after down payment to get the popular EV200 model.

Tesla, which already has 10 stores in China, told Xinhua it would open at least one more before the end of this year.

Regulators and carmakers are also pushing to build more charging stations for electric cars. BAIC is planning to build charging stations in SINOPEC petrol stations in Beijing. The charging process should take about three minutes, it said.

Xu Heyi, chairman of BAIC Group, has forecast that China will become the world's biggest electric car market in 2016, or probably this year.

3.4.2.3 BYD REPRESENTS INFLUENCE IN CLEAN GREEN VEHICLES

http://news.xinhuanet.com/english/2015-05/01/c_134201488.htm

The excitement of Chinese automaker BYD was palpable when the company announced an electric bus order from the United States this week.

"Positive energy will always win! Finally, we won the Long Beach Trans order—the only difference now is that the order is for 60 instead of 20! Cheers!" Li Ke, senior vice president of BYD posted on WeChat.

Long Beach Transit, which serves parts of the Los Angeles metropolitan area, announced an order for 10 BYD electric buses, with options for its partner agencies to buy as many as 50 more.

This is not BYD's first success overseas. The company has a reputation for top quality new energy vehicles (NEVs).

"We have been in the global market for a long time. We've been fighting for a place in the Japanese market for 10 years," Li Wei, marketing director of BYD's overseas business division, told Xinhua.

At present, BYD electric vehicles are marketed in more than 30 countries and regions. The company has sold more than 30 electric buses to the Netherlands since 2012 and will deliver to Los Angeles in the first half of this year.

Wang Jie, manager of the commercial vehicle sales, said it was hard for Chinese car makers to compete in the traditional vehicle sector, but they can catch up or even do better with NEVs through their own efforts.

Established in 1995, BYD specializes in information technology, automobiles and new energy, with products ranging from batteries and solar cells to vehicles. In 2010, the company joined with Daimler AG to create Shenzhen BYD Daimler New Technology Co. Ltd., which markets luxury electric car brand Denza.

"When BYD first entered the global market, our brand recognition was very low," Li Wei. Now, the company's electric vehicles are certified in Europe, Canada and United States.

BYD's rise in the NEV sector comes as China is pushing use of such vehicles to save energy and cut pollution. The government started subsidizing NEVs in 2010 and last year announced plans to raise those subsidies. BYD sold more than 20,000 NEVs in China last year, 28 percent of total NEV sales.

"Our customers are mostly convinced by seeing electric cars and buses in the streets. Even the most strict administrative authority cannot find any fault with our products," Li Wei said.

BYD has also shaped itself into a provider of urban new energy transport solutions, designing several charge stations, including a tower that can contain 400 NEVs, with each floor of less than 600 square meters.

"We have the capability to provide distinctive urban transit solutions for the whole world," Wang said.

3.4.3 CHINA TO BUILD 12,000 NEV CHARGERS BY 2020

 http://news.xinhuanet.com/english/2015-10/12/c_134707002.htm

China will build a network of 12,000 charging stations to meet the power demands of 5 million electric vehicles by 2020, a National Energy Administration official said in October.

In addition to the 12,000 chargers, 4.8 million power poles, 3,850 charging stations for public buses and 2,500 for taxis will be built in the same period, Tong Guangyi, vice-director of the NEA Power Department, told a meeting in Changzhou city, east China's Jiangsu Province.

China's State Council, the Cabinet, announced a guideline last week on a nationwide charging network.

The move is the latest effort by the government in the new energy vehicle sector, which has grown steadily in the past two years due to subsidies and tax cuts.

According to the guideline, new residential complexes should have charging points or assign space for them, while no less than 10 percent of parking spaces in public parking lots should have charging facilities. There should be at least one public charging station for every 2,000 NEVs, the guideline said.

To finance the project, the government will encourage private investment, allow charger manufacturers to issue corporate bonds, and seek investment from pension funds

China's State Grid is responsible for building a large part of the new charging facilities. Yang Qing, the company's vice president said at the meeting, that more than 6,000 public fast-charge stations and 59,000 chargers to power some 3.68 million electric passenger vehicles will be installed.

The State Grid will make public charging facilities available in 202 cities. In some major cities, including Beijing, Tianjin and Shanghai, a charging facility will be found within a circle of less than 1 km.

This year, the company plans to start construction of 1,888 fast-charge stations with the aim of putting them into service by the end of June 2016. Currently, 618 stations and 24,000 chargers are operated by the company, actually serving 49,000 NEVs.

3.4.3.1 BEIJING TO DOUBLE CHARGING STATIONS BEFORE 2016

http://news.xinhuanet.com/english/china/2015-02/11/c_133987422.htm

The number of electric-vehicle charging stations in Beijing will be doubled by the end of 2015 to encourage the use of new-energy vehicles, local authorities said in February.

Beijing currently has 1,425 public charging stations at 188 sites. They are expected to be open to the public ahead of the Spring Festival on Feb. 19, said Xu Xinchao, head of the new energy and materials department with the municipal science and technology commission.

The charging stations are located at shopping malls, office buildings, parking lots, airports, highway service areas, parks, technology parks and transportation hubs.

Xu said a charging station can now be found within a radius of five km from anywhere in the city.

However, the official called for more private investment in charging facilities to help increase their number in the capital city.

About 6,800 new-energy vehicles had been sold to private owners in Beijing by the end of 2014, according to the municipal commission of economy and information technology.

The Chinese government has been encouraging consumers to buy electric vehicles as one of the solutions to the country's pollution problems. But the plan has been hindered by limited charging infrastructure.

3.4.3.2 ELECTRIC CAR CHARGERS INSTALLED ON BEIJING-SHANGHAI EXPRESSWAY

http://news.xinhuanet.com/english/china/2015-01/16/c_127390937.htm

The construction of electric vehicle charging stations along the 1,262-km expressway that links Beijing and Shanghai finished in January.

State Grid, one of China's two grid corporations, built 50 quick-charging stations along the route, making it the country's first cross-city charging network.

Each of the stations has eight charging poles capable of fully charging an electric car in 30 minutes. All electric cars that meet Chinese standards can use the charging facilities.

State Grid built 133 quick-charging stations with 532 charging poles along three major expressways with total length of 2,900 km in 2014.

The company aims to build charging station networks along eight major expressways with total length of 19,000 km in China by 2020.

Electric vehicles are gaining popularity in China amid its "green" drive, but buyers are hesitant as they worry about a lack of charging stations.

3.4.3.3 EXPRESSWAYS IN BEIJING AND NEIGHBORING REGION TO ADD ELECTRIC CHARGING POSTS

http://news.xinhuanet.com/english/2015-07/30/c_134464411.htm

Beijing and neighboring Hebei Province and the coastal city Tianjin will build electric vehicle charging posts on four expressways in the region this year as part of a campaign to promote electric vehicles, authorities said in July.

According to Gao Peng, deputy director of Beijing Municipal Commission of Development and Reform, these charging posts will be placed at least every 50 km along four expressways linking Beijing, Tianjin and Hebei Province, a region jointly referred to in China as "Jingjinji," where authorities are pushing for greater integration in transportation, economic development and environmental protection.

More charging posts are expected to be built on other major transport arteries and parking lots in the region in the next two years.

The move came as governments in the Jingjinji area are promoting electric vehicles as an alternative to gasoline-fueled cars among the public to address air pollution in the region.

Emissions from cars have been blamed as one of several factors leading to the choking smog blanketing the region's skies.

3.4.3.4 BEIJING PILOTS STREET LAMP CHARGERS FOR ELECTRIC CARS

http://news.xinhuanet.com/english/china/2015-01/12/c_133913262.htm

Beijing has launched a pilot project to transform street lamps to serve as charging poles for electric cars.

Eighty-eight high-pressure sodium lamps on a road in Beijing's Changping District have been converted into energy-saving LED lamps. Eight charging poles have been installed and put into trial operation using the energy saved from the new LED lamps, said the Beijing Municipal Science and Technology Commission.

The charging poles work day and night, alleviating charging demand for electric taxis and private cars in the area, said the commission.

Beijing will expand the project to other areas.

Beijing has built charging poles at new energy car dealers, parking lots, high-tech industry parks and expressway service areas.

The city plans to build 10,000 public charging poles for electric cars by 2017, the municipal government said in June of last year.

The charging poles will be installed in airports and train stations, public parking lots, malls and supermarket parking lots, highway rest areas, electric car dealers and gas stations.

The Chinese government has been encouraging consumers to buy electric vehicles as a solution to the country's pollution problems. But the plan has been hindered by a bottleneck in the charging infrastructure.

A charging system for the Beijing-Shanghai expressway will soon open. Over the weekend, five electric cars started a 1,262-km test journey from east China's business hub of Shanghai to Beijing, with charging stations available every 50 km in each direction.

China's electric car production jumped fourfold to 83,900 vehicles in 2014, the Ministry of Industry and Information Technology said in January.

In 2014, output of pure electric passenger cars rose 300 percent from a year earlier to 37,800, with plug-in hybrid passenger cars reaching 16,700 units.

Measures including tax exemptions, price subsidies and requirements for government organs to buy green cars are in place. However, new energy cars still account for only a tiny proportion of total output. In the first 11 months of 2014, China's automotive industry produced 21.1 million vehicles.

3.4.3.5 TESLA TEAMS WITH PROPERTY DEVELOPER TO EXPAND CHARGING POLES

http://news.xinhuanet.com/english/2015-08/03/c_134476254.htm

U.S. electric car maker Tesla announced in August it will work with a Hong Hong property developer to build more charging poles at shopping malls in six Chinese cities.

Tesla said it agreed to build the public charging facilities at shopping malls operated by Hang Lung Properties in Shanghai, Tianjin, Wuxi, Dalian, Jinan and Shenyang.

Apart from the destination charging poles, Tesla will also build supercharging stations, as well as charging poles at the homes for customers.

Zhu Xiaotong, president of Tesla China, said the U.S. car marker hopes to provide convenient charging services for Chinese customers in a bid to encourage more people to love their cars.

On June 25, Tesla announced that it would establish seven supercharging networks in major cities and popular travel destinations in China in the second half of this year.

The new charging stations will be in the Yangtze River Delta, Beijing-Tianjin-Hebei region and at east China's Mount Huangshan, a UNESCO World Natural Heritage site.

Tesla has its second largest charging network in China — second only to the United States — with hundreds of supercharging stations and more than 1,400 public charging poles in operation across China.

Tesla superchargers, jointly powered by grid electricity and solar energy, can charge Tesla Model S in minutes instead of hours.

3.4.4 CHINESE FIRM TO PRODUCE SOLAR-POWERED CARS

http://news.xinhuanet.com/english/china/2015-02/02/c_133965178.htm

Hanergy Holding Group Ltd., the world's largest thin-film solar power company, will launch as many as five models of solar-powered cars in October, its chairman announced in February.

Hanergy is cooperating with three overseas and two domestic partners on the vehicles, board chairman Li Hejun told a press conference. Hanergy announced in late January that it had acquired Alta Devices, an American competitor, with charging stations for Tesla in Beijing and Shanghai.

The new models will have a range of 80 to 100 km once fully charged, he said.

"There are currently only 400,000 electric cars in the world but the market is expected to hit 10 million by 2020," said Lin.

3.5 CHINA'S FIRST ELECTRICITY-POWERED AIRCRAFT GETS PRODUCTION APPROVAL

http://news.xinhuanet.com/english/2015-12/04/c_134884955.htm

China's first domestically developed electricity-powered aircraft has been approved for production by civil aviation authorities.

The two-seat RX1E aircraft can fly for 45-60 minutes with a maximum speed of 120 km per hour after an hour and a half of charging, according to its developer, the Liaoning General Aviation Research Academy in northeast China.

The environmentally friendly model has strong market potential, especially in pilot training and tourism. There has been 28 orders for the aircraft, according to the academy.

3.6 CHINA RAISES CONSUMPTION TAX ON OIL PRODUCTS

http://news.xinhuanet.com/english/china/2015-01/12/c_133913905.htm

China's finance and taxation authorities raised the consumption tax on oil products from January.

The tax on gasoline, naphtha, solvent oil and lubricating oil will be increased to 1.52 yuan (about 25 U.S. cents) per liter from 1.4 yuan. The levy on diesel, jet fuel and fuel oil will be increased from 1.1 yuan per liter to 1.2 yuan, according to the Ministry of Finance (MOF) and the State Administration of Taxation (SAT).

This will be the third increase in as many months, following one on Nov. 29 and another on Dec. 13.

The retail prices of gasoline and diesel will be cut by 180 yuan and 230 yuan per ton after taking the higher tax into consideration, the National Development and Reform Commission announced in a separate statement.

This the 12th retail fuel prices cut since July 2014, as the government reacts to lower global crude oil prices.

Proceeds from the higher taxes will mainly be allocated to

counter-pollution initiatives and the new energy sector, according to the MOF and the SAT.

However, experts warn that the drop in oil prices is bad news for the new energy sector. For example, new-energy cars will see reduced sales, said Liu Shangxi, director of the research institute for fiscal science at the MOF.

China's energy consumption accounted for about 22.4 percent of the world's total in 2013, but its energy consumption per gross domestic product (GDP) was 3.5 times of that of the United States and seven times of that of Japan, according to Liu.

Fuel tax and pricing reform measures began five years ago, and have featured consumption tax hikes and the introduction of a pricing system more closely linked to the international market.

Consumption tax was first imposed in 1994 on consumer goods with a high energy cost and high pollution to make production and consumption more environmentally-friendly and promote sustainable growth.

Over ten countries including Russia, Australia, New Zealand and France have raised their oil product consumption tax since 2012 to ensure green development.

3.7 CHINA TO CAP COAL CONSUMPTION

http://news.xinhuanet.com/english/2015-10/28/c_134759673.htm

China will enforce a strict limit on total coal consumption, and continue to cut production, said a senior energy official in October.

Li Haofeng, deputy director of the coal office under the National Energy Administration, made the remarks at an international coal summit. He said that measures were needed to ensure the sustainable development of the coal industry.

To this end, he said, China will promote the clean, efficient usage of coal by using some of the world's most advanced process to support the industrial upgrade.

The country will step up coal market reform, and strengthen cooperation between China and other countries with huge coal production and consumption.

China will reduce the ratio of coal in primary energy consumption from 66 percent this year to around 50 percent by 2050, said the National Coal Association.

In the first three quarters this year, China produced 2.72 billion tons of coal, down 4.62 percent year on year, according to data by China Coal Transportation and Sale Society.

3.7.1 SLUMP IN SHANXI'S COAL INDUSTRY

http://news.xinhuanet.com/english/2015-07/28/c_134455957.htm

Coal mines in north China's Shanxi Province face a bleak future, with a continued slump in the fortunes of an industry that was once the backbone of the local economy.

Shanxi's coal industry lost more than 4 billion yuan (644 million U.S. dollars) in the first half of 2015 as government curbs on the polluting sector took their toll, official statistics indicated.

Coal production reached 463 million tons during the first six months, a year-on-year decrease of 3.2 percent. Meanwhile, coal storage climbed to 47 million tons, up 35 percent compared with the beginning of 2015 and accounting for almost half of China's total inventory.

The industry has now suffered losses for 12 consecutive months.

The Shanxi government has controlled the growth of coal production in recent years in the hope of shaking off the economic mode of relying heavily on coal resources. The provincial government is approving no new coal mines for the next five years to tackle overcapacity.

Meanwhile, banks in China have issued a variety of restrictive financing measures for coal-related industries, including raising the financing threshold for coal producers and lowering loan scales.

"It will be difficult to reverse the situation in the coal market," said Pan Yun, deputy head of the Shanxi Academy of Social Sciences.

"On one hand, the economic slowdown will cap demands for coal. On the other, the country has increased efforts to save energy and reduce emissions. The rising proportion of alternative energies including hydropower and natural gas will also reduce demand for coal," Pan added.

3.7.2 TOP CHINESE COAL MINING COMPANY REPORTS SHARP PROFIT DROP

http://news.xinhuanet.com/english/2015-07/29/c_134460422.htm

China Shenhua Energy Co. Ltd., the country's largest coal mining group, reported in July that its net profits dropped 45.6 percent to 11.73 billion yuan (1.9 billion U.S. dollars) in the first half of the year.

During the January-June period, the company's business income came in at 87.78 billion yuan, down 32.1 percent year on year.

Shenhua attributed the drop to weak demand that affected both sales and prices. Coal sales by China Shenhua Energy slipped 24.2 percent during the period.

Government policies to encourage the use of non-fossil fuels have also affected sales, the company added.

Coal accounts for about 66 percent of China's primary energy consumption, 35 percentage points higher than the world average.

The country's coal output fell in 2014 for the first time this century as a result of slowing economic growth, government efforts to reduce air pollution and increased investment in renewable energy.

China's economy expanded 7 percent year on year in the second quarter, unchanged from the first quarter but still much slower than the previous double-digit growth.

Overall coal production in China slipped 6.1 percent in the first four months this year to 1.15 billion tons, with the pace of decline accelerating from a 3.5-percent fall registered in the first three months of the year, official data revealed earlier.

3.7.3 CHINA'S MOST POLLUTED PROVINCE CUTS COAL USE

http://news.xinhuanet.com/english/2015-04/08/c_134134279.htm

Hebei Province, known for the worst air condition in China, vowed in April to clear the smog by reducing coal-related pollution.

Hebei Vice Governor Zhang Jiehui said the province would cut emissions from coal-fired power stations by half.

Stations that can not meet the goal will be shut down, according to the provincial government.

The government also plans to close all solid clay brick kilns as they cause heavy pollution.

Coal emissions contribute half of the air pollution in Hebei, the vice governor said at an air pollution control meeting.

3.7.4 COAL-RICH CHINA SEES SHIFT IN POWER MIX: FITCH

http://en.xinfinance.com/html/Industries/Utilities/2015/95329.shtml

Electricity consumption alone is becoming an increasingly unreliable gauge of China's economy, as the economy will gradually shift toward tertiary industries that are less energy dependent, an analyst with global ratings agency Fitch said in May.

There will be a subsequent reduction in the need for power and the power sector moves toward a cleaner future, said Jenny Huang, associate director of Fitch's Corporate Research. The structure of the Chinese economy is changing as growth slows, with the service sector and domestic consumption coming to the fore, according to the China Power Sector Blue Book, released by Fitch in May. Data from the National Energy Administration (NEA) showed electricity consumption growing in April, picking up 1.3 percent year on year.

Generation capacity had more than tripled to 1,360 GW in 2014 from 2002 levels, average annual growth of 12 percent. Such growth is unlikely in the future, Fitch said. Annual power capacity growth will slow to 7 percent between 2013 and 2020, based on the NEA's preliminary 2020 target of around 2,000 GW installed capacity, according to Fitch.

The government is focused on energy efficiency and reducing emissions to cut overall energy intensity by 16 percent in the 2010-2015 period, along with phasing out many heavy industries. The shift in China's energy mix toward cleaner fuels demands aggressive expansion of clean power capacity to nearly 40 percent in 2020 from 33 percent in 2014.

Greenhouse emissions are set to peak around 2030. China overtook the U.S. to become the world's top electricity consumer in 2011, accounting for 22 percent of global electricity use, but for each unit of GDP output, its power consumption is 1.4 times that of the Republic of Korea and 2.3 times that of the U.S. By the end of 2014, 67 percent of China's power generation capacity came from thermal power plants, but dependence on coal has raised environmental concerns.

Coal is the most carbon-intensive fuel and contains many pollutants. China burns more than 3.5 billion tons of coal each year, half of which is for power and heating. By comparison, the U.S. burns less than 900 million tons and the EU uses 1 billion tons. Coal-fired power stations generate more than 60 percent of nitric oxide, about 40 percent carbon dioxide and 25 percent of dust pollutants, in China's pollution mix.

3.7.5 CHINA PAYS POWER STATIONS TO CUT EMISSIONS

http://news.xinhuanet.com/english/2015-12/09/c_134900833.htm

China plans offer financial incentives to those coal-fired power plants that are least polluting over the next two years.

From Jan. 1, coal-fired generators that emit pollutants below the maximum permitted levels of natural gas-fired generators will receive government money per kilowatt-hour of electricity produced, the National Development and Reform Commission, the country's top economic planner, said in a statement. Local environmental protection authorities will be responsible for monitoring emission levels.

Coal-fired generators installed before 2016 will receive 0.01 yuan for per kilowatt-hour of electricity they generate, while those installed in after 2016 will get half that amount.

The announcement comes as severe smog persists in parts of north China, bringing traffic restrictions, closure of construction sites and suspension of schools. Coal contributes most of the pollutants.

On Dec. 2, the State Council, China's cabinet, decided to upgrade coal-burning power plants nationwide to reduce pollutants by 60 percent in the next five years.

3.8 CHINA'S CRUDE STEEL OUTPUT IN LANDMARK DIP

http://news.xinhuanet.com/english/2015-08/13/c_134513216.htm

China's half-year crude steel output has dropped for the first time in nearly 20 years, data from the country's top economic planner showed.

Crude steel output in the first half of 2015 dipped 1.3 percent year on year to 409.97 million tons, while crude iron output declined 2.3 percent year on year to 356.94 million tons, according to the National Development and Reform Commission data.

Zhang Guangning, president of the China Iron and Steel Association (CISA), said that "China's crude steel output probably reached a peak in

2014," when the country's per capita crude steel output exceeded 600 kg.

Zhang encouraged iron and steel producers to "accelerate industrial transformation and upgrading while promoting innovation as the economy adjusts to a new normal featuring slower but more balanced and sustainable growth."

In the Jan.-June period, 43 steel companies, or nearly half of the CISA member enterprises, posted a total deficit of 18.55 billion yuan in primary businesses, nearly double the losses registered in the same period last year.

CASE STUDY

GLOOM FOR HEBEI AS STEEL LOSES SHINE

http://news.xinhuanet.com/english/2015-02/27/c_134024029.htm

Steelmakers in north China's Hebei Province, which produces at least one fifth of the country's total crude steel, are struggling to survive through industrial reforms amid overcapacity and pollution concerns.

A slight yet nerve-wracking 0.6-percent drop in crude steel output last year, the first drop since the year 2000, has left companies pessimistic about their destiny in the Chinese Year of the Ram, which began in February.

Backed by its rich iron ore reserves, Hebei has for decades been a leading steel producer in China. Its annual output has surpassed that of Japan, the world's second-largest steel-producing country.

Last year, crude steel output in Hebei added up to 185 million tons, 22 percent of China's total 823 million tons.

As demand keeps shrinking and signs of overcapacity become more apparent, the central government has decided to cut China's steel and iron production by 80 million tons in three years.

The decision came as a heavy blow to local steelmakers, who were already struggling with deficits and pollution accusations: of the 10 most polluted Chinese cities last year, seven were in Hebei Province.

Gone are the days when the steel mills' production lines were compared to "banknote printers" as steelmaking was more lucrative than any other trade, said Kong Delin, a steel plant manager.

His company, once a cash cow in Qianan, a county-level city in Hebei, has been closed for more than a year. Its former workshops are deserted and the 450-cubic-meter furnace that used to be a great source of pride for locals has been reduced to a pile of waste iron.

DOWN AND OUT

Kong, 40, had tears in his eyes as he recalled the company's short-lived glory.

Jianyuan Steel and Iron Co. Ltd. was founded in 1992 amid soaring global demand. Kong joined the company in 2002, working his way up from a young engineer to deputy general manager.

"In our heyday, the market was so hungry for steel that billets were loaded onto container trucks immediately after they came out of the furnace," he said.

"People joked that steel company bosses carried huge sacks of cash to buy luxury cars, and if the sales assistant did not show due respect, they'd buy the car showroom."

By the time Kong joined Jianyuan, the company had helped the under-developed Qian'an County to shake off poverty and become one of the 100 richest counties in China.

But its glory did not last long. Business began to slump in 2008, under the impact of the international financial crisis. In 2012, steel prices dropped drastically to the 1990s level.

Locals applied gallows humor to the degree to which profits generated by each ton of steel had shrunken over the past decade.

"Ten years ago, it was equivalent to the price of a cell phone [about 3,000 yuan or 480 U.S. dollars]. After 2010, it was worth about the same as one kg of pork [about 30 yuan] and today, it is dirt cheap," said Kong.

By 2013, his company was deep in the red, reporting losses of at least 10 million yuan every month.

Kong himself was in charge when the company was forced to close down all its facilities, dismantle the furnace and put an end to its steel legend in 2013.

SACRIFICE

The central government has demanded China's steel output be cut by 80 million tons by the end of 2017. Hebei, as the largest producer, should cut production by 60 million tons.

The production cut would shake many related industries and affect the livelihoods of at least 600,000 people.

In Shucun Township of Wu'an City, a leading steel base, the past two years have seen the closure of 237 lime kilns, about 70 percent of the city's total.

Lime is a major ingredient in steelmaking, but lime kilns are heavy polluters.

Almost the entire Shucun Township was fed by limemaking. When kilns were bulldozed one after another, thousands of workers were left not knowing where they should go for a living.

The government, too, paid a price. Last year, Hebei Province posted a GDP growth of 6.5 percent, the third-lowest growth rate among all Chinese provinces.

By the end of 2017, production cuts in the steel sector will have reduced the province's tax revenue by 50 billion yuan.

SEEKING SURVIVAL

Ye Jinbao, founder of the first private steel plant in Qianan, evaded the steel industry's recession: he sold the plant in its heyday and tried his luck in biomedicine.

"It's still too early to tell if I've jumped from the frying pan into fire," said Ye, whose 400-million-yuan investment in vaccine and drug development has not yielded any profit. His first vaccine product, developed in 2006 and costing 20 million yuan, is still waiting for the clinical tests needed before it is approved for sale.

Though some plants have closed down altogether, the absolute majority of steelmakers are still clinging on, struggling to survive by upgrading their products and seeking new revenue streams.

Jinan Steel in Wu'an City has seen a ray of hope in teaming up with Fermat Machinery to produce digitally-controlled machine tools. But the city government's decision to move it and five other plants from downtown into a suburban industrial park by 2017 was a heavy blow.

Relocating is an expensive business for steel plants, as 90 percent of their facilities can not be moved and have to be rebuilt from scratch in the new location.

"I hope we can survive with financial and policy support from the city government," said Wei Kaozeng, a senior executive with Jinan Steel.

The industry's gloomy outlook has forced companies and governments to seek more sustained development.

"The city's iron ore reserves may last for another 50 years," said Li Zhong, Party chief in Qianan. "It's crucial to find more rational ways of development without exhausting our resources."

Powerful state companies are rapidly upgrading technologies to cut emissions.

The Tangshan steel plant of Hebei Steel and Iron Group, a 72-year-old state firm, has set up one of the largest sewage treatment facilities in north China and stopped using groundwater in its steel production.

The plant has also applied new technologies to cut other waste emissions and reduce noise.

"Survival calls for transformation and involves great pain," said Zhou Benshun, secretary of the Hebei Provincial Party Committee. "But there's no turning back and we have to forge ahead."

Part 4

Internet Technology Reshapes China's Economy

http://news.xinhuanet.com/english/2015-09/29/c_134672555.htm

The Internet will play an increasingly important role in reshaping China's economy, as more people are online here than anywhere else in the world, experts said.

By the end of June 2015, China had 668 million Internet users, 48.8 percent of the population. Total e-commerce transaction volume in 2014 surged 59.4 percent to 16.39 trillion yuan (2.57 trillion U.S. dollars), nearing its goal of 18 trillion yuan by 2015.

China's cabinet unveiled its "Internet Plus" action plan at the beginning of July to mold information technology and traditional sectors into a cohesive, efficient force.

Lin Nianxiu, deputy head of the National Development and Reform Commission (NDRC), said at a conference in September that China needs the integration as it will address the problems of rising costs and overcapacity.

Internet Plus will help cultivate new engines for economic growth and upgrade economic structure, Lin said.

The action plan identified areas that can benefit from Internet Plus, including manufacturing, modern agriculture, energy, finance, services, logistics and e-commerce.

Entering the food delivery business one year ago, China's Internet giant Baidu has been combining its cutting-edge technology with the catering sector.

Zhao Cheng, editor-in-chief of Baidu, said the company had become a leader in the sector as analyzed orders and matched the positions of customers with food delivery personnel. With this technology, the company can process more orders, quicker, making the process more convenient for clients and making more profits for restaurants, Zhao said.

Chinese taxi-hailing and ride-on-demand provider Didi, a leader in the sector, also uses mobile and location technology.

"The Internet has made it easier for startups and slashed the costs associated with innovation," said Lin.

Lin urged companies to embrace the Internet for their management operations, too, as it would raise overall productivity.

The NDRC will reinforce policy support for companies to participate in the Internet Plus program and collaborate with other government departments to realize scientific decision making in promoting Internet Plus, Lin said.

Huai Jinpeng, deputy head of the Ministry of Industry and Information Technology (MIIT), said at the forum that companies should make good use of the Internet and look for opportunities from untapped areas.

The ministry will continue to improve Internet infrastructure and make broadband Internet accessible in every corner of China, according to Huai.

By the end of this year, the average broadband speed for users in major municipalities and provincial capitals will be increased to 20 megabytes per second (Mbps) from the current 9 Mbps, the MIIT announced earlier this year.

The ministry will press ahead with the overall implementation of the "Broadband China" strategy, which was floated in August 2013 by the State Council to boost information consumption and expand broadband coverage across the country.

4.1 CHINA'S ONLINE POPULATION REACHES 648 MLN

http://news.xinhuanet.com/english/china/2015-01/24/c_133943957.htm

China's netizen population, the world's largest, reached 648 million at the end of 2014, 16 million more than in June, according to an industry expert.

Jin Jian, deputy director of the China Internet Network Information Center (CNNIC), said that online economy accounts for seven percent of GDP, up from 3.3 percent the previous year.

More than 70 percent of Internet users are worried by Internet security problems, such as leaking of private information, Jin told the Beijing Daily.

Chinese consumers are eager to spend online. Internet retail sales totalled 331 billion yuan in the first ten months in 2014, up a stunning 55.6 percent over 2013.

4.1.1. CHINA TO GIVE WHOLE NATION 4G COVERAGE BY 2018

http://news.xinhuanet.com/english/2015-12/15/c_134916498.htm

China aims to cover all its urban and rural areas with 4G network by 2018, according to an action plan published by the Ministry of Industry and Information Technology (MIIT) in December.

The country also plans to install fiber optics in more than 80 percent of its villages, according to the MIIT's three-year action plan "Internet Plus."

With regard to the upgrading of network infrastructure, the ministry set the target of "basically completing a broadband-based, integrated, ubiquitous and secure next-generation national information infrastructure."

To achieve this, China will channel more energy into the promotion of 4G, and boost research and development of 5G, according to the action plan.

The MIIT's plan is part of the Internet Plus action plan, which was unveiled in July.

The action plan will integrate mobile Internet, cloud computing, big data and the Internet of Things with modern manufacturing to encourage the healthy development of e-commerce, industrial networks, and Internet banking, and to help Internet companies increase their international presence.

4.2 INTERNET-LED CONSUMPTION BOOM ALMOST UNNOTICED AMID CHINA'S STOCK MARKET JITTERS

http://news.xinhuanet.com/english/2015-09/09/c_134607791.htm

The volatility of the stock market in recent months has eclipsed a much more subtle transition that has geared China's economic growth toward consumption.

The market correction in China has wiped out nearly 40 percent of market value of its stock markets in its plunge over the past two months, stoking fears that weakness in the world's second largest economy will put a drag on the frail recovery elsewhere.

Though China's economic growth slowed to a six year low of 7 percent in H1, retail sales have held up relatively well at 10.4 percent. Meanwhile, online retailing has witnessed even higher growth of 39.1 percent during the same period.

Much of the resilience of retail consumption has come as a result of the internet, which are likely to play a part in half of the country's total consumption in the future from nearly 10 percent now, according to Rich Lesser, CEO of management consultants Boston Consulting Group.

Speaking at a discussion at the annual summer meeting of the World Economic Forum in the northeastern Chinese coastal city of Dalian, Lesser said the stock market's impact on the Chinese economy is overstated and the shift in growth drivers toward consumption is a much more noteworthy trend.

Wang Jianzhou, chairman of China Association for Public Companies who used to head China Mobile, the world's largest telecom firm by subscribers, said the rise of mobile internet has profound implications for businesses in China.

China is already the world largest smartphone market, where smartphone handsets are becoming increasingly affordable as Chinese manufacturers markers like Xiaomi, Huawei and Lenovo are fighting to capture more consumers with 4G smartphones selling at less than 200 dollars.

Chinese smartphone users are using their phones to do everything from shopping to hailing taxis and ordering takeouts in a trend launched by internet giants Alibaba, Tencent and Baidu to deliver better services through mobile internet.

"What we are watching right now is a transition of the economy to more consumption, more services and less dependency on investment," Lesser said.

"In most parts of the world," he said, "the service environment has developed over many decades and the online players are challenging a very established, very embedded offline retail infrastructure. But what sets China apart is that consumption is growing in a highly innovative online world almost in parallel with the growth in offline services."

Many of the changes brought by internet firms are disruptive to traditional retailers and other industries in the way they do business and make profits. Companies are at risk of becoming irrelevant if they fail to adapt to an increasingly mobile world.

Telecom veteran Wang said the innovations in China's online world are creating a wave of new demand and redefining the entire telecom industry.

Revenue from telecommunications is being surpassed by that of mobile phone manufacturing, which will in turn be topped by revenues grossed from internet-based services.

But whether traditional players who used to hold dominance in China's retail scene can thrive in the shift to mobile consumption is just as uncertain as betting on the country's volatile stock market.

That, according to Lesser, is what China and companies doing business here, both domestic and foreign, should expect as authorities want the market to play a more decisive role in the economy.

4.3 CHINA TO DELIVER 50 BLN EXPRESS PARCELS BY 2020: OFFICIAL

http://news.xinhuanet.com/english/2015-11/04/c_134784025.htm

China aims to deliver 50 billion express parcels annually, generating 800 billion yuan (126.3 billion U.S. dollars) in business revenue, by 2020, a postal official said in November.

The target is equal to the annual sum of deliveries across the globe today, said Ma Junsheng, head of State Post Bureau in an online interview.

Total express deliveries would near 20 billion pieces with business revenue reaching 400 billion yuan in 2015, Ma said, adding that the sector has registered an annual growth rate of over 50 percent in the past five years, according to Ma.

The country plans to build an efficient and safe express delivery system with nationwide coverage, advanced technology and services and international connections by 2020, according to a policy document released last week by the State Council, China's cabinet.

Despite a slowing economy, express delivery services have grown steadily. The amount of express delivery packages has increased 8.2 times over the past six years. In the first half of 2015, express deliveries jumped by more than 43 percent year on year.

On average, each Chinese person received more than 10 parcels last year, even with only half of the country covered by the delivery network.

4.4 WHEN THE INTERNET MEETS AGRICULTURE

http://news.xinhuanet.com/english/2015-08/02/c_134472388.htm

Being a farmer in China no longer means eking out a living in a backward industry. Farmers nationwide are adopting new business practices made possible by the Internet, boosting their earnings and modernizing the sector.

For Zhang Guoqin, growing crops sometimes simply needs a few clicks of the mouse.

In northeast China's Heilongjiang Province, he monitors his rice fields on computer screens. He uses a system of sensors and automatization which takes a lot of the toil and inefficiency out of his business. For example, his fields are irrigated automatically if sensors detect that they need it.

"Thanks to the data, we are able to track the conditions of crops, assess nutrient levels and forecast disasters," Zhang said.

Such innovation is a new trend in Chinese farming, a welcome change of direction for a rural economy that has long been seeking modernization.

China's cabinet unveiled an "Internet Plus" action plan at the beginning of July targeted at integration of the Internet with traditional sectors to make them smarter and more efficient. Along with manufacturing, agriculture was on the top of the list.

Farming in China has been booming for over three decades. The summer grain output reached a record high of 141.07 million tons in 2015 after 11 consecutive years of increases.

Though harvests were good, inefficient sales channels, a shrinking labor population and lack of access to loans have been squeezing farmers' earnings and dragging down the rural economy.

In 2014, the per capita disposable income of rural residents rose 9.2 percent year on year to 10,489 yuan (1,720 U.S. dollars), less than half of that of urbanites, and 70.17 million rural Chinese earned an annual sum less than 2,300 yuan, the official poverty line.

However, the Internet, especially mobile networks, have provided agriculture with a new vision. By the end of 2014, nearly 30 percent of China's rural population were online.

E-commerce enables farmers to sell goods quickly, conveniently shop around for materials and obtain small loans more easily. The Internet has made intensive mechanized production achievable, boosted yields with fewer laborers and made agriculture greener and food safer.

Given the bright outlook, Internet companies and e-commerce giants are thronging to take a bigger share of the agricultural pie.

Taobao.com, China's largest online shopping platform, has launched an agricultural channel.

Its Internet conglomerate owner, Alibaba, also ambitiously plans to invest 10 billion yuan into 100,000 new service centers in Chinese villages in the next three to five years to help train farmers in Internet use.

"Following the new generation of farmers, online stores selling farm produce have witnessed explosive growth and e-commerce is reshaping the whole industry," said Chi Fulin, director of the China (Hainan) Institute for Reform and Development.

Internet firms don't need the might of Alibaba to get involved. Beijing Tianchen Cloud Farm Co., developed Cloud Farm, an app designed as a one-stop shop for farming business.

It has amassed over a million registered users as it requires no more than a mobile phone and a SIM card, simplicity which is crucial in the Chinese countryside, where Internet infrastructure lags behind the situation in cities.

Han Guiyin, a farm owner in east China's Shandong Province, turns to Cloud Farm whenever he needs to source fertilizer or logistics services, apply for loans or even technological support.

However, there are still bottlenecks that have to be addressed to facilitate the national ambition of upgrading agriculture.

Analysts agree the government needs to improve infrastructure and logistics in mountainous regions, cultivate IT professionals and provide more information services to help farmers access the web.

4.4.1 CHINESE FARMERS TURN TO E-COMMERCE TO RID POVERTY

http://news.xinhuanet.com/english/2015-10/15/c_134716966.htm

Huo Liang earns about 1,000 yuan a month (158 U.S. dollars) running an online shop to sell millet, a humble but nutritious food popular among Chinese.

His earnings are remarkable for a financially disadvantaged family in Tongyu county, northeast China's Jilin Province.

In the county, nearly a third of the agricultural products including millet are sold online. Sun Hongjun, secretary of the county Party committee, said to further alleviate poverty through Internet, the government needs to improve infrastructure and logistics in rural regions, cultivate IT professionals and provide more information services to help farmers access the web.

Tongyu is not the only place to do so. The Ministry of Finance and the

Ministry of Commerce have announced 200 counties as demonstration bases for rural E-commerce.

In the lead up to China's 2nd National Poverty Relief Day on Oct. 17, the State Council unveiled plans in October to upgrade its Internet infrastructure and the development of its logistics industry in rural areas.

The government decided to allocate more central government funds to building Internet infrastructure and also advocated funding from local governments and social organizations. It plans to invest up to 140 billion yuan by 2020 to provide at least 50,000 villages with Internet access.

By then, about 98 percent of the nation's rural areas will be hooked up to the Internet.

It coincides with another of China's 2020 target to help about 70 million rural residents out of poverty.

China still had 70.17 million people in the countryside living below the country's poverty line of 2,300 yuan in annual income at the end of 2014. If using the new international poverty line of 1.9 U.S. dollars a day as benchmark, the number will see a substantial rise.

October 17 also marks the 23rd International Day for the Eradication of Poverty. In preparation, Beijing will host the Global Poverty Reduction and Development Forum on October 16, during which around 300 worldwide representatives will gather to share their experience in combating poverty.

Many provincial governments, such as Shandong and Gansu, have announced policies to fight poverty with the help of e-commerce, said Qu Tianjun, an official with the State Council Leading Group Office of Poverty Alleviation and Development.

Farming in China has been booming for over three decades. The summer grain output reached a record high of 141.07 million tons in 2015 after 11 consecutive years of increases.

Though harvests were good, inefficient sales channels, a shrinking labor population and lack of access to loans have been squeezing farmers' earnings and dragging down the rural economy.

In 2014, the per capita disposable income of rural residents rose 9.2 percent year on year to 10,489 yuan, less than half of that of urbanites.

The Internet, especially mobile networks, has provided agriculture with a new vision. E-commerce enables farmers to sell goods quickly, conveniently shop around for materials and obtain small loans more easily.

4.4.2 CHINA'S RURAL AREAS TO BENEFIT MORE FROM E-COMMERCE

http://news.xinhuanet.com/english/2015-11/09/c_134798610.htm

Chinese rural areas will benefit from e-commerce as online businesses combine with brick-and-mortar stores in rural areas.

The State Council, China's cabinet, released a guideline in November on development of e-commerce in rural areas until 2020 to promote rural entrepreneurship, expand rural consumption and bring poor rural residents out of poverty.

A rural e-commerce system will feature openness, orderly competition, good faith, security, reliability and environmental protection. An online rural shopping platform will enable rural areas to access e-commerce.

The government will promote Internet technology in agriculture, and use big data analysis to guide production.

Better broadband access and better roads will raise the logistics capacity of rural areas.

In 2014, online retail sales rose 49.7 percent to 2.79 trillion yuan (439 billion U.S. dollars), compared with a 12 percent growth for total retail sales of consumer goods.

4.5 E-BOOKS OVERTAKE PAPER IN CHINA

http://news.xinhuanet.com/english/2015-04/20/c_134167260.htm

Digital media have overtaken books as the most read media in China, according to a national survey released in April.

About 58.1 percent of Chinese adults read digitally in 2014, up 8 percent, while 58 percent read books, only 0.2 percent up, said an annual survey on reading habits polling about 35,500 adults in 29 provincial divisions.

The survey, conducted from September by the Chinese Academy of Press and Publication, revealed that 51.8 percent of the respondents read on their mobile phones while 49.4 percent on ordinary computer and 5.3 percent on e-reader such as a Kindle.

Tablet computers were first listed this year and 9.9 percent of those surveyed used them.

Digital reading has picked up quickly. In 2008, only about 24.5 percent of respondents read digitally. About 22.3 percent of Chinese adults read e-books in 2014, up from 19.2 percent in previous year.

Each person read 3.22 e-books on average, up from 2.48 in 2013, while 4.56 books were read per capita in 2014, slightly down from 4.77 in 2013.

The Chinese also spent much more time on digital reading than traditional. About 55 minutes was spent on reading online and 33.82 minutes on reading on mobile phone each day, compared with 18.76 minutes on books and 18.8 minutes on newspapers.

However, the amount of time Chinese spent on reading books, newspapers and magazines all increased in 2014.

According to the survey, 67.6 percent of Chinese aged between 18 and 39 were engaged in digital reading.

4.5.1 CHINA'S E-BOOK REVENUES SURGE IN EIGHT YEARS

http://news.xinhuanet.com/english/2015-07/15/c_134415689.htm

China's e-book revenues have grown from 150 million yuan (24.5 million U.S. dollars) in 2006 to 4.5 billion yuan in 2014, with an increase of 20.5 percent annually since 2012.

The revenue of digital magazines grew from 500 million yuan in 2006 to 1.43 billion yuan in 2014, said Wei Yushan, head of the the Chinese Academy of Press and Publication (CAPP).

China's digital publishing industry grossed 338.8 billion yuan in 2014, according to Wei.

Another national survey done by the CAPP showed that in 2014, digital reading has become the main type of reading. Of digital readers, more than half were reading on mobile devices.

Sun Shoushan, deputy chief of the State Administration of Press, Publication, Radio, Film and Television, said that favorable state policies, market needs and technological innovation are main reasons for the development of digital reading.

As China promotes its "Internet Plus" strategy, first presented by Premier Li Keqiang in March this year, Sun said that the national plan to promote reading and large online population will continue to boost the industry.

By the end of 2014, China has an online population of 649 million, with 557 million accessing the Internet through a phone or other mobile devices.

Part 5

China to Boost Sustainable Growth in Agriculture

http://news.xinhuanet.com/english/2015-03/20/c_134084800.htm

The State Council has issued a plan to boost sustainable development of agriculture by 2020, said vice minister of agriculture Chen Xiaohua in March.

Speaking at a routine briefing on government policies, Chen said that China's agricultural growth should shift from the extensive mode, which features high resource consumption, heavy input and disregard for the ecological environment, to the intensive mode that emphasizes improving quality and efficiency.

According to the plan, the country will promote scientific and technological advance in agriculture, protect farmland, raise irrigation efficiency, fight environmental pollution and restore agricultural ecology,

It says that China's forest coverage shall exceed 23 percent by 2020.

5.1 CHINA STRIVES FOR ECO-FRIENDLY FARMING

http://news.xinhuanet.com/english/2015-07/25/c_134446328.htm

China will cap fertilizer and pesticide use and better water conservation in the next five years as it pushes for greener agriculture, the Ministry of Agriculture said in July.

By 2020, the utilization rate of irrigation water should rise to 55 percent from the current 52 percent level, and the use of fertilizer and pesticide should be capped, said Agricultural Minister Han Changfu during a working conference held in Chengdu.

He said manure and waste, agricultural films and crop straw resources should be managed properly to achieve eco-friendly farming.

Currently, one cubic meter of water only produces a kilogram of grain harvested in China, lower than the average of 1.2-1.4 kilograms in advanced countries.

China has seen a record summer grain output for 12 straight years this year, but problems including soil acidification and hardening are raising costs while reducing yields.

Official statistics showed that at least 16 percent of China's soil contains more pollutants than national standards allow; less than one third of fertilizers and pesticides are absorbed by crops; less than two thirds of plastic film is recycled; less than half of livestock and poultry waste is processed; and straw burning is still widespread.

5.1.1 CHINA'S FARMLAND WELL ABOVE "RED LINE"

http://news.xinhuanet.com/english/2015-04/22/c_134175085.htm

China is on track to meet its target of having 1.818 billion mu of farmland (121.2 million hectares) by the end of 2015, the Ministry of Land and Resources (MLR) said in April.

China's total area of arable land stood at 2.027 billion mu at the end of 2013, showed the most up-to-date MLS data.

The 2015 "red line" target was set to ensure grain security as accelerating urbanization has threatened to encroach on farmland.

On April 22, the Chinese Academy of Social Sciences forecast that grain production would rise 0.5 percent on an annual basis this year, down from a 0.9-percent rise last year, indicating an increasing challenge for the country to maintain development in agriculture.

The central government allocated 24.59 billion yuan (3.9 billion U.S. dollars) in 2014 to improve the quality of farmland and boost grain production, said the MLR.p China saw an increase in new farmland of 3.83 million mu in 2014, and the amount of land approved for urban construction last year reached 6.06 million mu, down 24.4 percent year on year.

The ministry pledged to continue rigorously protecting farmland and to do more work to curb worsening soil pollution.

5.1.2 CHINA ADJUSTS SUBSIDY POLICY TO HELP FARMERS

http://news.xinhuanet.com/english/2015-05/01/c_134200726.htm

China will improve agricultural subsidy policies in an effort to deepen rural reform, promote agricultural modernization and increase peasants' income, the Ministry of Agriculture (MOA) announced in May.

A total of 14 billion yuan (2.3 billion U.S.dollars) will be given directly to grain farmers. Another 20.4 billion yuan will go to farmers to promote good crop varieties. A total of 23.4 billion yuan will be used to support the appropriate management scale of grain, with a focus on big professional bodies such as family farms and farmer cooperatives.

The ongoing trial program on land use reform announced by the MOA in March, will be adjusted. The number of pilot regions, including the three experimental regions in Jiangsu, Sichuan and Guizhou and 27 counties, will be increased by 9 in Jiangsu and Jiangxi provinces.

There are two kinds of land ownership in China—urban land is owned by the state and rural land is normally under collective ownership.

Farmers are part of the collective community and enjoy land use rights, but with restrictions.

Under the pilot scheme, farmers will be allowed to turn their land-use rights into shares in farming enterprises or cooperative societies.

5.1.3 CHINA TO STRENGTHEN FINANCIAL SUPPORT TO AGRICULTURE

http://news.xinhuanet.com/english/2015-03/03/c_134034477.htm

China's banking regulator in March urged financial institutions nation-wide to channel more financial support to rural areas to help modernize the agriculture sectors.

Chinese commercial banks should increase the number of loans and financial bonds they give to rural regions, the China Banking Regulatory Commission (CBRC) said.

Agricultural infrastructure, including water conservation projects and road construction, in under developed areas will be prioritized.

The China Development Bank should improve services and funding channels, strengthen medium and long-term lending, while the Postal Savings Bank of China should expand its petty loan business, the CBRC said.

Banks will be encouraged to set up branches in rural areas and develop village and town banks. Small loan companies and trust institutions were also urged to make their contribution.

The CBRC also urged to strengthen support of major grain producing areas and help high-tech enterprises with research and development.

The central government issued a top-down central document in February, outlining that the transformation of agricultural development must be accelerated to build a strong and modernized industry.

China feeds more than a fifth of the world's population on only 10 percent of arable land. However, agriculture has been dwarfed by its enormous manufacturing industry.

5.1.3.1 CHINA'S 2014 LOAN FOR AGRICULTURE HITS 23.6 TRLN YUAN

http://news.xinhuanet.com/english/2015-03/25/c_134097176.htm

China's loan for agriculture stood at 23.6 trillion yuan (3.84 trillion U.S. dollars) in 2014, up 13 percent year on year, according to a central bank's report released in March.

The volume took up 28.1 percent of the country's year-round total loans, and its growth rate is 0.7 percentage point higher than the average growth speed of other loans, the People's Bank of China (PBOC) said.

Lu Lei, head of the PBOC's research department, said the two cuts to reserve requirement ratio (RRR) have greatly boosted development in rural areas.

The RRR was cut twice last year for banks engaged in lending to agriculture, by 2 percentage points in April and 0.5 percentage points in June.

The central bank will encourage commercial banks to provide more credit to small businesses without a sharp expansion in total loan volume.

Lu said supporting rural finance should include payment and settlement networks, rural bank cards, property records and mobile connectivity.

"One of the major problems is lack of information and Internet,necessary in developing modern agriculture," Lu said.

More institutions and companies are expanding their coverage to achieve mobile transactions without banks or ATMs, he said.

"Fewer outlets cut costs for both institutions and customers." Lu explained. "This will boost Internet finance."

He said there is no conflict between traditional financial institutions and Internet enterprises.

5.1.4 XINJIANG CIVIL SERVANTS BOOST RURAL DEVELOPMENT

http://news.xinhuanet.com/english/2015-07/07/c_134389792.htm

Su Guoping was working for days to help farmers divert water from wells to parched fields in Kumkuduk, a village on the edge of the Taklimakan Desert in northwest China's Xinjiang Uygur Autonomous Region.

One of the officials dispatched to Xinjiang's rural areas to help improve the livelihood of local residents, Su mixed his sweat among farmers and village officials to get the task done.

"Water shortage can affect this year's harvest. There is no time to delay. We must help the farmers," said Su, deputy director of Xinjiang Economic and Information Commission.

Su lives in Urumqi, capital of Xinjiang, before joining a program that began in March last year to send 200,000 civil servants to live and work at over 8,000 villages, 700 state farms and pastures, and 1,000 communities in the vast region for a one-year term over the course of three years.

He and eight more peers became neighbors with Uygur villagers in Kumkuduk, trying to understand what the villagers need and then give assistance.

Su said working in rural villages is a good way for cadres to accumulate grassroots experience and help improve the life quality of the local residents, though it's not always easy.

Emer Abla said the fields in his village have had an acute lack of water after the wells dried up a few years ago. Su and his colleagues turned to construction workers and local electric power department for help. With the help, a new well was built and irrigation ditches built, bringing water to the otherwise barren fields.

At the beginning, villagers were reluctant to trust the newcomers. An elderly man named Musataji turned a cold shoulder on Su multiple times when he tried to talk with Musataji.

"He was not willing to tell us his troubles, as he thought it was useless and may result in troubles," Su said.

Su then changed their working methods and started to have talks with the farmers in the fields and help them clean yards and roads.

"These cadres are modest, hardworking, and hardy. We are like brothers," said Dawut, head of Kumkuduk Village.

Now, more and more villagers are willing to turn to these officials for help. "The rural life has also provided an opportunity for us to understand grassroots living conditions and their demands," Su said.

Civil servants sent to the rural areas are expected to help local residents solve problems and improve their living conditions. The three-year-long campaign aims at enhancing the relationships among different nationalities while improving the cadres' abilities and cultivating good virtues, according to Pu Shiyu, deputy director of the organization department of the regional committee of the Communist Party of China.

The cadres also help farmers and herdsmen increase income, maintain social stability and promote religious harmony during their rural experience, Pu said.

With their expertise, Su Guoping and his colleagues have helped the villagers obtaining financial aids to raise sheep, and to open a textile mill and a clothing plant.

So far, the first batch of the designated civil servants, including 262 provincial level officials, have finished their service in the rural areas.

5.2 CHINA TO CURB FARM POLLUTION

http://news.xinhuanet.com/english/2015-04/14/c_134150522.htm

The Ministry of Agriculture urged in April farmers to do more to address water and soil pollution.

Annual water consumption in agricultural irrigation should not exceed 372 billion cubic meters by 2020, said Zhang Taolin, vice minister of agriculture, at a press conference held at the State Council Information Office.

Currently, one cubic meter of water is needed for every kilogram of grain harvested in China, lower than the average of 1.2-1.4 kilograms in advanced countries, Zhang said.

Zhang urged farmers to reduce the use of chemical fertilizers and pesticides by limiting waste and switching to organic alternatives.

Chemical fertilizer use hit 59 million tons in 2013, up 5.2 percent on average when compared with the past three decades, according to earlier reports.

Pesticide consumption should be cut to 300,000 tons, from the current 320,000 tons, said Zhang.

Fecal residue and waste, agricultural films and crop straw resources should be managed properly, he added.

5.2.1 CHINA CAPS FERTILIZER, PESTICIDE USE

http://news.xinhuanet.com/english/2015-07/24/c_134444571.htm

Fertilizers and pesticides have done so much damage to China's ecosystem and brought an array of food safety issues that their use is to be capped from 2020.

China feeds its huge population with very limited agricultural resources.

Annual grain output has grown for 11 straight years, but achievements have come at great cost. The target is part of the national drive for efficient, eco-friendly farming.

BALANCING ACT

The northeastern province of Heilongjiang produces about one tenth of China's grain but acute problems including soil acidification and hardening are raising costs while reducing yields. Farmers blame overuse of fertilizers and pesticides but face the dilemma that cutting down on chemicals will cause an even sharper fall in yields.

According to the Ministry of Agriculture, at least 16 percent of China's soil contains more pollutants than national standards allow; less than one third of fertilizers and pesticides are absorbed by crops; less than two thirds of plastic film is recycled; less than half of livestock and poultry waste is processed; and straw burning is still widespread. This all adds up to an agronomic nightmare and an environmental situation staggering from bad to worse.

The ministry is also concerned about desertification, water resources, industrial contamination, and maintain sufficient arable land.

The State Council, China's cabinet, announced in July plans to improve low-yield farmland and increase irrigation. Less water must be used in agriculture and treatment of sewage and waste must improve. Fertilizers and pesticides are just a small part of a big problem.

BIGGER IS BETTER

Much of China's agricultural production comes from small farmers or groups of small farmers working communal land. Large, well established agricultural concerns are seen as one way of boosting food production and processing. Better use of technology, another feature of large commercial endeavors, is another prerequisite to better efficiency.

The development pattern of agriculture in developed countries focused first on yields before any thought was given to environmental protection,and China is now heading down that same path. Natural resources are limited and moderate economies of scale can cut the cost of management and reduce fertilizers and pesticides, according to Li Guoxiang, a researcher with the rural development institute under the Chinese Academy of Social Sciences.

A sustainable development plan released by the ministry this May is a general guideline for the agricultural development over the next 15 years. By 2030, resources should be used more efficiently and frugally and the natural environment in agricultural regions should be sound, with yields stable.

DUCKING THE ISSUE

Since the beginning of this year, China has been experimenting with self-sufficiency by combining crops with livestock in some northern regions.

According to Li Guoxiang, planting feed instead of grain has proved a great success in Inner Mongolia, where farmers started to cultivate alfalfa and corn to feed livestock. Subsidies and technological assistance be in place to motivate local government officials and farmers.

Instead of using fertilizer and pesticide, a company in Heilongjiang has experimented with raising ducks in rice paddies. The ducks eat weeds and pests while stimulating the growth of rice as they swim. The ducks' droppings are also an organic fertilizer that provides everything rice needs.

This "duck rice" has been a limited success on the market with a sale price of 60 to 80 yuan (13 U.S. dollars) per kilo, ten times the price of rice grown with fertilizers and pesticides.

5.2.2 MAPS REVEAL EXTENT OF CHINA'S ANTIBIOTICS POLLUTION

http://news.xinhuanet.com/english/2015-07/14/c_134411007.htm

Farmer Lao Liao keeps more than 2,000 pigs in south China's Guangdong Province, but he worries about the cost of keeping them healthy.

It's not just the economic cost, but price paid by the environment.

"It worries me giving the pigs so many veterinary drugs to prevent them from getting ill," says Liao.

His worry is reflected in a series of maps drawn by scientists, which have also sparked concern among the wider public.

New research by scientists at the Guangzhou Institute of Geochemistry of the Chinese Academy of Sciences (CAS) shows that China consumed 162,000 tons of antibiotics in 2013, or more than half of the global total. About 52 percent was used on livestock and 48 percent by humans. More than 50,000 tons ended up in the water and soil.

Based on the data of antibiotics usage and emissions along 58 major river basins in China, scientists drew a series of maps showing antibiotic pollution. They were recently published in the academic journal, Environmental Science & Technology.

The maps show that developed provinces such as Guangdong, Jiangsu, Zhejiang and Hebei are seriously polluted. The antibiotics emissions concentration in the densely populated east China is six times that in west China.

The average in Chinese rivers is about 303 nanograms per liter, compared with 9 nanograms per liter in Italy, 120 nanograms per liter in the United States, and 20 nanograms per liter in Germany.

"China lacks supervision on the use of antibiotics, with insufficient information about usage and emissions into the environment," says Ying Guangguo, a lead scientist on the study.

The research, which is aimed at gathering comprehensive data on antibiotics usage and emissions, has lasted for 10 years, focusing on 36 frequently used antibiotics types, Ying says.

The antibiotics in the environment mainly come from sewage, medical wastewater, animal husbandry and aquaculture wastewater, experts say.

"During the research, we found that some pig farms, especially large-scale farms with more than 10,000 pigs, add more than a dozen antibiotics in the fodder and water. It's really horrible," Ying says.

5.2.3 WASHING AWAY SOIL EROSION WORRIES

http://news.xinhuanet.com/english/2015-05/12/c_134232818.htm

Thirty-eight years ago, torrential rain swept masses of soil and sand from the bare hills above Lan Linjin's new house, destroying the building and throwing his family into destitution.

It was a common tragedy in Changting, a southeastern Chinese county known for its severe soil erosion, but it prompted the then 15-year-old Lan, whose heart-broken father died soon after, to make a vow to fill the barren hills with trees and stop the terror of flooding.

Lan is pushing towards meeting that pledge. Even after he lost both hands and his left eye in a quarry explosion, Lan has managed to plant over 100,000 tea-oil trees on the once-barren hill Hongqiling since 2010.

He is one of the tens of thousands of farmers in Fujian Province's Changting who are rescuing one of China's most erosive regions from the grip of natural disasters.

After much success in the past few decades, they are now eyeing an upcoming survey which will tell how far they have come. According to research by remote-sensing satellite technology in 1985, the amount of land suffering soil erosion in Chanting at that time amounted to 97,467 hectares, or 31.5 percent of the county.

When the survey was repeated in 2012, Changting's soil-eroded areas had dropped 70 percent to 30,000 hectares, while forest coverage had increased by 19.6 percent. The next remote-sensing survey is due in October.

ROOTING FOR CHANGE

Experts predict it may take decades to find a cure for the pollution and environmental degradation China faces. However, Changting's story suggests this can be accelerated—with government support, and also the entrepreneurial spirit that Chinese authorities have lately been so keen to encourage.

The trees on Hongqiling contribute to water and soil retention. Lan, who is studying e-commerce, sees vast business potential in them as well. "In a few years, these trees will yield tea oil worth more than 2 million yuan (322,000 U.S. dollars) a year," he says.

This picture of security and profits is a far cry from the recent past. Changting sits in a region of red soil, susceptible to erosion due to poor water retention. The problems began about 200 years ago as a result of deforestation, and by the 1940s, Changting was one of the worst counties in China for soil erosion.

In 1940, the ruling Kuomintang government set up China's first pilot zone conserving soil fertility in Changting's Hetian Town, but researchers then were pessimistic.

"The mountains and hills all glow blood-red. Trees are a rare sight!" they wrote in a report, predicting that soil erosion was unstoppable and would reduce Hetian to ruins within decades.

That this prediction has proved wrong is largely a result of locals' hard work tending the soil since the founding of the People's Republic of China in 1949. It has come at a heavy cost though—the barren mountains and frequent floods have been blamed for grinding poverty in the county.

Rays of hope appeared in 2000, when the provincial government led by Xi Jinping, now the Chinese president, approved an annual fund of 10 million yuan to aid Changting's soil erosion control.

"That was a fortune for an impoverished county like Changting," says Lin Yufeng, director of the county's water and soil conservation bureau.

"It elevated our cause to an unprecedented level."

In the same year, the county government severely restricted building and farming developments in the mountains to prioritize afforestation.

"The biggest challenge was to persuade villagers to abandon the habit of burning wood or grass for fuel. So we subsidized their use of coal and marsh gas," Lin says.

Now the fuel subsidies, surpassing 14 million yuan a year, are mainly spent on electricity. For every kilowatt they use, locals are refunded 0.2 yuan, about one third of the market price.

Changting residents have also adapted the traditional afforestation pattern to suit local conditions. With the land too barren to accept trees straight away, planting in Changting usually starts with grass, which takes root easily, then bushes and then trees like Masson's pines.

In Luodi Village of Hetian, where such "backward planting" experiments have been conducted since the 1980s, the red hills are now covered in Masson's pines.

"The river used to rise and turn muddy the moment the rain fell," says 65-year-old villager Liu Ronggao. "Now, thanks to the forests, it only rises after a few hours of rain and the water remains clear."

The afforestation has also alleviated water shortages. Nearly all local households dig wells and have access to good-quality groundwater.

While there has been much progress, there is still room for improvement in the afforestation drive. Experts and local officials are far from satisfied with the fact that coniferous trees, mainly Masson's pines, make up about 80 percent of the 247,000 hectares of woodland in the county.

"Masson's pines are easy to grow but inefficient in retaining water and soil," says Wu Chenghuo, director of the county's forestry bureau. "Broadleaf species are much better in this regard."

Through government-sponsored projects, broadleaf trees such as maple, soapberry, tung and cherry have been introduced into existing coniferous forests since 2011. Wu says they will eventually replace coniferous trees to create an ideal eco-system.

BUDDING BUSINESS SENSE

In addition to the government's ecological campaign, farmers' economic motivation has played an equally important role in treating soil erosion.

Huang Jinyang, a 62-year-old farmer in Sanzhou Town, was one of the first in his village to plant red bayberry, believing the plant can both reduce soil and water loss and increase income.

Inspired by his success, Sanzhou farmers have planted red bayberry on over 800 hectares of the hills since the 1990s, growing it into a lucrative industry.

Lin Muhong, 66, came back to his home village of Hongdu to grow tea-oil trees after retiring as a doctor in 2009. He invested more than 16 million yuan after selling his house and borrowing from friends and relatives.

Lin also started a pig farm that has produced manure to fertilize the hills. "There used to be little grass; now we have to get overgrown weeds cut," he says.

The improved ecosystem also brought back young natives who used to flee their poor hometowns to work or study in cities.

Lan, Lin and Huang have all seen their children return home to help with family business or start their own. Better educated and more ambitious, the young generation have introduced new ideas in the forests, including medicinal herb cultivation, eco-tourism and e-commerce.

Lin says of the remote-sensing survey due in October that "the figures will certainly look better."

However, Changting still has 250,000 hectares of untreated land, including 5,000 hectares that are categorized as highly erosive, and the forests need constant maintenance.

"There's no end to soil erosion control," says county head Li Shanchang. "We're always half way up the mountain."

And medical abuse of antibiotics is also common. Prescription of antibiotics in China's large hospitals is basically well controlled, but medium-sized and small hospitals and the animal husbandry industry lack supervision, Ying says.

Some doctors depend on antibiotics as an immediate remedy, and hospitals encourage doctors to use them because their sale brings more profit.

"Antibiotics can cause drug-resistance in the human body and the ecological system. The use of antibiotics must be strictly controlled," Ying says.

The research will provide data and theoretical support for government regulation of antibiotics use and pollution, says Ying.

The per-capita antibiotics use in China is five to eight times that of Western countries, the research shows.

"Although the residual antibiotics in the environment will not directly harm people, the real danger is intensified bacterial resistance," Ying says.

Experts say the emergence of "superbacteria" and "multi-drug resistant bacteria" is a result of antibiotic pollution, killing microflora in the environment.

Li Lanjuan, an infectious diseases expert at the 1st Hospital Affiliated to the Zhejiang University and an academician of the Chinese Academy of Engineering, says China is on the verge of extensive drug resistance. This would lead to a greater risk of surgical infection, even in routine operations such as cesareans and hip replacements.

Children are the most vulnerable. Shanghai Fudan University tested more than 1,000 children aged 8 to 11 in Shanghai, and Jiangsu and

Zhejiang provincecs in April, and found that almost 60 percent of urine samples contained antibiotics.

About a quarter of the samples contained two or more antibiotics. Some showed as many as six kinds of antibiotics. The tests also found three kinds of antibiotics normally only used on livestock and poultry in the samples.

Antibiotic resistance is recognized as a major threat to public heath everywhere in the world, and urgent actions are needed, the World Health Organization (WHO) warned in a statement released in June.

"This limits our ability to treat infectious diseases and contributes to the deaths of hundreds of thousands of people globally every year caused by diseases that were easily treatable before," the WHO statement says.

5.3 PRODUCERS HOPE POTATOES TAKES ROOT IN CHINA

http://news.xinhuanet.com/english/2015-07/29/c_134460371.htm

Potatoes seem like an unlikely ingredient for ice cream, but the allure of tasting the strange concoction had dozens of visitors lining-up at the China Kitchen exhibition at the 2015 World Potato Congress in Beijing.

The 1,000-square-meter stall was serving up to 100 potato-based foods, from noodles to sweet purple drinks, developed by Xisen Potato Industry Co. Ltd., the country's biggest potato producer. By combining potatoes with traditional Chinese cuisine, the company is at the congress looking for partners to promote their new products being tested at the China Kitchen.

With China promoting potato acreage and encouraging the vegetable as one of the country's staple foods, more companies like Xisen want to take a bigger slice of the growing market.

Around 500 km away from Beijing, Linkage Potato Co. Ltd., based in Inner Mongolia, China's major potato production base, is expanding its product portfolio to satisfy people's appetite.

With five farms and a 70,000-mu (around 4,667 hectares) high standard planting base, the company produces potatoes and seeds and processes potato flakes.

Yan Hongxin, vice president of Linkage, told Xinhua that the company will set up a new production line in autumn to increase its annual output of potato flakes from current 3,000 tons to 15,000 tons.

In addition, they are eyeing the frozen French fry market as domestic demand grows, driven by expanding fast food chains.

In March this year, it has established a joint venture with Farm Frites, a Dutch enterprise with over 40 years experiences in potato processing, in Wudan Town, Chifeng City in Inner Mongolia.

The new production line will have a capacity of 70,000 tons frozen French fries annually with consumption of 140,000 tons of fresh potatoes. The fries will be put into the market by 2017 and expansion will continue after that, Yan said.

NO SMALL POTATO

His confidence in the domestic potato market is justifiable.

China is the largest potato producer in the world with a planting area of 5.5 million hectares. However, average Chinese consumption of potatoes is 41.2 kilograms, far below the consumption level of European and American countries, data from China's Ministry of Agriculture showed.

"Its nutritious value is often overlooked," said Bi Yang, professor of Gansu Agricultural University.

He pointed out that an average-size potato contains as much protein as an egg, and 10 times more vitamin C than an apple.

With the country's gross domestic product (GDP) per person surpassed 7,000 U.S. dollars last year, people's need for improving food nutrition patterns has grown. Bi said potato is a good option to improve nutrition.

In addition, potato is more resistant to the cold and the drought compared with wheat and rice. China is boosting its acreage to make potato as one of the country's staple foods to better ensure its food security under the pressure of less farmland, water, labor and chemicals.

After years of research, steamed buns made from potato flake made their debut in more than 200 supermarkets in Beijing last month, one step closer to make it a centerpiece of people's dining table.

LONG WAY TO GO

Seed quality, production cost and eating habits all pose a challenge for potato companies.

Kiremko, a food processing equipment company from the Netherlands, has cooperated with 15 Chinese potato companies for over 30 years.

Joost Miltenburg, area sales manager of Kiremko, said two kilograms of European potato can make one kilogram of French fries with the company's processing equipment, but some Chinese potatoes fail to produce the same amount of French fries owing to poor quality.

He sees a lot of potential in China but also a lot of waste in potato storage and transportation, inefficient planting and irrigation.

Companies are also seeking ways to lower cost. The potato yield per hectare is 16 tons in China, while the number is around 50 tons in developed countries, making potato flakes three times more expensive than wheat flour, said Lu Xiaoping, director of International Potato Center's branch in Asia and the Pacific area.

"Only by establishing a high-tech breeding base and producing in a mechanized way can we guarantee high-quality seeds," said Liang Xisen, chairman of Xisen Potato Industry Co. Ltd.

But the most difficult problem facing potato companies is to change Chinese people's long-standing diet habits and give potatoes similar role as rice and wheat.

Miltenburg said Chinese potato noodles and steamed buns are new for him. Although it takes time to change people's habit, he believes that providing more choices can earn potato fans sooner or later.

Part 6

China Vows to Promote Low Carbon Urban Development

http://news.xinhuanet.com/english/2015-06/15/c_134328231.htm

China will continue to promote green and low carbon development in urban areas to achieve efficient and high quality growth, the country's top economic planner said in June.

"China will push forward energy-saving and environment-friendly urban development to provide citizens with a sustainable living environment," said Zhang Yong, deputy head of the National Development and Reform Commission (NDRC), during National Low-carbon Day on June 15.

Acknowledging the previous economic growth came at the expense of environmental destruction, Zhang said China has been making concrete contributions to address climate change and prioritizing green, low-carbon economic development. China's energy consumption and carbon dioxide emissions per unit of gross domestic product dropped 29.9 percent and 33.8 percent respectively in 2014 compared to the levels in 2005.

In a joint statement issued during a visit by U.S. President Barack Obama to Beijing in November last year, China pledged to achieve peak carbon dioxide emissions around 2030, and increase the share of non-fossil fuels in primary energy consumption to around 20 percent by 2030.

The introduction of the National Low-carbon Day beginning in 2013 is aimed at promoting awareness about climate change and low-carbon development policies, encouraging public participation and facilitating the country's commitment to reduce greenhouse gas emissions.

National Low-carbon Day falls on the third day of the National Energy Efficiency Promotion Week in June every year.

6.1 GROWTH IN FARMER-TURNED-LABORERS SLOWS

http://news.xinhuanet.com/english/2015-02/28/c_134027073.htm

Growth in the number of former farmers pursuing non-agricultural work has slowed as more people are reluctant to leave their hometowns, official data showed.

China had 274 million farmer-turned-laborers as of the end of 2014, and 168 million of them had moved to cities to seek work, according to data released in February by the Ministry of Human Resources and Social Security (MHRSS).

However, growth in the number of total non-agricultural workers and migrant workers slowed to 1.9 percent and 1.3 percent respectively in 2014, from 2.4 percent and 1.7 percent the previous year.

China has the world's largest population of farmers.

But their willingness to grow crops has waned as returns from the land are typically much smaller than those from working in cities, posing threats to the country's food security. The trend is slowing, however, thanks to the government's efforts to boost agricultural production.

The number of new workers coming from rural areas has been shrinking since 2011, said Vice Minister Yang Zhiming.

The annual increase of workers' wages has also slowed down. Monthly salaries of migrant workers increased less than 10 percent to 2,864 yuan (around 470 U.S. dollars) in 2014, down from 13.9 percent registered in 2013 and much lower than the 20-percent increase five years ago.

SKILLED WORKERS NEEDED

Despite a growing population rushing to cities, experienced laborers are still badly needed in China, which is trying to move up the global value chain by stimulating high-tech sectors with high value added.

The majority of migrant workers in China lack skills — only one third of workers have received training before employment. Workers that can be counted as having expertise in their field accounted for 19 percent of all those employed nationwide, while highly-skilled talent made up merely 5 percent, the MHRSS data showed.

Chinese factories have started to meet trouble in finding qualified workers, while former farmers are familiar with the experience of being turned for jobs on the grounds that they lack skills.

The structural contradiction has become a normal state, Yang said.

The problem has emerged as a hurdle to industrial upgrading in China, which is mulling measures to reverse the situation.

The country plans to launch a mass training program to train 20 million migrant workers each year, according to Yang. "As of 2020, all young migrant workers will be able to learn a trade with subsidies from the government," he said.

Measures including tax reduction will also be maintained to support companies in the tertiary sector, small and medium-sized enterprises and labor-intensive factories, usually generous employers of workers from the countryside.

In addition, seasoned migrant workers will be encouraged to return to their hometown and set up their own businesses, Yang said, estimating the size of this group at two million currently.

6.2 BEIJING TO SHIFT CITY ADMIN TO EASE "URBAN ILLS"

http://news.xinhuanet.com/english/2015-07/13/c_134408425.htm

Beijing will move some of its city administration out of the city center to the eastern suburbs as part of the capital's contribution to the national Beijing-Tianjin-Hebei integrated development plan, it was officially announced over the weekend.

The decision to build a new municipal subsidiary administrative center in Tongzhou, about 40 minutes drive from the city center, is one of several moves to ease "urban ills" and follow through on the regional development plan.

While the move has long been anticipated, it was officially announced at a meeting of the Communist Party of China (CPC) Beijing Municipal Committee in July.

"Remarkable progress" will be made on the center in Tongzhou by 2017, a statement from the meeting said.

GOOD START BUT NOT ENOUGH

Hu Gang, head of the South China Urban Planning Institute under the Urban Planning Society of China, said the decision is a good beginning.

"After a subsidiary administrative center is established, state-owned enterprises and public services will move out as well," he said, adding it can help set a good example for regional development in other areas.

The population explosion in Beijing during the urbanization drive has led to a host of problems, including traffic congestion and air pollution. The city is now trying to readjust its population growth, aiming to move 15 percent of its population out of the city center and keep the total population below 23 million by 2020.

However, simply moving government functions is not enough to address the city's bigger problems.

"Administrative and residential regulations are far from enough," said Liu Zhiyan, a research fellow with the Institute for Urban and Environmental Studies in the Chinese Academy of Social Sciences.

"Only after concerns for public services, such as education and medical care, are addressed in these areas, will be people be willing to move out [of the city center]," he said.

Lin Xiaohui, 38, who is employed with a foreign company and moved to an apartment in Tongzhou in 2010, said that so far, such services are lacking.

"Medical services here are really poor," she said.

Lin recently went to a hospital to get vaccinated after being scratched by a cat. "Later I learned that the vaccine they gave me is not proper at all," she said.

AVOID REPETITION OF URBAN ILLS

But Lin is most worried about the traffic, which is already bad in the east of Beijing. Commuting from Tongzhou normally takes around two hours, she said.

"At its worst, the traffic stops for half an hour without moving," she said. "Will the traffic get worse in the future?"

If all goes according to plan, the latest move could help avoid such woes in the future, according to Zhao Hong, vice president of the Beijing Municipal Academy of Social Sciences.

Over the past few decades, the Beijing expansion model has focused on developing urban sprawl from the city center outward. But with the rapid growth of the city, this model is no longer effective due to overcrowding.

"The construction of the subsidiary administrative center should avoid the previous expansion model to prevent the repetition of urban problems," he said.

Another concern is housing prices.

As more people move into Tongzhou, the cost of living there is also increasing.

Statistics from the Tongzhou district government showed the number of permanent residents grew from 880,000 in 2005 to 1.3 million at the end of 2013. The annual increase rate was 6.23 percent, higher than Beijing's average of 4.69 percent.

A salesman with a real estate agent in Tongzhou told Xinhua that housing prices have been rising in Tongzhou since late April.

The price of some apartment buildings has increased by 2,000 yuan or more per square meter, forcing groups of people to purchase apartments before the prices rise too high, he said.

The construction of a new city administration center in Tongzhou is expected to further increase the price of real estate.

"This is very good news for us," said the salesman.

VANGUARD OF INTEGRATED DEVELOPMENT

The move is also designed to benefit Tongzhou's neighboring areas in Hebei Province and Tianjin Municipality.

Currently, more than 200,000 people live in Yanjiao, Hebei, but work in Beijing.

Tongzhou's development could be a pioneering step in the national plan for coordinated development between Beijing, Tianjin and Hebei, helping create long-term urban planning solutions, Zhao said.

If development in Tongzhou goes well, it can absorb a portion of the commuting population from Hebei and help reduce pressure on Beijing's city center.

A guideline for coordinated development of the Beijing-Tianjin-Hebei region was approved by the Political Bureau of the CPC Central Committee in late April.

The primary goal for the project, which has not been made public yet, stresses adjustment of the economic structure to create new growth sectors and control Beijing's population.

Traffic infrastructure, environmental protection and industrial upgrading are the top priorities as Beijing looks to move some industries to Hebei.

In July, an intercity rail line linking Beijing with Jixian county in Tianjin started operation, following the start of passenger trains between the capital and Yanjiao in Hebei in January.

More intercity rails between Beijing and areas nearby are under construction.

In the past two years, air quality in the region has seen improvement with the joint treatment efforts of Beijing, Tianjin and Hebei as well as nearby provinces.

6.3 EMBRACING GREEN CONSTRUCTION ON A LOCAL LEVEL

http://news.xinhuanet.com/english/2015-03/28/c_134105226.htm

Green construction has been widely recognized in China as an important step toward energy efficiency amid efforts to fight pollution, but the concept does not always translate to the Chinese market.

The concept of "green construction" was first introduced to China in 2000 as an efficient way to reserve resources, protect the environment and cut pollution.

Green construction incorporates design, building, and operation practices that use sustainable materials in construction, achieve energy efficiency, save water, and improve indoor air quality, among other measurable targets.

According to the guidelines on raw material industry transformation and development in 2015 published by the Ministry of Industry and Information Technology (MIIT), the country will set up a green building material service platform, establish an industry development alliance, refine downstream industry as well as advance polymer materials' utilization in rail traffic and high-end equipment areas.

However, blind imitation of foreign techniques and real estate developers' unwillingness to promote green construction by sacrificing their profits have become major obstacles as the country to adopts the idea.

"The government has been promoting green construction by offering subsidies for real estate developers, but we worry that most developers do not use the subsidies in the right way," said Ye Qing, CEO of Shenzhen Institute of Building Research Co. Ltd.

"The subsidies should be used to hire professionals from the industry to publicize the green construction concept in those under developed areas," Ye added.

In April 2006, China became one of the few countries in the world to establish their own green construction standards. Ye suggests building another set of standards from the people's perspective to educate people about the standards using big data.

"The purpose of the second standard is to force real estate developers to promote green construction under the supervision of both the government and the general public," Ye said.

Using complicated and expensive high-tech materials to build green is another mistake that China is now making, according to Lin Wusheng, technology director of green technology research and application center of China Merchants Property Development Co. Ltd.

"The development of green construction should be based on our actual conditions, pure imitation of foreign developed countries' experiences might cost us more," said Lin. "Green construction means to control energy and resource consumption in the very details of the building rather than using expensive green technology and materials."

Offering an example, Lin introduced a window shade that was installed in every conference room at the headquarter building of China Merchants Property Development Co. Ltd.

"Without the window shade, only one third of rooms can be covered in sunlight. A low-cost window shade will make every corner of the room bright," Lin said. "This is a good example of how we should approach green construction in our own way."

6.4 MORE THAN 97% OF CHINA'S HOUSEHOLD GARBAGE TREATED PROPERLY

http://news.xinhuanet.com/english/2015-03/06/c_134044480.htm

More than 97 percent of China's household garbage was disposed of properly last year, according to a report released in March.

The 2014 report on the impact of solid waste on the environment in large and medium-sized Chinese cities was released by the Ministry of Environmental Protection.

The first-ever report said that China produced 161 million tons of household garbage and nearly 2.4 billion tons of industrial solid waste in major cities.

Shanghai produced more household garbage than any other city last year, according to the report.

Industrial solid waste was mainly produced in northern China, with Hebei and Shanxi provinces as well as Inner Mongolia Autonomous Region being the top three industrial waste producers, it said.

6.5 INDUSTRIAL CITY FACES POLLUTION CONTROL CONUNDRUM

http://news.xinhuanet.com/english/2015-07/09/c_134398256.htm

China's Ministry of Environmental Protection has downplayed a controversy revolving around pollution control measures in an industrial city in eastern China, saying the forceful measures were legal and affordable to the local economy.

According to a report published by China Environment News, a newspaper run by the ministry, air quality at Linyi, a coastal city in east China's Shandong Province, has improved greatly thanks to a series of measures since late last year, including suspending production at dozens of steel mills and other factories.

Though the measures have gained support among the public, they have also met opposition by some who say the steel sector, which employs more than 100,000 people locally, was badly scathed.

The report cited an inspection team from the ministry as saying that pollution control in the city was not "shock therapy," or a sudden change in economic policy, as alleged in a previous report by Southern Weekly. Rather, the measures are legitimate and valid as the suspended factories were given ample time to prepare.

Some steel mills were only suspended after they failed to rectify illegal waste discharge activities, it noted.

Instead of simply shutting down energy-intensive factories, the measures also helped transform the economic structure locally, it said, adding fiscal revenue and other financial indicators for the city had not changed significantly because of the factory closures.

The measures came after the ministry summoned the city's leaders in March, urging them to strengthen inspections and impose severe penalties on polluters. A new environmental law, which went into effect on Jan. 1, also gives the environmental watchdog more power to manage

GDP-obsessed officials.

The pollution control conundrum at Linyi revealed another challenge in China's war on pollution, in which local government leaders have to put up with more economic loss if they want to curb pollution.

The Linyi government has ordered 412 factories to rectify their practices, including 29 that will be relocated.

Case Study

CHINA EYES INFRASTRUCTURE PROJECTS TO RELIEVE POVERTY, POWER ECONOMY
http://news.xinhuanet.com/english/2015-10/14/c_134713949.htm

The land surrounding Qicun, a small township in north China's Hebei Province, used to be infertile and barren. Now, the once-bare hills shimmer with farms that require no water.

Thousands of solar panels laid by local workers, who joke they are "planting the sun", are offering a ray of hope for the region's impoverished farmers who see it as a ticket to prosperity.

Qicun remained one of the country's least developed regions for years, with villagers completely unaware of the huge untapped resource all around them — 2,599 hours of sunshine a year.

It wasn't until state-owned China Three Gorges Corp., a new energy conglomerate, stepped in three years ago that they began to see the region's potential.

The company rented land from residents and employed local workers to erect photovoltaic (PV) installations. Li Jinru, a villager, said he was paid 120 yuan (nearly 20 U.S. dollars) per day during construction and 80 yuan for equipment maintenance after the PV power plant began operation.

Li is not the only one who benefitted from the project, which is already China's largest PV power station in mountainous areas with installed capacity totaling 99 megawatt. It created 7,000 jobs in the township and, more importantly, brought hope for prosperity to the remote area.

The project was only one small step in the government's plan to combat national poverty, currently in focus as the country prepares to celebrate its second National Poverty Relief Day on Oct. 17, also the date for the 23rd International Day for the Eradication of Poverty.

Hong Tianyun, deputy director of the State Council Leading Group Office of Poverty Alleviation and Development of China, said poverty relief will remain a top priority for China in the next five years at a press conference.

Hong said the government will carry out more effective and targeted measures to enrich a total of 70.17 million people in the countryside living below the country's poverty line of 2,300 yuan, including launching education campaigns, encouraging financial support and building public platforms to mobilize more people to join the fight.

China's anti-poverty funds from central authorities maintained 18.1 percent of annual growth from 2011 to 2014. In 2015, China further increased the budget to 46.75 billion yuan.

Qicun's story illuminated a previously overlooked path for more effective poverty relief amid a lingering economic slowdown—promoting major construction projects in rural areas which will improve living environment, boost employment and power regional growth.

As a result, the government has accelerated infrastructure, irrigation work and energy projects in poverty-stricken regions.

Northwest China's Gansu Province is engaged in a 7.45-billion-yuan water diversion project that will channel clean water to more than 2.5 million people plagued by drought. Jiao Yong, vice minister of water resources, said the government has planned 172 water conservation projects nationwide with 27 scheduled to break ground this year.

"Those projects have a huge demand for labor, equipment and raw materials and will significantly drive upstream and downstream industries," Jiao said.

Transportation projects are another driver for poverty alleviation. China Railway Corporation, a state-owned railway operator and contractor, invested 265.13 billion yuan in railway construction during the first half of the year, up 12.7 percent from a year ago, with projects in central and western China prioritized.

China has made remarkable progress in poverty relief. It was the first developing country to meet the Millennium Development Goals target of reducing the population living in poverty by half ahead of the 2015 deadline.

In the past 15 years, China has lifted more than 600 million people out of poverty, accounting for about 70 percent of those brought out of poverty worldwide.

Part 7

China's Ecological Footprint Expected to Peak in 2029: Report

http://news.xinhuanet.com/english/2015-08/28/c_134566489.htm

The average ecological footprint per capita in China is expected to peak at 2.9 global hectares in 2029 amid fast-paced urbanization, according to a report released in August.

The report, released by the Beijing branch of the World Wide Fund for Nature (WWF), noted the ecological footprint could reach its peak three years early if the country adopts a green development path, potentially lowering it to 2.7 global hectares per capita.

An ecological footprint measures the amount of resources humans use and the waste they generate. It is used to gauge whether they are outpacing what their local ecological system can provide.

A global hectare is a standardized hectare of land able to produce resources and absorb waste at world average levels.

China is experiencing the fastest urbanization in the world, with 54.77 percent of its 1.3 billion people living in urban areas in 2014, according to the report.

Consumption by urban residents accounted for more than 80 percent of the national total last year, compared to 40 percent in 1980, it said. The per capita ecological footprint of urban residents is 1.4 to 2.5 times higher than that of rural residents.

The WWF's Living Planet Report 2014 said the ecological footprint was continuing its upward climb and that humanity's demand on the planet is more than 50 percent larger than what nature can renew.

Seeking sustainable urbanization by promoting development of green industries, green production, green consumption and investment could be a better choice for China's development, said Li Lin, executive director of programs with WWF China.

The report was jointly compiled by the WWF and the Institute of Scientific and Technical Information of China.

7.1 CHINA TO STOP COMMERCIAL LOGGING OF NATURAL FORESTS IN KEY ZONES BY 2020

http://news.xinhuanet.com/english/2015-03/18/c_134077570.htm

Commercial logging of natural forests in key zones will be stopped by 2020 as part of a slew of reform steps to promote ecological progress, Chinese authorities announced in March.

State plantations are also asked to reduce harvesting from man-made forests for business purposes by 20 percent by 2020, the central government said in an announcement on the reform management of national forest farms and zones.

China logs about 49.94 million cubic meters of natural forest each year and started a landmark pilot program in key forest zones in northeastern China's Heilongjiang Province to ban all commercial logging of natural forests last April.

The pilot program is expected to be gradually applied in other key state forest zones to stop similar logging practices, according to the announcement.

Forested areas will also be increased by 100 million mu (6.7 million hectares) and more than 600 million cubic meters of forest growing stock will be added to state forest farms. National forest zones will be increased by 5.5 million mu and will see a 400 million cubic meter increase of growing stock.

The announcement also urged national forest farms and zones to separate government functions from enterprise management and called for more fiscal, financial and infrastructure support to facilitate sustainable development and improve employees' livelihoods.

China has 4,855 state forest farms designed to promote forestation on uncultivated land and about 87 key forest zones in forest-rich areas to supply logs and manage forests.

7.1.1 CHINA TO KEEP ON GREENING

http://www.china.org.cn/china/Off_the_Wire/2015-03/19/content_35105053.htm

China has big plans for its forests as environmental protection takes center stage after great achievements in "greening" the nation.

Protecting and developing forest reserves is now a central tenet of policy, deputy head of the State Forestry Administration (SFA) Zhang Yongli said during a tree-planting activity ahead of the International Day of Forests on March 21.

"China will continue environmental rehabilitation projects, including returning marginal farmland to forest, controlling sources of sandstorms in regions around Beijing and Tianjin and growing shelter forests," Zhang said.

There have been some eye-catching achievements in forestry with more than 6 million hectares of wood stock added each year since 2011.

While global forest resources keep shrinking, China has been increasing its forested area for over 30 years, Zhang said.

Worldwide, forests are now at about 50 percent of the ideal level, figures from the United Nations showed.

An SFA survey last year revealed that China had 208 million hectares of forest, an area bigger than Mexico, covering 21.6 percent of the country, up 1.3 percentage points from that five years before.

A VALUABLE INHERITANCE

"To save Earth," Chinese President Xi Jinping once said, "we have to save our forests first." "We have inherited the forests from our ancestors and we should pass them on to our offspring," he said on another occasion.

Beyond the rapid economic growth that has awed the world, China is now doing everything it reasonably can to preserve, protect and restore the environment.

A forestation project, due for completion in 2050, plans to weave an enormous green belt across 13 desert regions in the arid northwest. The project has another 35 years to increase coverage to around 15 percent.

The latest measures demand that commercial logging of natural forests in key areas cease by 2020 and promises to reduce harvesting from man-made forests by 20 percent in the same timeframe. China currently extracts about 50 million cubic meters of timber each year.

This year, over 600,000 hectares of marginal farmland will be returned to forest or grassland, and a further 6 million hectares of new forest will be planted.

7.2 CHINA TO SPEND 1.6 BLN ON WETLANDS PROTECTION

http://news.xinhuanet.com/english/2015-08/07/c_134491963.htm

The central government plans to spend 1.6 billion yuan (262 million U.S. dollars) to preserve and restore China's wetlands, the Ministry of Finance said in August.

The planned investment includes 680 million yuan for protection and restoration projects, 405 million in compensation for services that benefit the environment, 400 million in incentives for those who help protect the environment and another 115 million used to revert agricultural lands to wetlands.

China ranked the fourth in the world in terms of wetland surface, with important wetlands such as Poyang Lake and Dongting Lake. The government vowed to protect the wetlands with 1.59 billion yuan in fiscal spending last year, helping them expand in many parts of the country.

7.2.1 BEIJING TO EXPAND GREEN SPACES, WETLAND

http://news.xinhuanet.com/english/2015-07/21/c_134433506.htm

Beijing is set to get 2,300 more hectares of green space in the next five years, with municipal authorities planning new parks for areas vacated by businesses being pushed outside of the city.

Deng Naiping, head of the Beijing Municipal Bureau of Landscape and Forestry, said in July that it will make green belts out of suburban land once occupied by markets and logistics centers, with these moved to neighboring Hebei Province to reduce traffic congestion and population density in the capital.

The capital will also make use of idle land to build 300 more small parks by 2020, Deng promised.

Meanwhile, Beijing will cooperate with Hebei Province and Tianjin Municipality on wetland construction.

By 2020, Beijing will have 3,000 hectares of wetland in the three suburban districts of Fangshan, Daxing and Tongzhou and 8,000 hectares of wetland recovered from the Yongding River, Chaobai River and Guanting

Reservoir, Deng said. If the city reaches this target, it will have 54,400 hectares of wetland, accounting for 3.3 percent of the country's total.

Thirty forest parks and five national wetland parks will also be added by 2020, according to Deng.

7.3 CHINA TO FURTHER PROTECT DESERTIFIED LAND

http://news.xinhuanet.com/english/2015-06/02/c_134291316.htm

The State Forestry Administration of China rolled out guidelines on protecting the country's desertified land in June.

The guideline advised more than 1.2 million square kilometers of desertified land in China be closed off as a protection zone so as to control drifting sand and improve the environment.

The guidelines, effective from July to the end of 2020, demand that activities including cutting down trees, cultivating land, animal grazing, resource exploration, mining, and misuse of water be prohibited in the protected zones. Construction of railways and highways are not allowed. No immigrants should be settled in the areas.

According to the guidelines, the protected areas should be important locations that have an impact on regional and national ecology and have suffered from frequent human activity.

Desertified land, which is land that has become barren due to constant water shortages and excessive exploitation, makes up more than half of the total desert area.

According to statistics from the State Forestry Administration, China had a desert area of around 2.62 million square kilometers, which accounts for 27 percent of its total land area.

7.3.1 DESERTIFICATION IN CHINA REVERSED OVER PAST DECADE

http://news.xinhuanet.com/english/2015-12/29/c_134961111.htm

China has experienced less serious desertification over the past decade, as data revealed desertified areas have been shrinking, China's forestry authority said in December.

By the end of 2014, desertified areas in China totaled 2.61 million square kilometers, about 27.2 percent of the country's territory, down 12,120 square kilometers from the previous survey in 2009, according to research by the State Forestry Administration.

7.4 CHINA'S NATURE RESERVES FLOURISHING

http://news.xinhuanet.com/english/2015-10/06/c_134687168.htm

The ecological systems in China's natural reserves are stable with numbers of some endangered animals and plant species growing, the Ministry of Environmental Protection announced.

A ministry press release said that nature reserves at various levels are providing protection to more than 85 percent of rare species.

China has 428 natural reserves at national level, covering over 96 million hectares. The population of endangered and rare species, such as golden monkeys, Asian elephants and dawn redwood trees, have been growing in these areas.

China has over 60 natural reserves for giant pandas and the number of wild giant pandas has increased from about 1,100 in 2000 to around 1,600.

Efforts to protect the crested ibis (Nipponia nippon) and its habitat have helped the population grow from only seven in 1981 to about 1,000 today.

7.4.1 WHO PAYS FOR WILDLIFE "CRIME"?

http://news.xinhuanet.com/english/indepth/2015-02/17/c_134004095.htm

For farmers and herders around Changtang nature reserve in Tibet Autonomous Region in southwest China, there are two sides to the wildlife coin.

Tashi Wangyel from Nyima Township in the north of Tibet only sleeps well in the winter, while local brown bear are hibernating in caves.

Several months ago, he found more than 20 dead sheep in his yard and several others were missing. The forestry department confirmed that the killer was a brown bear.

"The wolf usually bites the sheep's neck, while bears peels the skin off their hindquarters," he said.

A growing number of herders in Tibet are having similar unwelcome encounters with wild animals, whose populations are on the increase. Tibet is home to 795 vertebrate species, 125 of which are protected.

Local governments paid 419 million yuan (about 68 million U.S. dollars) in compensation for losses caused by wildlife between 2006 and the end of 2014.

"Wolf, brown bear, snow leopard and wild yak are often troublemakers," said Mao Shiping, head of the wildlife protection office of Nagqu Prefecture. They take livestock, damage buildings and crops, and sometimes hurt people. Twelve people were killed by wild animals around the reserve in 2012.

"We do not know how to deal with protected wildlife. A bear once took over a house for three or four days. Finally, we used firecrackers and strong lights to scare it away," Tashi Wangyel said, adding that he does not allow his children or parents to stay at home alone.

COMPENSATION PROGRAMS

Tashi Wangyel was lucky. Tibet's government has a compensation program for losses caused by wild animals. The amount of compensation varies according to the value of the livestock.

Tashi Wangyel received 250 yuan for each sheep, but an adult sheep sells for roughly 700 yuan in local markets.

Legally, local governments must compensate victims wildlife "crime" but most local governments have no compensation standards or specific budget, so enforcement has been poor.

The Siberian tiger, one of the world's most endangered animals, can be a big troublemaker in northeast China's Heilongjiang Province.

Last November, a tiger took dozens of goats for Guo's farm, but he did not report the incident.

"There is no compensation program in the province, so we just have to put up with it," he told Xinhua.

Hundreds of such cases are reported each year in Heilongjiang and losses are substantial.

"Many local governments are neither willing nor able to pay," said Jiang Guangshun, executive deputy director of the state feline research center.

It can be difficult for local governments to pay compensation due to economic pressure. The challenge is to find creative solutions that protect wild animals, as well as the people who share the land with them, he added.

CREATIVE SOLUTION

Southwest China's Yunnan Province may have the answer, at least in part. Wild elephants pillage or trample crops, damage trees and houses and are a threat to people's lives.

From 2005 to 2013 in Yunnan 1,324 deaths and about 390 million yuan of losses were attributed to wild animals .

In 2010, Yunnan began to purchase commercial insurance for people in some regions. The government pays the premiums, and the insurers investigate and compensate people when animals cause trouble. The commercial mechanism is clearly more effective. Compensation is higher and paid more quickly.

As the environment has improved, more of these cases are likely, said Zhang Minghai of Northeast Forestry University.

One way to help humans and wildlife co-exist and thrive in harmony is to maintain the integrity of protected parks, but if "tragedies" do happen, someone should be responsible, said Zhang.

"A sustainable future depends on the health of both the ecosystem and the people," he said.

7.4.2 CHINA'S WILD TIGER, LEOPARD POPULATION IN RECOVERY

http://news.xinhuanet.com/english/2015-05/23/c_134263633.htm

The population of once-endangered wild Siberian tigers has achieved recovery growth in northeast China over the past decade, research has found.

Approximately 28 Siberian tigers and 42 Amur leopards have been spotted in the forests in northeast China's Jilin Province, according to a decade-long survey by the Jilin Provincial Forestry Department and Beijing Normal University unveiled in March.

Whereas, a 1998 project by U.S. and Russian scientists showed there were only six to nine Siberian tigers and three to seven Amur leopards in the area.

The country's crackdown on poaching and recent wild animal protection measures have contributed to the growth, said Lang Jianmin, director of the scientific research and publicity center of the Hunchun National Siberian Tiger Nature Reserve in Jilin.

But the increase of wild animal populations has also caused damage to the local people's interests. To solve the problem, the Jilin provincial government has rolled out a series of measures to compensate for personal injuries or property damage.

"We got compensation from the government after our cornfield was damaged by wild boars. Other villagers were compensated after their cattle was killed by tigers. We appreciate the policy," said Zhang Jincheng, a villager from Chunhua Town, Hunchun City.

As an increasing number of wild Siberian tigers roam the China-Russia border, experts have suggested a cross-border nature reserves to provide a favorable environment for the tiger migration.

The barbed wire on the border should be removed and a state-level Siberian tiger nature reserve should be jointly built by China and Russia so that the tiger population would continue to grow, said Jiang Guangshun, deputy director of the feline animal research center under the State Forestry Administration.

Siberian tigers, also known as Amur or Manchurian tigers, mainly live in east Russia, northeast China and northern parts of the Korean Peninsula. Less than 500 Siberian tigers are believed to survive in the wild, with an estimated 18 to 22 in Heilongjiang and Jilin. The world population of Amur leopard is less than 60, and most of them live in Russia. The species has been on the verge of extinction in northeast China as a result of poaching and deforestation.

Case Study

PROTECTING YANGTZE RIVER AT SOURCE

http://news.xinhuanet.com/english/2015-06/14/c_134325408.htm

The Chinese government has been controlling herding, downsizing industrial production, and remodeling towns in an effort to protect the source of the Yangtze River on the Qinghai-Tibet Plateau.

Billions of dollars have been rolled out to reverse the once deteriorating environment in the Sanjiangyuan Nature Reserve in northwest China's Qinghai Province.

Kunga Namje, who was a herdsman for five decades, moved out of a grassland in the nature reserve 11 years ago to live in a suburb of Golmud. Another 406 herdsmen moved with Namje. In return, they received 20,000 yuan (3,200 U.S. dollars) from the government every year.

"We moved out on our own will. We just want to protect the environment and the plateau," Namje said.

Tangula Mountain Town, with an altitude of 4,500 meters, is located inside the Sanjiangyuan Nature Reserve.

To conserve the environment and the source water of the Yangtze River, the township government has been issuing quotas for herding based on each year's growth of the grasslands. Many mines were also shut down.

The town itself is also undergoing an infrastructure facelift, said Tang Haiping, deputy head of the Tangula town government.

Local people have also volunteered to help protect the Sanjiangyuan Nature Reserve.

Tsring, a local Tibetan man, joined an environmental group after witnessing the growing amount of trash that came along with the population increase.

Since 2012, he has been campaigning to raise local residents' environmental awareness.

"Local Tibetan people are glad to protect the source of the Yangtze River," Tsring said.

A large number of bar-headed gooses come to breed in the Sanjiangyuan Nature Reserve every April. In the past, people would take their eggs for food and that prompted the environmental volunteers like Tsring to act.

Tsring said he and fellow group members would camp during the two-month breeding season and prevent people from taking away the birds' eggs.

The number of bar-headed gooses that came to breed nearly tripled in the last three years, Tsring added.

As environmental protection efforts continue, residents in the Sanjiangyuan Nature Reserve are in closer contact with wild animals.

A town official said he received reports from herdsmen that a bear rushed into their home and took away all their food.

According to an official report on Sanjiangyuan Nature Reserve protection, in the last decade, the area of wetlands in Sanjiangyuan increased 279.9 square kilometers and the area of grasslands grew 123.7 square kilometers.

In January 2014, 16 billion yuan was allocated for further protection of the nature reserve.

Part 8

New Environmental Protection Law Shows Its Teeth

http://news.xinhuanet.com/english/2015-04/10/c_134141352.htm

China's new environmental protection law has added claws to the usually weak enforcement efforts, helping reap roughly 12.3 million yuan (1.99 million U.S. dollars) in fines from big polluters in the first two months thanks to a newly designed provision.

The provision allows environmental protection agencies to impose fines on a daily basis as long as problems remain. The Ministry of Environmental Protection (MEP) said in April it used the new provision in 26 cases at the start of the year.

In the past, heavy polluters would rather pay a one-time penalty than fix pollution problems or buy pollution discharge equipment because the penalty was too cheap.

A local oil refinery in northeast China's Jilin Province was fined one million yuan in 2005, the utmost limit at that time, when it was found guilty of contaminating a major river, though the incident caused heavy economic losses and even threatened the lives of thousands of local residents.

Zou Shoumin, director of the MEP bureau of environment supervision, said the new law has shown its formidable force thanks to joint enforcement by environmental protection agencies and the police.

The ministry also handled hundreds of other cases that saw polluters' production halted, suspects detained or their property seized, said Zou, adding such cases are on the rise as seen in the two months.

8.1 TOUGHER PENALTIES FOR CHINA'S AIR POLLUTERS

http://news.xinhuanet.com/english/2015-06/15/c_134328210.htm

Polluters were given unprecedented penalties in the first four months since the new Environmental Protection Law took effect, said a statement by the Ministry of Environmental Protection in June.

The law imposes heavy fines for polluters. Since January, companies have been fined 112 million yuan (18.3 million U.S. dollars) in 160 cases, with Shaanxi Coalification and Energy fined 15.8 million yuan for refusing to reduce its emissions, the highest penalty so far on a single company.

The four months have seen 1,186 cases of companies having their doors sealed, 698 cases resulting in limitations or suspensions on production, 437 cases of administrative detention and 429 cases of alleged environmental crimes, it said.

Around 40 percent of all cases occurred in Zhejiang Province, east China.

March and April saw a sharp increase in cases, the statement said.

Zou Shoumin, head of the environmental inspection bureau at the Ministry of Environmental Protection, said companies were spending more on environmental protection under the pressure of large fines.

8.1.1 CHINESE COURT ACCEPTS FIRST LAWSUIT FROM ENVIRONMENTAL ORGANIZATION

http://news.xinhuanet.com/english/2015-03/25/c_134096103.htm

A commonwealth organization has demanded an industrial polluter in Shandong province receive hefty penalties when filing the country's first environmental lawsuit under a new law that came into effect on Jan.1.

On March 25, the Intermediate People's Court in Dezhou City, east China's Shandong Province, confirmed it accepted the lawsuit lodged by the All-China Environment Federation. In it, the federation demands 30 million yuan (4.8 million U.S. dollars) compensation for damages from air pollution discharged by the Zhenhua Co. Ltd., an affiliated branch of Dezhou Jinghua Group.

The case arose after Zhenhua Co., which produces glass, neglected warnings by environmental watchdogs that they were emitting excess sulfur and dust.

The company was placed on a blacklist by the Ministry of Environmental Protection in October last year after failing to treat the emission.

Experts from the federation received several strong complaints from residents living near the company's plant, which regularly discharges foul-smelling yellow smoke.

"Neither fines by the local environmental watchdog nor the blacklist warning by the ministry pushed the polluter to take effective measures in the pollution control. The litigation is a new attempt to check head-strong violators like Zhenhua," said Ma Yong, a litigation director with the federation.

It is the first case after amendments to the environment protection law were enacted by China's national legislature in April 2014. The new law makes it much easier for environmental NGOs to file lawsuits against polluters for public good.

The new environment law must be a powerful, effective tool to control pollution instead of being "as soft as cotton candy," Premier Li Keqiang said while speaking at a press conference following the annual national legislative session which concluded last week.

Fu Qiang, a lawyer with the Shandong Pengfei Law Firm, said big industrial polluters are often protected by the local government, which makes pollution control difficult. Non-governmental organizations will play a bigger role in representing public interests for environmental cases in the future.

The federation's involvement has also triggered more government efforts.

The Dezhou municipal government urged Zhengzhou Co. to immediately overhaul emission treatment facilities to meet pollution control requirements before the end of the month. Otherwise, it would be ordered to suspend production on April 1.

8.1.1.1 CHINA NGOS WIN LANDMARK ENVIRONMENTAL LAWSUIT

http://news.xinhuanet.com/english/2015-10/29/c_134763719.htm

Two NGOs won an environmental damage lawsuit in October against a quarry in the east China's Fujian province. It is believed to be a landmark case made possible by China's strengthened environmental law.

The case, filed by Friends of Nature and Fujian Green Home, opened in Nanping Municipal Intermediate People's Court of Fujian months ago, and the verdict was delivered in October.

The two NGOs have accused four people of severely damaging vegetation on a hillside in Nanping City.

The court ordered the defendants to clear work sheds, mechanical equipment and waste at a quarry within five months, and to restore vegetation they had damaged by planting trees over the next three years.

They were also asked to pay 1.27 million yuan (200,000 U.S. dollars) in compensation.

According to the court, defendant Li Mingshuo transferred possession of his quarry without approval of authorities to the other three defendants in July 2008, who expanded the mining area, illegally occupied forest and damaged local vegetation.

The total area of vegetation damaged by the four defendants, including land damaged by Li before the transfer, reached around 28.33 mu (1.9 hectares), the court said.

"This is the first case filed by NGOs over non-pollution-related environmental damage since the amended Environmental Protection Law took effect on January 1, 2015. It offers a good example for future cases," said Lin Dongbo, deputy head of the court.

The law allows any NGO of sufficient size specializing in environmental protection for more than five years to file civil cases over pollution and environmental damage for the good of the general public.

China only has about 80,000 officials to enforce environmental laws, and they must oversee 1.5 million companies, not including unregistered ones. With the new law, about 700 organizations can join the fight.

8.1.2 CHINA PROSECUTORS FILE LAWSUIT AGAINST ENVIRONMENTAL DEPARTMENT

http://news.xinhuanet.com/english/2015-12/21/c_134938567.htm

Prosecutors in east China's Shandong Province have lodged a lawsuit against a county-level environmental protection department in the first ever prosecutors vs. administration public interest case, according to the Supreme People's Procuratorate (SPP).

The Qingyun Environmental Department is accused of "illegal acts" during its supervision of a local sewage firm and "failing to fulfil its duty" even after it was issued with a warning, the SPP said December in a statement.

The lawsuit comes after an investigation by Qingyun County People's

Procuratorate into the sewage company over allegations that it lacked adequate environmental protection facilities, it said.

According to the SPP, despite residents' ire and pressure from the county-level Communist Party of China committee, the department failed in its capacity of supervisor and imposed only nominal administrative punishments.

The lawsuit was filed on Dec. 16. Details concerning how the department acted illegally were not included in the statement.

China's top legislature in July approved a draft legal document that allowed prosecutors to institute public interest litigation in civil and administrative cases against acts that compromise public rights and interests by pollution or food and drug safety.

8.1.3 PROSECUTORS FAST-TRACK POLLUTION CASE IN EAST CHINA

http://news.xinhuanet.com/english/2015-08/03/c_134476566.htm

The Supreme People's Procuratorate (SPP) has pressed local prosecutors to fast-track a pollution investigation in east China's Anhui Province, an SPP statement announced in August.

China's national broadcaster CCTV reported in June that a river near an industrial park in Chizhou City, Anhui is heavily polluted, cutting off the water supply for many nearby farms.

Local prosecutors looked into the case immediately after the media report and opened a joint investigation with the environment department and police, according to the SPP statement.

Investigations into eight local firms found that a chemical company and a pharmaceutical company were discharging unprocessed waste water into a nearby river.

Evidence suggested that the two companies may have broken criminal law. Local police have opened a criminal case against the chemical firm and the Chizhou procuratorate has also started to investigate possible graft, according to the SPP.

The SPP has instructed the provincial procuratorate to closely follow the development of the case and fast-track prosecution if the evidence is solid, the statement said.

The SPP also informed the Ministry of Environmental Protection about the case and requested its assistance.

8.1.3.1 OIL GIANTS SUED OVER BOHAI SPILL

http://news.xinhuanet.com/english/china/2015-07/27/c_134449223.htm

A landmark lawsuit has been filed against two oil giants in a maritime court over the oil spill in 2011 that polluted a huge area of Bohai Bay in Northeast China.

The suit, filed against ConocoPhillips and China National Offshore Oil Corp, is the first public interest litigation brought by a nonprofit organization over marine environmental pollution to be accepted by a court.

Such a move was not possible until a new environmental protection law took effect on Jan 1.

The China Biodiversity Conservation and Green Development Foundation said in July it had been told by the maritime court in Qingdao, Shandong province, that the suit had been filed.

The law allows any environmental organization registered with a civil affairs bureau at city level or above and that has been operating for at least five years to bring public interest litigation.

Before this case, in June, the Dalian Environmental Protection Volunteer Association demanded 645 million yuan ($105 million) for damage it says resulted from pollution caused by China National Petroleum Corp in July 2010. The claim, the largest made in an environmental case in China, is still under review by Dalian Maritime Court.

The association is a nonprofit organization founded in June 2003 in Dalian, Liaoning province.

The China Biodiversity Conservation and Green Development Foundation is not suing Conoco Philips and CNOOC for compensation, of which the companies have paid about 1.7 billion yuan to the State Oceanic Administration, a government body that supervises and administers maritime affairs.

The foundation said that on public interest grounds it is calling for the two companies to accept responsibility for the damage they caused because four years after the oil spill, remedial work has still to begin.

In a series of spills between June 4 and July 12, 2011, oil in the Penglai 19-3 field in Bohai Bay polluted more than 6,200 square km of water — an area about nine times the size of Singapore.

It caused huge losses to the tourist and aquatic farming industries in Liaoning and Hebei provinces, a report by the State Oceanic Administration said in June 2012.

Penglai 19-3 is one of China's largest offshore oil fields, producing about 160,000 barrels of oil a day.

ConocoPhillips China is a joint venture in which CNOOC, the country's largest offshore oil producer, holds a 51 percent stake, with ConocoPhillips holding the rest.

Under a damage compensation agreement, ConocoPhillips China offered 1.09 billion yuan for ecological losses, while CNOOC paid 480 million yuan and ConocoPhillips China 113 million yuan for environmental protection efforts in Bohai Bay.

The compensation for fishermen has been sent to the governments in Hebei and Liaoning provinces, according to a statement by the oceanic administration.

However, disputes remain as oil spills continue to affect the area. In December, 21 aquaculture farmers sued the two oil giants in Tianjin Maritime Court over the oil spill.

Sea cucumber farmers from Leting county in Hebei province demanded compensation of 148 million yuan to cover their economic losses and litigation costs. They said the oil spill destroyed a large number of sea cucumbers, with losses amounting to 140 million yuan. The result of this case is still pending.

Ma Jun, director of the Institute of Public and Environmental Affairs, an NGO that researches water pollution, said it is hard to predict the outcome of the ongoing public interest litigation.

8.1.3.2 CHINA ARRESTS FOUR FOR DUMPING INDUSTRIAL WASTE WATER

http://news.xinhuanet.com/english/2015-05/05/c_134212665.htm

Four people have been arrested in north China's Tianjin municipality for dumping 10,000 tons of unprocessed industrial waste water, according to a statement released in May by the Supreme People's Procuratorate (SPP).

Among the suspects, three worked at a chemical plant in the city and allegedly received waste water from another company to extract copper sulfate, the SPP said. With no processing procedures, the water was then illegally discharged for two years, totaling more than 10,000 tons, the statement said. The fourth suspect was the middle man between the two groups.

The case is among 12 on an SPP's priority list of environmental crime.

8.1.3.3 CHINESE FIRM PUNISHED FOR POLLUTING DESERT

http://news.xinhuanet.com/english/2015-03/27/c_134103998.htm

"Tengger" means "sky" in Mongolian; however, the Tengger Desert is not as clear as its namesake, due to the negligence of companies that choose to dump their untreated waste.

A private enterprise in Wuwei City in the northwest province of Gansu was found to have dumped more than 80,000 tons of waste water in the desert.

Ronghua Industrial and Trade Company, a company with businesses ranging from agriculture, mineral products to medical service, was fined more than 3 million yuan (about 480,000 U.S. dollars) in March.

Two employees were detained, and its chairman and officials at local environmental protection departments are under investigation.

The company relocated near the desert to enable it to expand production in 2011. It began to produce corn starch and glutamic acid in 2014 but failed to install the equipment needed to prevent and control pollution.

The company secretly built pipes to dump the industrial waste water in the desert.

Preliminary investigation showed that Ronghua had discharged 83,715 tons of waste water through the pipes into areas below the desert between May 2014 to March 2015.

Images collected by unmanned aerial vehicle showed that the pollution has caused 23 sewage water pools in the desert. The polluted area covered 266 mu (about 18 hectares).

The majority of the waste water has been transported to treatment plants, while the remaining problems will be handled after the environmental impact assessment, said the city's publicity department.

This is not an isolated case. Companies in Gansu Province, in north China's Inner Mongolia Autonomous Region and Ningxia Hui Autonomous Region have been reported to have also dumped waste in the desert.

Last September, Mingsheng Dye Chemical Co. in Zhongwei City in Ningxia was shut down after it dumped waste water in the Tengger Desert. Media reports said the contamination threatened groundwater in the area.

Local governments and experts blamed desert pollution on lax supervision, covert factory locations and a lack of responsibility on behalf of the companies.

Ronghua's waste water dumping happened despite an ongoing provincial crackdown on desert pollution.

The incident revealed holes in supervision and inspection, said an official with the local environmental department, who also added that high-tech monitoring methods like unmanned aerial vehicles were needed to help supervision efforts.

In addition, half of Gansu's cities and prefectures border the desert. A vast territory with a sparse population as well as hidden pipes make it difficult to supervise enterprises, said Ma Jianmin, an environmental protection expert with Lanzhou University.

The revised Environmental Protection Law, which came into effect in January, brought with it heavier punishments. "But the law needs stronger enforcement," said Ma.

Compared with urban pollution, desert pollution, which is an important part of the ecosystem, is often ignored.

"A string of such cases have sounded the alarm," he said.

8.1.3.3.1 ANOTHER CHINESE FIRM PUNISHED FOR POLLUTING DESERT

http://news.xinhuanet.com/english/2015-05/06/c_134216013.htm

A chemical factory and its legal representative in northwest China's Ningxia Hui Autonomous Region have been punished for dumping untreated waste in the Tengger Desert.

According to a court statement, Mingsheng Dye Chemical Co. in Zhongwei City was fined 5 million yuan (about 817,580 U.S. dollars), and the company's legal representative, Lian, was given an 18 month sentence with a two-year reprieve and fined 50,000 yuan.

The company was found to have illegally dumped industrial waste since 2007, and was shut down last September. Media reports said the contamination threatened groundwater in the area.

Since beginning of the year, companies in Gansu, Inner Mongolia and Ningxia, which border the desert, have been investigated for dumping waste in the desert.

In March, a private enterprise in the northwest province of Gansu was fined more than 3 million yuan for dumping over 80,000 tons of waste water in the desert.

The revised Environmental Protection Law, which came into effect in January, brought with it heavier punishments.

8.1.4 CHINA IMPOSES GREATER FINES FOR ENVIRONMENTAL VIOLATIONS IN 2014

http://news.xinhuanet.com/english/2015-04/14/c_134150496.htm

China dealt with 73,160 environmental violation cases in 2014, a year on year increase of 10 percent, according to the Ministry of Environmental Protection.

Fines imposed on violators implicated in these cases totaled more than 3.16 billion yuan (510 million U.S. dollars), up 34.4 percent from 2013, a ministry statement revealed in April.

Sentencing in 81 percent of these cases has been passed.

Guangdong in south China and Zhejiang in the east, both economically advanced coastal provinces, reported more than 10,000 administrative cases each.

While vowing to publicize all administrative punishments for the scrutiny of disciplinary and judicial organs as well as the public. The ministry warned that any regions that were late declaring their violation cases or their law enforcement was proven to be ineffective would face questioning and possibly punishment.

"The covering up of environmental crimes and severe dereliction of duty will be passed on to the Supreme People's Procuratorate," the statement said.

8.1.4.1 CHINA RULES THAT ALL POLLUTERS HELD ACCOUNTABLE REGARDLESS OF FAULT

http://news.xinhuanet.com/english/2015-06/01/c_134288599.htm

China's top court in June ruled that all polluters will be liable for any damage they have on the environment even if they do not breach regulations.

According to a legal explanation issued by the Supreme People's Court, which will be enforced from June 3, polluters will be held accountable for any discharge, even if it is within national or local standards, that causes damage.

The SPC said the ruling would also apply to public-interest litigation on environmental issues.

One year after the world's second-largest economy "declared war" on pollution — following decades of pursing growth at the expense of air, water and soil quality — pollution remains a key challenge in the country.

The revised Environmental Law was adopted last year, bringing with it heavier punishment for those that break environment-protection legislation.

The new law stipulated that polluting enterprises should be "named and shamed".

As an incentive for companies to expedite costly modifications to reduce pollutants, a daily fine system was introduced. No limit was set on the fine, meaning that polluting companies that fail to rectify problems will accumulate higher fines.

Executives at polluting companies could face up to 15-days detention.

8.1.5 CHINA CLEANS UP 1,790 ENVIRONMENT CRIMES FROM JANUARY TO JULY

htt//news.xinhuanet.com/english/2015-09/14/c_134622997.htm

China has cleaned up 1,790 crime cases involving environmental pollution from January to July this year, vice minister of environmental protection Wu Xiaoqing said in September.

Addressing a symposium on environment and development, Wu said that since the new environmental protection law came into effect, the environmental protection authorities have been very busy.

The ministry conducted inspections and warned local officials with serious environmental problems in their area, Wu added.

The ministry has strengthened work on pollution. Among the 161 cities implementing new air quality standards in the first half of this year, 8.2 percent more days met the standard compared to the same period last year.

An action plan for water pollution has been fully implemented, while the authorities are devising action plan on soil pollution, Wu added.

The ministry has assisted local governments and centrally administered state-owned enterprises to make plans for emission cuts. Chemical oxygen demand and emissions of ammonia, sulfur dioxide and nitrous oxides dropped by 2.9 percent, 3.18 percent, 4.63 percent, 8.8 percent year-on-year respectively in the first half of this year.

8.1.5.1 ENVIRONMENTAL VIOLATIONS SEEN IN CHINA IN FIRST HALF OF 2015: 25164

http://news.xinhuanet.com/english/2015-08/05/c_134484557.htm

China has imposed punishment in 25,164 environmental violation cases in the first half of 2015, with 9,325 companies having their doors sealed, the Ministry of Environmental Protection said in August.

Violators were fined more than 230 million yuan (37.6 million U.S. dollars), and 740 cases of suspected environmental crime have been transferred to the police for criminal investigations.

Since the Environmental Protection Law took effect this year, environmental authorities have closed down companies, limited or suspended on production, and detained wrong-doers.

The ministry has given administrative punishment to ten cities, and people in charge of polluting companies in four of the ten were warned or sacked.

The ministry said it will cooperate with other ministries to tighten environmental inspection with increased awareness from local governments, enterprises and the public.

8.1.5.2 CHINA FOCUS: 8,500 ARRESTED FOR ENVIRONMENTAL CRIMES IN 2014

http://news.xinhuanet.com/english/2015-06/29/c_134366082.htm

Chinese police arrested around 8,500 suspects in more than 4,500 environment-related criminal cases in 2014, as the country waged war against pollution, environment minister Chen Jining said in June.

Addressing lawmakers during a bi-monthly session of the National

People's Congress (NPC) Standing Committee, Chen said stricter enforcement of tough environmental laws was a key factor in curbing air pollution.

Environmental authorities transferred more than 2,000 cases of suspected environmental law violations to the police, more than double the figure for the past 10 years combined.

Close to 3,400 companies and 3,700 construction sites were also found to have violated environment laws and more than 3,100 workshops were closed following air quality inspections by Ministry of Environmental Protection (MEP) officials and drones, Chen said.

The announcement came amid a spell of heavy smog in Beijing and the neighboring Tianjin municipality and Hebei Province for the better part of a week.

One year after the world's second-largest economy "declared war" on pollution after decades of pursuing growth at the expense of the environment, air pollution has become one of the top concerns for Chinese citizens, particularly those living in big, industrial cities in the central and eastern regions of the country.

According to an MEP communique released earlier this month, only 16 of the 161 major cities subject to air quality monitoring met the national standards for clean air in 2014.

But Chen — who was appointed environment minister just this March amid hopes to breath some new air into the uphill battle against pollution — said that China's overall air quality improved in 2014 and early this year.

Average PM10 readings in 338 cities monitored by the MEP dropped by 2.1 percent year on year in 2014, and by 5.3 percent in the first four months of 2015.

Readings of PM2.5 — smaller particulate matter which can penetrate deep into the lungs, thus posing a greater health threat than

PM10—dropped in 74 cities by 11.1 percent in 2014 and 15.2 percent from January to April this year, the minister said.

Air quality changes were particularly evident in the notoriously smoggy Beijing-Tianjin-Hebei region, where PM2.5 readings recorded faster-than-average drops: 12.3 percent in 2014 and 20 percent this year, according to Chen.

He attributed the decrease to additional government financial support and enforcement of its policies, new technology and better coordination between ministries and among cities in the Beijing-Tianjin-Hebei region, the Pearl River Delta and the Yangtze River Delta.

The government earmarked 9.8 billion yuan (1.6 billion U.S. dollars) for air pollution prevention and control in 2014 in addition to 2.5 billion in budget investment arrangements, Chen said, adding that government funds helped leverage private investment worth some 300 billion yuan.

He noted that China had managed to meet its target set in the 12th Five-Year Plan (2011-2015) to cut outdated capacity in the polluting steel, cement and glass sectors one year ahead of target, and that optimization of the country's energy structure is already in motion.

Nationwide consumption of coal fell for the first time in 15 years in 2014, when it declined 2.9 percent. Clean energy sources such as hydroelectricity, wind energy, nuclear energy and natural gas, meanwhile saw their total share in the power mix rise by 1.3 points to 16.9 percent.

Discharges of key pollutants including sulphur dioxide, oxides of nitrogen (NOx) and volatile organic compounds (VOC) have been checked, whereas vehicle emissions have been curbed by pulling heavy-polluting vehicles off the road while promoting new energy automobiles.

The next step is to further optimize the country's industrial and energy structure and cut back on discharges of air pollutants, Chen said.p Authorities will go on slashing outdated capacity this year, shut down 1,000 small coal mines, improve the quality of coal on the market, ensure stable supply of natural gas, and promote the use of clean energy and energy-saving buildings.

They will aim to reduce discharges of SO_2 and NO_x by 3 and 5 percent respectively, and to "strictly control" that of VOC.

Chen said efforts will also be made to improve the evaluation of governments' implementation of air pollution control measures, deepen regional coordination, step up technological research and sharpen laws and regulations in the field, to make polluters pay the "unaffordable price".

China put into force a new Environmental Protection Law this year. A daily fine system was incorporated to punish offenders and motivate companies to expedite the costly modifications needed to reduce pollutants. In cases where fined violators fail to rectify the problem, the fine can increase without limit.

Chen said environmental authorities would "bring new tools introduced in the law into full play, conduct more covert inspections and seek heavier penalties for companies guilty of illicit or excess emissions and those which forge pollution data."

Government officials who neglect their duties or abuse their power will be investigated in line with law, he said.

8.1.6 CHINA PASSES LAW TO CONTROL AIR POLLUTION

http://news.xinhuanet.com/english/2015-08/29/c_134568483.htm

China's top legislature in August adopted an amendment to the Air Pollution Control Law that will restrict various sources of smog and make information on environmental cleanliness more readily available to the public.

Members of the Standing Committee of the National People's Congress (NPC) passed the bill through a vote at the close of the bi-monthly legislative session.

The law stipulates that a gasoline quality standard should be established and matched with the country's restriction requirements for major pollutants.

Although China's gasoline has roughly the same standard as in Europe in terms of sulfur content, the permitted content of olefin, arenes and benzene in diesel is far higher.

Li Mengliang, of the China Automotive Technology & Research Center, suggested environmental authorities work with other departments to compile the gasoline quality standard.

The amended law also provides that China should promote clean and efficient use of coal, obliging local governments to ban low-quality coal for residential use.

Meanwhile, it bans dispersing toxic pesticides into trees and bushes in densely populated areas, which will be good news for people with asthma and lung diseases.

The law gives the green light for remote sensors to be positioned on streets to check the emissions of moving vehicles.

This technology will test the intensity of carbon monoxide, carbon dioxide, carbon hydrate and nitrogen oxide.

Beijing plans to install about 150 such surveillance devices along key roads, said Li Linnan, vice director of the city's vehicle emission control center.

Air quality in coastal areas is heavily impacted by ships fueled by sulfur-intensive heavy oil. In response, the adopted version stipulates that a control area for pollutant discharge of ships be designated.

Ships entering the area must conform to emission requirements.

The law also provides greater environmental transparency to the public. It stipulates authorities of the State Council should evaluate provincial-level governments on their attainment of air quality improvement targets.

Likewise, provincial-level governments will assess cities within their jurisdictions in this regard, and assessment results should be made public.

Moreover, air pollution following environmental emergencies should be monitored and details made public, a revision adopted based upon legislators' proposals during this bi-monthly session.

A warehouse explosion in Tianjin on Aug. 12 not only killed at least 146 people but also endangered the environment of surrounding areas with toxic chemical.

The law also specifies other items to be disclosed publicly, including air quality standard, catalogue of major polluters, contact information of environmental authorities and supervisors, test results on the emissions of new vehicles, and sources and fluctuations of air pollution in important areas.

Another prominent revision adopted is the removal of clauses allowing local governments to restrict or ban vehicles to fight air pollution.

Hao Ruyu, vice chairman of the NPC Financial and Economic Committee, supported the revision on the ground of protecting citizens' rights to property.

People pay to buy cars and pay taxes for the cars. Banning people from driving on certain days equates to deprivation of citizens' rights to property, Hao said.

In a bid to control smog, Chinese cities have begun to restrict the use of vehicles. In Beijing, vehicles are restricted one out of five weekdays based upon the last numbers of their license plates.

As lawmakers discussed the draft amendment, half of Beijing's cars were off the road, as a traffic restriction is imposed to keep air clean before the World War II victory parade on Sept. 3.

8.2 ENVIRONMENT TAX LAW ON FAST TRACK

http://news.xinhuanet.com/english/2015-03/26/c_134097387.htm

The State Council, China's cabinet, said in March that it would review the draft environment tax law "as quickly as possible."

The State Council adopted a plan for its legislative work in 2015 at an executive meeting presided over by Premier Li Keqiang.

Economic management, social and cultural development, environmental protection and government reform will be prioritized, according to a statement issued after the meeting.

Last November, the draft environment tax law was submitted to the State Council for review, which will levy tax on polluters. The bill will not be tabled at the legislature until the State Council approves it.

Sun Youhai, an environment expert with the Counselors' Office of the State Council, told Xinhua earlier this month that the draft law planned to tax sulfur dioxide, nitrogen oxides, ammonia nitrogen and fine dust emission as well as activities that cause an increase in chemical oxygen demand, a key index of water quality.

The new tax is expected to help deter polluters and fund environmental protection efforts.

Also on the fast track are regulations on government investment, affordable urban housing, agricultural irrigation and management of residence permits, the statement said.

The State Council pledged at the meeting that the government will try to prevent policies from overpowering the law.

It will incrementally reduce the number of regulatory documents issued by ministries and commissions under the State Council and limit government approvals, the statement said.

The State Council will also comb through existing regulatory documents and abolish outdated ones.

8.2.1 CHINA FOCUS: CHINA PROPOSES DOUBLE TAXES ON EXCESS EMISSIONS

http://news.xinhuanet.com/english/2015-06/10/c_134315536.htm

The State Council, China's cabinet, released in June for public opinion a draft law on environmental taxes, which proposes business taxes for pollutants, solid waste and noise.

The draft proposed rates ranging from 350 yuan (57 U.S. dollars) to 11,200 yuan on various industrial noises according to the decibels level. It also set rates of 1.2 yuan on a stipulated quantity of air pollutants, 1.4 yuan on a stipulated quantity of water pollutants, and a range of 5 to 30 yuan for each ton of different kinds of solid waste. Rates will be doubled for emissions in excess of the stipulated amount.

Taxes may also be halved if emissions are below half the national standard.

Provincial governments may "appropriately" raise rates taking local environmental conditions into account.

The draft was drawn up by the Ministry of Finance, State Administration of Taxation and Ministry of Environmental Protection to promote an "energy saving, and environmentally friendly" industrial system, according to the Legislative Affairs Office of the State Council.

Instead of taxing polluters, China currently collects a "pollutant discharge fee" that almost equals the standard tax amount in the draft law.

For each outlet for waste air and water, authorities can tax at most three major pollutants, but that number could reach five if the pollutants are all heavy metals. This still allows provincial governments to increase the categories of pollutants subject to taxation based on their "special needs."

Environment Minister Chen Jining said, "the Chinese environment is reaching or has reached its limit."

Chen characterized the overall Chinese environment as "poor." with high pollutant emissions, serious ecological damage and high risks, which are all very far from public expectations.

He said the government will take "more forceful" measures in the next five years to protect the environment and promote green development.

According to the draft, the tax will exclude pollutants from agriculture except those from large-scale animal husbandry and mobile pollution sources including motor vehicles, locomotives, non-road mobile machinery, ships and aircraft as long as the pollutants are within national standards.

Normal emissions by urban sewage and refuse treatment plants will also be exempted.

No punishment is specified for tax evasion or fraud, merely that tax authorities should report such violations to the Ministry of Environmental Protection.

8.2.2 CHINA LEVIES CONSUMPTION TAX ON BATTERIES, PAINT

http://news.xinhuanet.com/english/business/2015-01/27/c_
133950846.htm

China announced in January that it will impose consumption tax on some types of batteries and paint to encourage environmental protection.

A four-percent tax will be levied on the production, processing and import of batteries and coating from Feb. 1, according to an online statement by the Ministry of Finance (MOF).

But cleaner batteries including mercury-free, nickel-hydrogen, lithium and solar cell varieties will be exempted and taxation on lead storage batteries will be postponed till Jan. 1, 2016.

Coating that contains volatile organic compounds of less than 420 grams per liter will also be excluded from the list, the statement said.

China firstly imposed consumption tax in 1994, on consumer goods with a high energy cost and high pollution, to promote a sustainable economic growth model.

Jia Kang, head of the Research Institute for Fiscal Science under the MOF, said China would impose consumption tax on merchandise including luxury products such as private jets and yachts in the future.

Consumer goods including cigarettes, alcohol, cosmetics and jewelry are currently subject to consumption tax in China.

8.3 CHINA PUSHES HARD FOR CLEANER ENVIRONMENT; TOUGHER REQUIREMENT ON OFFICIALS

http://news.xinhuanet.com/english/2015-09/17/c_134634759.htm

Beijing in September asked about 1,000 industrial and polluting companies in the new administrative center of Tongzhou District to either move out or upgrade their businesses in 2016.

It is part of China's efforts to forge ahead with a new environment action plan despite persistent economic headwinds.

Rather than being a drag on growth, the environmental campaign offers China "tremendous development opportunities" to upgrade and become a green and carbon-efficient economy, Yang Weimin, a member of the Central Leading Group for Deepening Overall Reform, said in September.

"China has laws and regulations on environmental protection, but it lacks a 'top-level design' that can unite and coordinate them," Yang said.

The master plan, adopted at a key meeting last week and due to be released in a few days, is expected to resolve the "too many cooks" problem and make cleaner environment a realizable goal.

TOUGHER RULES

The plan laid out a fundamental framework, including a clear ownership system of natural resources, an ecological compensation system and a responsibility-tracking system on officials.

"Clearly-defined ownership of the natural assets will enable the compensated and more efficient use of natural resources," noted Zhang Xiaode, a professor with the Chinese Academy of Governance.

One of the key constraints on environment protection is overlapping supervision, which has made the implementation of regulations time-consuming and inefficient.

According to Yang, the latest reform plan was a result of "vehement" discussions and debates among 12 ministries and departments, including the Ministry of Environmental Protection and the National Development and Reform Commission.

The Office of the Central Leading Group for Financial and Economic Affairs will coordinate all opinions and a team has been set up to push for the reforms.

The plan also called for increased environmental protection weighting on officials' assessments. This would mean that those deemed to have pursued economic growth at the cost of the environmental will be unlikely to be promoted.

China's environmental protection lags far behind its economic status, with prominent problems such as limited resources and severe pollution becoming major bottlenecks for sustainable growth.

Decades of breakneck growth in China has dried up resources and left problems including smog and contaminated water.

In 2014, only eight of 74 major Chinese cities subject to PM 2.5 air quality monitoring met the national standard, according to data released by the Ministry of Environmental Protection (MEP).

Another MEP report released in June 2014 revealed that some 60 percent of ground water checked by 4,778 monitoring stations was rated as "bad" or "very bad."

To strike a balance between growth and the environment, China declared a "war against pollution" last year, calling for tougher regulations.

In his annual government work report in March, Premier Li Keqiang pledged to take "a firm and unrelenting approach to ensure blue skies, clear waters, and sustainable development."

BALANCING ACT

While China endeavors to ditch the growth-at-all-costs economic model, balancing growth and environmental protection in times of economic slowdown will inevitably be fraught with challenges.

Last year marked the weakest annual expansion in 24 years due to a housing slowdown and falling external demand and a tepid global recovery. Growth further slowed to 7 percent in the first half of 2015.

According to a report published by the MEP last week, measures to combat pollution, including closure of outdated production facilities and caps on pollutant emissions, have a negative, albeit short-term, influence on economic growth.

The report estimated that gross domestic product (GDP) had decreased 186.9 billion yuan (29 billion U.S. dollars) due to the closure of outdated facilities, 0.12 percent of GDP, during the 11th Five-Year Plan period from 2006 to 2010.

The clean-up process, though painstaking, is an inevitable path China must take to achieve sustainable growth in the long run.

"Though the move curbed the growth of traditional industries like thermal power, steel and concrete over a short time, it boosted some emerging industries such as services and environmental protection in the long term," it noted.

The advantages of an improved environment for economic development overweigh the disadvantages, said the report.

"In the past, we are only preoccupied with 'gold mountain, silver hill,' but we must realize that lush hills are themselves valuable treasures," Yang said.

8.3.1 LIFELONG LIABILITY FOR POLLUTING OFFICIALS IN CHINA: REGULATION

http://news.xinhuanet.com/english/2015-08/17/c_134527310.htm

Environmental hazards caused by poor official decision-making will be traced back to whoever was originally responsible, and they will be punished with lifelong retroactive effect, under a new Communist Party of China (CPC) regulation.

Leading officials should bear primary responsibility for environmental damage in their jurisdiction and will be held accountable for major pollution incidents, it said.

Announced in August, the regulation took effect on Aug. 9, days before the massive deadly warehouse explosions in Tianjin, which are thought to have dispersed dangerous chemicals into the surrounding area.

The rules cover all leading members of CPC committees and governments above county level.

Punishments include sacking, demotion and public apology, and records of environmental misconduct should be disclosed to the public, the CPC said.

8.3.2 MINISTRY NAMES AND SHAMES NORTHERN CITY FOR POLLUTION

http://news.xinhuanet.com/english/2015-08/03/c_134476814.htm

China's environmental watchdog in August named and shamed Hohhot, capital of North China's Inner Mongolia Autonomous Region for poor air and water quality.

The Ministry of Environmental Protection said various violations were found in the city, including excessive emissions, inadequate pollution treatment facilities and lax supervision by local regulators.

Inspection teams had been sent to Hohhot in May and June to check on pollution prevention and control. It is one of the 30 cities targeted in a nationwide environmental inspection this year.

The problems of excessive pollution and waste are easy to see in the city, according to the inspectors.

The lack of sewage treatment facilities has led about 100,000 tons of untreated dirty water flowing out of the city each day.

The ministry ordered local environmental authorities to harshly punish the polluters and submit rectification measures to the ministry within 20 work days.

Inspection teams have also been sent to Hebei, Henan, Shanxi, Beijing and Tianjin.

8.3.3 CHINA'S ALL PROVINCIAL REGIONS REACH POLLUTANTS EMISSION CUT TARGET

http://news.xinhuanet.com/english/2015-07/22/c_134437334.htm

All provincial regions in the Chinese mainland reached their targets for pollutants emission cut last year, China's Ministry of Environmental Protection (MEP) said in July.

Except Taiwan, Hong Kong and Macao, which are not included in the statistics, the other 31 provinces, municipalities and autonomous regions in the Chinese mainland and Xinjiang Production and Construction Corps reached their targets, according to a report issued by the MEP.

All of the eight centrally-administered state-owned energy enterprises, including PetroChina, Sinopec, Huaneng, Datang, Huadian, China Power Investment Corp. and Shenhua, also reached their targets for annual cuts in emissions.

The evaluation included four indicators, chemical oxygen demand, ammonia nitrogen, sulfur dioxide and nitrogen oxide. Statistics showed that in Beijing the four indices dropped significantly, down 5.4 percent, 3.82 percent, 9.35 percent and 9.24 percent year-on-year, respectively.

The nation's total emission of the four pollutants also dropped last year compared to 2013. Compared to 2010, the emission of all the four pollutants dropped around 10 percent, according to the report.

8.4 EXTRA EFFORTS NEEDED TO BATTLE SMOG: MINISTER

http://news.xinhuanet.com/english/2015-03/07/c_134046871.htm

China needs to make "extra efforts" to battle the grave air pollution that has raised public concern, the newly appointed Environmental Protection Minister said in March.

About 80 percent of more than 300 cities failed to meet the official standard of air quality last year, with smog frequently choking the Yangtze River and Pearl River deltas as well as the Beijing-Tianjin-Hebei region, said minister Chen Jining, an environmental scientist and former president of Tsinghua University.

The Chinese government issued the Air Pollution Prevention and Control Action Plan in September 2013 to control PM2.5, or airborne particles with a diameter of less than 2.5 microns, and reduce the number of smoggy days.

China has been promoting desulfurization and denitration of newly installed power plants. More than 6 million old vehicles and heavy-polluting vehicles were weeded out last year, exceeding the total figure of the previous three years, he said.

Environmental protection authorities transferred 2,080 cases of suspected violation of laws to public security agencies, which doubled the total figure of the previous 10 years, he added.

"No country in the world is making such great efforts as China to combat air pollution within so short time," he told a press conference.

"We can achieve the goal of greatly improving air quality, but the difficulty is formidable," he said. "We need to make extra efforts."

The government would strengthen the implementation of the revised environmental protection law and raise the capacity of pollution control in a scientific and systematic way, he said.

The ministry summoned leaders from the cities of Linyi in east China's Shandong Province and Chengde in the northern province of Hebei, urging them to strengthen inspections and impose severe penalties on polluters.

A good law should not become "paper tiger." We must use it as a sharp weapon, Chen said.

Local governments found slack in supervision or inactive in pollution control would face punishment, he said.

The government would also ensure information transparency and protect the public's right to know, participate in and supervise the fight against air pollution.

8.4.1 CHINA SEES LESS ACID RAIN IN THE FIRST OF 2015

http://news.xinhuanet.com/english/2015-07/27/c_134452139.htm

China observed less acid rain in the first half of this year, according to a communique released by the Ministry of Environmental Protection in July.

Of 470 cities nationwide that observe precipitation, 164 have been affected by acid rain, and acid rain cities with average PH value of rainfall lower than 5.6 dropped by 4.5 percent year on year, said the communique on environmental condition in the first half of 2015.

The total area of regions with acid rain accounted for 7.6 percent of the country's land area, which decreased by 2.4 percentage points year on year, according to the communique.

Acid rain is mainly detected in the south of the middle and lower reaches of Yangtze River, the southwestern part of Chongqing, the Yangtze River Delta and the Pearl River Delta.

The two delta regions refer to the economically-developed eastern and southern areas encompassing Shanghai and Guangzhou respectively.

Compared with the same period last year, the Beijing-Tianjin-Hebei region, the Yangtze River Delta region and the Pearl River Delta region all witnessed improved air quality, said the communique.

Six Hebei cities were featured on a list of the 10 most polluted Chinese cities.

Authorities also conducted surface water quality tests at 956 monitoring points.

Only 2.7 percent of the monitored sites reached "excellent" water quality, dropping by 1.1 percentage points year on year, while 17 percent of them had "poor" or "extremely poor" water quality, said Luo Yi, head of the environmental monitoring division with the ministry.

8.4.2 MINISTRY PLANS FIVE-YEAR AIR POLLUTION CONTROL PROJECT

http://news.xinhuanet.com/english/2015-03/03/c_134033233.htm

China's Ministry of Science and Technology has started planning for a five-year air pollution prevention and control project, the ministry announced in March.

A draft blueprint for the project has been published on the ministry's website and the ministry is soliciting public comment.

According to the draft, the focus of air pollution control in China should be shifted from simply responding to heavy smog to a coordinated scheme to prevent both PM2.5, or airborne particles measuring less than 2.5 microns in diameter, and ozone (O3).

Air pollution monitoring and management practices will be shifted from the city level to a regional scale, the draft said.

Authorities will promote joint scientific and technological research and sharing of achievements to support air pollution control efforts, the document said. The research will focus on the cause and spread of pollution, its impact on health, monitoring and warning systems, as well as pollution management and air quality improvement technology and strategy.

The research will also help promote the diagnosis and prevention of pollution-related diseases, the draft added.

According to the draft, the project will be carried out starting this year until 2020.

The ministry said it will improve the plan after listening to opinions from government departments and experts.

8.4.2.1 CHINA ENVIRONMENT COMMUNIQUE EXPOSES POOR AIR, GROUNDWATER QUALITY

http://news.xinhuanet.com/english/2015-06/04/c_134297940.htm

China's Ministry of Environmental Protection released its 2014 Environment Condition Communique in June, revealing serious air and groundwater pollution.

Only 16 of the 161 major Chinese cities subject to air quality monitoring met the national standard for clean air in 2014, statistics from the communique showed.

The other 145 cities, or more than 90 percent of the total, failed to meet the new standard, which was implemented in 2013 and includes a PM2.5 index for monitoring airborne particles measuring less than 2.5 micrometers in diameter.

Authorities observed precipitation in 470 cities and detected acid rain in 29.8 percent of them last year, according to the communique.

Authorities also conducted groundwater quality tests at 4,896 monitoring points. Results showed that only 10.8 percent of the monitored sites had "excellent" water quality, while 61.5 percent of them had "poor" or "extremely poor" water quality.

The communique also showed that the quality of 96.2 percent of the nation's drinking water met standards.

8.4.3 BEIJING PM2.5 LEVEL DOWN 20%

http://news.xinhuanet.com/english/2015-11/02/c_134775744.htm

Beijing's environment authority said in November that the capital city's PM2.5 density, an indicator of air pollution, has dropped by over 20 percent during the first 10 months of the year from the same period last year.

The average density of PM2.5, airborne particles smaller than 2.5 microns in diameter, was 69.7 micrograms per cubic meters in Beijing, down 21.8 percent year on year. Meanwhile, the density of PM10, sulfur dioxide, and nitrogen dioxide fell by 21 percent, 39.8 percent and 17.1 percent respectively, according to the Beijing environmental protection bureau.

During the first nine months, Beijing's number of days with good air quality grew by 31 from last year, and the number of days with heavy pollution dropped by 16.

The bureau attributed the improvement to air pollution control measures and favorable weather conditions.

The city has removed some 280,000 old cars from roads, closed 315 polluting companies, and increased green area by 6,000 hectares during the first 10 months.

Fang Li, deputy head of the bureau, said the city will intensify its monitoring of air quality and enhance controls on activities such as burning leaves, barbecues, and fireworks during the last two months of the year.

8.4.3.1 BEIJING BREATHES CLEANER AIR IN FIRST HALF 2015

http://news.xinhuanet.com/english/2015-07/03/c_134380646.htm

Beijing breathed cleaner air in the first half of this year as the Chinese capital's average PM 2.5 reading dropped 15.2 percent from the same period a year earlier, environmental watchdog said in November.

The average PM 2.5 reading registered in the first six months stood at 77.7 micrograms per cubic meter, which is still more than double the national standard of 35 micrograms per cubic meter, said Beijing Municipal Environmental Protection Bureau.

In the first six months, Beijing residents had to endure 16 days of heavily polluted air as PM2.5 readings shot up to more than 300 micrograms per cubic meter, according to the bureau, seven days less than the same period a year earlier.

Other air pollutants have also been reduced. Sulfur dioxide dropped by 41 percent, nitrogen dioxide by 15 percent and PM 10 by 13 percent, according to the bureau.

8.4.3.2 BEIJING SHUT DOWN NEARLY 400 POLLUTING FACTORIES IN 2014

http://news.xinhuanet.com/english/china/2015-01/23/c_133942352.htm

Beijing closed or removed 392 polluting factories in 2014, according to the municipal people's congress, which opened on January 23.

A total of 30 industrial relief and cooperation platforms and 53 related programs were launched to pull the polluting companies out of Beijing in the past year, mayor of Beijing Wang Anshun said in a government work report.

An additional 36 low-end wholesale markets were also shutdown.

The municipal industrial and commercial authorities have turned down 3,760 applications for new businesses because they were on the list of prohibited or restricted operations.

According to the report, relocating non-core functions from Beijing has become a priority in the coordinated development of municipalities of Beijing and Tianjin and Hebei Province. Another 300 factories are expected to be closed in 2015.

8.4.3.3 OVER 300 FURNACES DISMANTLED AROUND BEIJING IN ONE DAY

http://news.xinhuanet.com/english/2015-07/31/c_134469036.htm

A total of 319 furnaces and 74 chimneys were dismantled in Beijing's neighboring province of Hebei on July 31, a move authorities say could reduce annual coal consumption by 210,000 tons.

The province has already removed nearly 700 furnaces so far this year in a bid to fight air pollution in the Chinese capital and its surrounding regions.

Along with the furnaces and chimneys dismantled on the day will come a reduction of 430 tons of fumes, 2,380 tons of sulfur dioxide and 640 tons of nitrogen oxide, all major pollutants that help form the thick smog that blankets northern China in winter.

Authorities say they are also upgrading existing coal-fired power plants to reduce emissions and aim to cut coal use by 5 million tons.

In the morning of the day, a decade-old chimney was dismantled in a university in the province, which burned 20,000 tons of coal for heating last year. Now the university has installed a solar heating system to replace coal.

The steel industry, which the province has relied on for much of its economic growth, has also been forced to shrink amid the ongoing battle against pollution.

8.4.3.4 BEIJING CLOSES 185 FIRMS TO FIGHT POLLUTION

http://news.xinhuanet.com/english/2015-07/17/c_134423047.htm

Beijing closed or relocated 185 firms in the first half of 2015 in a battle against pollution, local authorities said in July.

The capital city is expected to shut down or move 300 polluting companies by the end of this year, according to a meeting held in July to discuss the city's economic situation in the first half of 2015.

In order to curb "urban ills," including congestion and air pollution, Beijing has also shut down 60 low-end wholesale markets and upgraded another ten markets to alleviate congestion, according to information released at the meeting.

More than 8,500 booths in wholesale markets are expected to be relocated by the end of the year.

Relocating non-core functions from Beijing has become a priority in the coordinated development of Beijing and Tianjin municipalities and Hebei Province.

8.4.3.5 BEIJING FIGHTS POLLUTION THROUGH REGIONAL COOPERATION, PLANT CLOSURES

http://news.xinhuanet.com/english/2015-03/23/c_134090774.htm

On a Friday morning in March, Li Zhu (a pseudonym) and his

colleagues stood in front of a distinctive chimney on Chang'an Avenue in downtown Beijing, waiting to take one last group picture.

Li was about to bid farewell to Guohua Beijing Thermal Plant, once a major pillar in Beijing's heating system. The plant, whose chimney soars 240 meters into the sky, was shuttered under a government plan.

"I have been working here for more than three decades, so it's hard to say goodbye," Li told the Beijing News.

Beijing has renewed its pollution-fighting efforts, including closing a series of coal power plants, to bring back "APEC Blue" — a phrase coined by Chinese netizens to describe the city's clear skies during the Asia-Pacific Economic Cooperation (APEC) meetings in November.

The efforts are badly needed in Beijing, a city frequently enveloped in acrid smog, particularly as the capital and Zhangjiakou in neighboring Hebei Province pursue a joint bid for the 2022 Olympic Winter Games.

According to official figures, the plant's closure will help slash Beijing's coal usage by 1.3 million tons, or 14 percent of Beijing's total goal for the year, and cut emissions of sulfur dioxide, nitric oxide and dust by 1,410 tons, 2,690 tons and 420 tons respectively.

Guohua is not the only thermal plant to fade into history. Its shutdown came a day after the closure of another 93-year-old thermal power plant run by Beijing Energy Investment Group in western Beijing. Of the four major coal-fired power plants in Beijing, three have been closed so far and the last is scheduled to be closed next year.

Acrid smog has caused public discontent in Beijing, prompting local authorities to take actions to prevent it from worsening, including closing high-polluting companies, banning substandard vehicles and increasing funding to fight pollution.

In 2014, Beijing shut down 392 companies that cause pollution, upgraded 116 types of environmental protection equipment and slashed 2.3 million tons of coal use by closing the Gaojing Thermal Power Plant, one of the four major coal-fired plants.

Meanwhile, regional cooperation is high on the agenda for Beijing authorities in tackling foul air.

On March 23, Wang Anshun, Beijing's mayor, said at the China Development Forum 2015 that Beijing will map out a long-term plan to combat smog and air pollution with neighboring Tianjin Municipality and Hebei Province. Tianjin and Hebei have also been shrouded in smog in recent years.

Regional cooperation to fight pollution has also won support from the central government. On March 20, the National Development and Reform Commission issued a circular stating that the central government will allocate a total of 1.5 billion yuan (241.5 million U.S. dollars) in funds to help six localities, including Beijing, Tianjin and Heibei, treat air pollution.

"All these efforts stand as solid proof that the government is taking the strictest measures, and I believe the blue sky and white clouds will come back to us more and more often," said Lyu Zhongmei, a professor with Hubei University of Economics.

For Li Zhu, it may be painful to say goodbye to the historic Guohua plant, but he said it is worth the loss as long as it benefits the environment.

"I know the closure is good for the environment, and that comforts my heart," he said.

8.4.3.6 BEIJING TO CHARGE EMITTERS OF PM2.5-FORMING POLLUTANTS

http://news.xinhuanet.com/english/2015-09/15/c_134626861.htm

Emitters of volatile organic compounds (VOCs), a source of air pollution, in Beijing will pay fees from October, the city's environment watchdog said in September.

Manufacturers of furniture, petrochemicals, automobiles and electronics; packagers; and printers will be subject to the charge, according to Wang Chunlin, director of pollution prevention and control with Beijing Municipal Environmental Protection Bureau.

Vehicle emissions, the use of solvents, storage and transport of gasoline may generate VOCs, which can form hazardous, breathable particles known as PM2.5 following chemical reactions in the atmosphere.

The polluters will be charged 10 yuan (1.57 U.S. dollars) for per kilogram of discharged gas if their VOC emissions do not exceed 50 percent of the city's limit. Those whose emissions are higher than half of the limit but do not exceed the standards will be charged 20 yuan per kg.

Those polluters whose VOCs emissions pass the limits will pay 40 yuan per kg. Those who do not have waste gas treatment facilities or those whose facilities malfunction will be charged the same amount.

The fees are higher than the treatment cost for polluters, so will stimulate polluters to adopt cleaner methods, Wang said.

The capital has become increasingly smog-bound in recent years, partly due to the rise of PM2.5. The central government has ordered the city to cut PM2.5 from 2012 levels by 25 percent by 2017.

8.4.4 POLLUTION CONTROL SLASHES GDP GROWTH IN BEIJING'S NEIGHBOR

http://news.xinhuanet.com/english/china/2015-01/08/c_133906168.htm

Beijing's neighboring province Hebei, known for its industrial pollution, has reported GDP growth of 6.5 percent in 2014, 1.5 percentage points below target and well behind the 7.7 percent seen in 2013.

GDP of the province stood at 2.9 trillion yuan (467 billion U.S. dollars) last year, governor Zhang Qingwei told the annual session of provincial people's congress in January.

Chen Yongjiu, director of the provincial development and reform commission, said lower market demand, eliminating excessive capacity and air pollution control were among the reasons for the slowdown. He estimated that the latter two factors had dragged 1.75 percentage points off growth.

Governor Zhang said the province reduced production capacity of iron by 15 million tons, steel by 15 million tons, cement by 39 million tons and flat glass by 25 million weight boxes, in 2014. The four industries are major sources of air pollution.

Benefitting from the reductions, the average density of PM2.5 fell by 12 percent in 11 cities in the province last year, and the number of days with heavy air pollution was 14 less than in 2013, according to Zhang.

To combat smog, the State Council, China's cabinet, targeted cutting iron and steel production by 80 million tons by 2017, and Hebei was ordered to bear three quarters of the cut. The province is also due to reduce cement production capacity by 60 million tons and coal by 40 million tons.

All things considered, the province set the GDP growth target at 7 percent in 2015.

8.4.4.1 CHINA'S HEBEI TO CLOSE 2,500 BRICK KILNS TO CUT POLLUTION

http://news.xinhuanet.com/english/2015-03/12/c_134062319.htm

Northern China's Hebei Province will close all 2,500 solid brick-tile kilns within one year as part of its effort to cut pollution, said the provincial government in March.

Authorities dismantled the first batch of 62 kilns across 11 cities on March 12. The move is expected to save 90,000 tons of coal and reduce emissions by 11,000 tons of dust, sulfur dioxide and nitrogen oxides per year.

The closure of kilns are one of the measures Hebei is using to cut coal consumption and pollution. New building materials, such as air bricks will replace the old solid bricks.

Solid brick kilns waste resources, destroy croplands and cause serious pollution because of their direct emissions, a provincial official said.

A total of 2,500 solid brick-tile factories in Hebei produce 12 billion bricks each year, but consume 2.2 million tons of coal and discharge 250,000 tons of pollutants.

Hebei, which neighbors Beijing and the northern port city of Tianjin, is often blamed for the notorious choking smog that often seeps into neighboring regions due to its heavy industry.

The province is taking steps toward limiting the excessive number of iron and steel, glass, and concrete factories to reduce pollution.

In 2014, Hebei cut coal consumption by 15 million tons, the first time that coal consumption in the province dropped year on year.

Beijing, Tianjin and Hebei will see coal consumption reduced by 13 million tons, 10 million tons, and 40 million tons from their 2012 levels respectively by 2017, said the National Development and Reform Commission in January.

8.4.5 INDUSTRIAL FIRMS AROUND SHANGHAI DISNEY SCHEDULED FOR CLOSURE

http://news.xinhuanet.com/english/china/2015-09/07/c_134596535.htm

A total of 153 industrial enterprises surrounding Shanghai Disney Resort are scheduled to be shut down by the end of next year, accompanied by industrial structure adjustment in the area, Jiefang Daily reports.

Most of these enterprises struggle with high-energy consumption, heavy environmental pollution, and low production efficiency.

The adjustment will involve an area of some 10 square kilometers. Following the move, ecological reclamation and public service facilities will become priority.

Shanghai has accelerated progress in industrial structure adjustment in several key areas this year. According to an unnamed director with the municipal Economic and Information Commission, when such adjustments end, some 2 square kilometers of land will be set aside and 40,000 tons of standard coal reduced annually.

8.4.6 60% OF HIGH-EMISSION VEHICLES REMOVED FROM CHINA'S ROADS

http://news.xinhuanet.com/english/2015-09/29/c_134671922.htm

From January to August, China removed 696,500 high-emission vehicles from roads nationwide, accounting for 60 percent of China's high-emission cars, said the Ministry of Environmental Protection.

China has only four months to remove the others to meet this year's target of pulling all high-emission commercial vehicles registered before the end of 2005 from roads. The target was set in a government work report in March in an effort to improve air quality.

According to statistics released by the ministry, north China's Tianjin Municipality has fulfilled its share ahead of schedule, while 13 provincial regions including Hunan, Shandong, Hainan and Fujian have fallen behind with less than 50 percent of their work completed.

To accelerate the removal of targeted vehicles, the ministry has filed monthly reports briefing the public on the latest developments in each provincial region since July.

8.4.6.1 CHINA SPEEDS UP FUEL QUALITY UPGRADING FOR BETTER AIR

http://news.xinhuanet.com/english/2015-04/28/c_134193303.htm

China introduced new measures in April to accelerate the quality upgrading of refined gasoline.

Quality upgrading is key to preventing and controlling air pollution and will help improve the environment and living standards, said a statement released after a State Council executive meeting presided over by Premier Li Keqiang.

The measures will also boost investment and promote the technological transformation of domestic enterprises, as well as increase consumption demand.

Starting from next year, all vehicles in the 11 provinces and municipalities of eastern China should use fuels, including gasoline and diesel, that adhere to China's leading '5th-phase' standards, with sulphur content within 10 ppm (parts per million), starting from next year.

Previously the regions only included Beijing, Tianjin and Hebei, and major cities in the Yangtze River Delta and Pearl River Delta.

Fuels in line with the standard should be supplied nationwide as early as January 2017.

From July 2017, provisions of 4th-phase automobile standard diesel, with no more than 50 ppm of sulphur content, will be available all over the country. Nationwide provisions with sulphur content within 10 ppm, will start from January of 2018.

To fulfil these tasks, oil refineries will have to increase their investment in technological upgrading by about 68 billion yuan (11.11 billion U.S. dollars), which will further mobilize investment and production of related industries such as refining equipment.

The State Council also vowed to enforce standards and strengthen supervision to support the acceleration of quality upgrading of oil products.

8.4.6.2 BEIJING UPGRADES DIESEL BUSES TO CUT AIR POLLUTION

http://news.xinhuanet.com/english/2015-07/06/c_134387353.htm

Beijing in July completed the renovation of its 8,800-strong fleet of diesel buses, which will now discharge significantly less emissions.

This latest effort, led by Beijing Municipal Environmental Protection Bureau, means that the buses will discharge 60 percent less nitrogen oxide, or 2,800 tons, annually.

The project follows standards on automobiles and their emissions, released by the city in 2013, that aimed to address loopholes in diesel vessel standards.

Observers and officials say vehicles are a major contributor to Beijing's air pollution. The city has 5.57 million vehicles, which churn out 700,000 tons of pollutants annually.

The city has promised to phase out 200,000 vehicles that fail to meet emission standards, as well as close more than 300 polluting factories this year.

8.5 CHINA TO INSPECT WATER POLLUTION PREVENTION, CONTROL

http://news.xinhuanet.com/english/2015-04/28/c_134192337.htm

China's top legislature will carry out a nationwide inspection on the implementation of the Water Pollution Prevention and Control Law.

Four or five teams will carry out inspections across provincial-level regions in May and June, the water pollution prevention and control committee of the National People's Congress (NPC) Standing Committee said in April.

The inspectors will visit Inner Mongolia, Heilongjiang, Anhui, Shandong, Hubei and Guangxi provinces, as well as others, to examine water resource measures.

They will inspect protection of water resources, water pollutant discharge, the legal system for permitting pollutants and pollution prevention measures for major rivers. Opinions on amending the current law will also be solicited.

In other regions, provincial-level legislators will conduct research and examination in preventing and controlling water pollution.

In late August, the NPC Standing Committee will hear and review reports on water pollution prevention and control.

A string of water pollution incidents have occurred in recent years, eliciting serious concern across China.

Chen Changzhi, vice chairman of the NPC Standing Committee, said inspections for the enforcement of the Water Pollution Prevention and Control Law will promote an anti-pollution drive and help amend the law.

8.5.1 COOPERATION BETWEEN GOVERNMENT, CITIZENS ENCOURAGED ON WATER POLLUTION PREVENTION

http://news.xinhuanet.com/english/2015-04/27/c_134189491.htm

Cooperation between the government and society to prevent water pollution will be advanced, according an announcement released by the Ministry of Finance (MOF) and the Ministry of Environmental Protection (MEP) in April.

The cooperation public-private-partnership (PPP) model will first be rolled out in regions where the waterways are on the national list of key support, as well as regions supported by water pollution prevention special funds.

A integration of methods including financial incentives, investment subsidies and fundraising allowances will be utilized to support the implementation of PPP projects concerning water pollution prevention.

Local governments should also encourage financial institutions to offer support for projects by raising the line of credit and improving credit ratings, the announcement said.

8.5.2 WATER POLLUTION PLAN TO BRING LONG-TERM GAIN

http://news.xinhuanet.com/english/2015-04/17/c_134160737.htm

A detailed action plan to fight water pollution in China bodes well for a nation troubled by dirty waterways.

Announced in April by the State Council, Chin re exacting requirements on polluting companies will probably force some of them to close. In the long term though, the plan is expected to fuel economic growth, not slow it.

A BLESSING AMID PAIN

Alarm bells are sounding for small, outdated factories in sectors including paper, insecticides and tanning, which have been ordered to shut down by the end of 2016.

However, calls for bigger facilities in these sectors to update their technology to meet emission requirements and a target for clearer water in major river valleys by 2020 present unprecedented business opportunities for companies related to environmental protection.

Li Jie, a researcher in environmental science and engineering with Shanghai's Tongji University, said the action plan will hurt polluting enterprises in the short term, but they must face up to an irreversible trend toward closer environmental scrutiny of their operations.

Many small plants operate without any pollution controls or treatment. It is these operations that will be hit hardest.

Meanwhile, Li said, the action plan will bring business opportunities to the green industry, as enterprises are pushed to take more responsibility for their emissions, driving demand for equipment designed to limit pollution.

According to the Ministry of Environmental Protection (MEP), implementation of the new measures will increase GDP by 5.7 trillion yuan (about 910 billion U.S. dollars) and create 3.9 million urban jobs.

Sewage treatment businesses will be the first to benefit, said Li, referring to the plan's target to see dark and odorous water in urban areas eliminated by 2030.

Xia Guang, director of the MEP's Policy Research Center for Environment and Economy, said the action plan will create new customers for both domestic green enterprises and foreign ones.

Foreign firms have already taken a sizable share of the pollution treatment market.

AN ARDUOUS TASK

Analysts have said that pollution controls are badly needed. After more than three decades of rapid economic growth, China's water pollution has become too serious to ignore.

Some 60 percent of ground water checked by 4,778 monitoring stations was rated as "bad" or "very bad," according to an MEP report released in June 2014.

It said 17 of 31 major freshwater lakes are moderately or slightly polluted, including China's two biggest lakes, Poyang and Dongting, both of which also have shrunk significantly compared with their peak.

The report also said that more than 300 of 657 cities sampled face water shortage problems.

In the Beijing-Tianjin-Hebei region, water per capita is even less than Israel, whose 300-cubic-meter standard is rated "extremely scarce."

As cities have expanded rapidly, even tap water has fallen victim to big polluters and mishandling of industrial chemicals. In recent years, panic buying of bottled water has occurred frequently in cities, where a rising middle class is increasingly concerned about water quality.

In 2013, Shanghai's drinking water came under threat after pig carcasses were found in the Huangpu River.

The Ministry of Supervision estimates that the number of people affected by substandard drinking water may be as high as 140 million.

The new action plan is part of China's efforts to wage war on all types of pollution. It follows a plan released in 2013 to tackle smog.

That plan seems to be working. The average reading of PM 2.5, airborne particles with a diameter small enough to penetrate the lungs, has declined more than 10 percent in Hebei and Tianjin while Beijing has had a 4-percent drop, according to figures from local governments.

HARSHER MEASURES WITH DEADLINES

Xia said one the strengths of the new action plan is that it defines the responsibilities of local governments.

Pollution checks will be conducted every year and the results will be part of performance reviews for provincial officials. Distribution of funds for the campaign will also depend on the results.

Meanwhile, the plan also targets businesses with concrete measures. From 2016, a blacklist will name businesses that exceed their pollutant quotas, with severe violators risking closure.

Li said concerns about their public image will pressure enterprises to make genuine efforts to reduce pollutants.

The action plan's other main strength is that it announces deadlines, according to analysts. The plan stipulates that more than 70 percent of water in the seven major river valleys, including the Yangtze and Yellow rivers, should be in good condition by 2020. It set the same target for offshore areas.

By the end of 2030, more than 75 percent of water in the seven major river valleys should be clear, with dark and odorous water in urban areas eliminated.

Li warned that national standards on water cleanliness have long existed without proper enforcement. With harsher rules in place, implementation is the key.

8.5.2.1 BEIJING CONSERVES MORE WATER IN 2014

http://news.xinhuanet.com/english/2015-10/04/c_134683703.htm

Beijing conserved 120 million cubic meters of water in 2014 as the city used multiple ways to fight water scarcity, the Ministry of Water Resources said.

The figure compared to 113 million cubic meters of water saved in 2012. said the ministry, without mentioning the figure for 2013.

Water consumption per 10,000 yuan of GDP growth fell 4 percent last year, it said.

Beijing has controlled underground water more strictly, and made rainfall collection and water reclamation more effectively. As it cracked down on private well-digging and improved agricultural water-saving, the city used 1.96 billion cubic meters of underground water last year, 48 million cubic meters less than that in 2013.

With the goal of transforming Bejing into a "sponge city," the city has invested more in projects collecting rainfall. Last year, 110 million cubic meters of rain was collected.

Beijing also put 860 million cubic meters of reclaimed water to reuse thanks to better sewage treatment.

8.5.2.2 SOCIAL CAPITAL ENCOURAGED IN WATER POLLUTION CONTROL

http://news.xinhuanet.com/english/2015-05/06/c_134215776.htm

China will encourage more social investment to team up with the government in water pollution prevention and control, according to a guideline issued in May.

The efforts will first focus on drinking water sources, and additional areas of water pollution prevention and control will be opened for public investment, said the guideline, jointly issued by the Ministry of Finance and the Ministry of Environmental Protection (MEP).

Water pollution prevention and control, including river protection, drinking water safety and environmental monitoring, currently depend on government investment.

The guideline said an investment-return system should be set up to attract social capital to expand financing channels.

Expanded investment will help intensify the government's fight against water pollution and implement the Action Plan for Water Pollution Prevention and Control, which was released on April 16, said Zhao Hualin, an MEP official.

8.5.3 CLEANING UP CHINA'S BIG RIVERS

http://news.xinhuanet.com/english/2015-04/17/c_134160642.htm

The health of China's rivers is due for a thorough examination, as an action plan for pollution control goes on stream.

A State Council plan on water pollution, released in April, aims to reduce pollutants and protect resources through new, strictly quantifiable targets.

Over 70 percent of the water in the basins of China's seven major rivers should be in "good" condition by 2020. The target applies to the Yangtze, Yellow, Zhujiang, Songhuajiang, Huai, Hai and Liao rivers.

Over the last few decades, industrialization, urbanization and rapid population growth have taken their toll on China's already rare freshwater resources. Half of China's major rivers and around 40 percent of important lakes are polluted.

The action plan is just one small step in the right direction, but it won't be easy to clean up China's "most polluted."

The Hai River in the heart of Tianjin Municipality is among the worst. According to a 2013 report by the city, 72.7 percent of water in the Tianjin section is "bad." Zhang Kai of a Tianjin hydrology institute said the river suffers from a severe water shortage.

"Per capita resources along the river have been just over 100 cubic meters for years, compared to 300 in Israel, a country famous for water shortages. Quantity and quality of water are closely related," he said.

Former chief Tianjin environmental protection engineer Bao Jingling said, "The small amount of water has led to accumulation of industrial, agricultural and household pollution in the river basin. The pollution is often washed into the city streets by torrential rain."

Pollution control on the river has been obstructed by a lack of collaboration between government departments. An unwritten rule states that water departments deal with problems of water, while the environmental protection departments take charge of pollution on the shore. When pollution in a waterway originates on the riverbank, the division of responsibility is problematic.

The 1,000-km Huai, which crosses five provinces, has been classified as "severely polluted" since the 1990s. Thanks to a national pollution control campaign in place for 20 years, water quality has improved somewhat, but the situation remains grave.

Wang Jiaquan of Hefe University of Technology in Anhui Province said that while water in the main stream of the Huai has become clearer, tributaries and lakes have not received enough attention, so parts of the river are still in a poor state.

On a recent fact-finding mission, a Xinhua reporter visited a tributary of the Huai in Anhui and found it covered in white foam and dead weeds with a foul smell. Local farmers said the smell is especially bad in summer and people who wade in the river develop a red rash.

The problem is nationwide. The main streams of rivers are often given more attention than tributaries and lakes. It will be important to attach just as much importance to tributaries in order to hit the new targets, Wang said.

"The response of the local governments to the plan matters," he said. "Can local authorities come up with detailed and feasible policies?"

8.6 CHINA TO DEPLOY SPACE-AIR-GROUND SENSORS FOR ENVIRONMENT PROTECTION

http://news.xinhuanet.com/english/2015-08/04/c_134480651.htm

China will build a space-air-ground integrated sensing system to detect and stop pollution, according to the Ministry of Environmental Protection.

China's central authorities decided in July to build a comprehensive ecological environment monitoring system that will have the ability for automatic early warning using surveillance sites across the country.

The ministry said it will retake the power of environmental monitoring from local authorities, so that the country will have a unified standard for pollution detection and punishment.

A total of 2.5 billion yuan (402.8 million U.S. dollars) has already been invested to build the system, the ministry said.

So far, there has been more than 2,700 surveillance sites with 60,000 professional staff spread all over the country, covering 338 cities.

The ministry said it will also utilize satellites for remote sensing and drones to conduct regular surveillance on air and water quality.

8.6.1 UAVS BRING NEW TRENDS IN ENVIRONMENTAL PROTECTION

http://news.xinhuanet.com/english/2015-04/02/c_134119197.htm

Unmanned aerial vehicles (UAVs) are playing an increasingly important role in China's battle against pollution.

During the latest air pollution inspections in Beijing, Tianjin, Hebei Province and surrounding areas, law enforcement officials of the Ministry of Environmental Protection deployed UAVs to check key places.

UAV's were responsible for the discovery of at least one environmental violator in Hebei's Handan City, where the air quality ranks among the worst in China. Two outdated pieces of machinery were found hidden in the Hexin Iron and Steel Company factory. Government inspectors came to the site immediately.

The sintering machines exceeded emissions standards and operation should have stopped before the end of 2013. Workers were also found improperly operating the desulfurization facilities installed in the machines, an inspector said.

Six enterprises including Hexin were found violating pollution control guidelines during the inspections.

With strong determination to fight pollution, UAVs have been frequently used to monitor pollution discharge and the operation of desulfurization facilities of companies related to steel, coking and electricity industries.

As a manufacturing hub, Foshan City of south China's Guangdong Province houses 40,000 sources of industrial pollution and nearly 900 industrial parks scattered in different villages, which are difficult to supervise.

The long-standing problem has pushed Foshan to seek innovative ways to prevent and treat pollution.

When law enforcement officials enter a plant, often illegal behaviors are stopped, making it hard to collect evidence, said Peng Cong'en, head of the city's environmental protection bureau.

The UAVs used for environmental protection collect information with installed remote sensors, including digital cameras in high resolution, infrared and laser scanners and magnetometer. Some are even installed with infrared thermal imager which can show the operation of facilities at night.

Peng told Xinhua that the drones can provide video evidence and record the law enforcement process. "In this way, polluting firms fail to conceal their illegal behaviors," he said.

In addition to Foshan, China's Jilin Province also uses UAVs to monitor the Mudanjiang River, a major waterway in northeast China, in a move to ensure water security.

East China's Zhejiang Province uses UAVs to supervise factories and prevent them from stealthily pumping waste water into rivers or lakes.

UAVs bring a new trend to environmental protection. They also provide technical support in dealing with major environmental emergencies as well as assessment for construction projects, said Wang Qiao, an engineer with the Satellite Environment Center.

Wang said a new system, which could monitor the types, density and diffusion process of pollutants with the help of UAVs once emergencies happen, will be put into use soon.

8.6.2 DRONES DETECT ENVIRONMENT VIOLATIONS

http://news.xinhuanet.com/english/2015-05/18/c_134249488.htm

Polluters need to watch out for an eye in the sky as drones have helped the Ministry of Environmental Protection (MEP) detect factories flouting environmental laws in one of China's most polluted provinces.

The ministry dispatched drones in March to Handan City in north China's Hebei Province, where they uncovered violations including excessive emissions and inadequate waste processing, the ministry said in May.

Several companies missed deadlines for putting anti-pollution facilities into operation, and others do not have any waste processing facilities, the ministry said, quoting monitoring results from the drones.

They are equipped with infrared devices which can allow them to work during the night.

The drones found a polyphenyl ether factory that was under construction without passing necessary environmental assessment and a stone factory pouring polluted water into surrounding rivers.

Local authorities have fined these violators, according to the MEP.

Ministry official Zou Shoumin said it will continue to use drones, which he called a "secret weapon", for random pollution inspections in more polluted areas.

The MEP also said that checks of construction sites, roads and coal storage yards in 52 cities since March had found 88 violations of laws designed to limit smog. The law-breaking included excessive emissions and faking of pollution data. East China's Jiangsu Province was found to have the most violations.

8.7 CHINA RECORDS 471 ENVIRONMENT EMERGENCIES IN 2014

http://news.xinhuanet.com/english/china/2015-01/23/c_133942741.htm

China recorded 471 pollution emergencies in 2014, 241 less than in 2013, the Ministry of Environmental Protection (MEP) announced in January.

The MEP disclosed the top three worst incidents of the year.

One in Maoming City, Guangdong Province, in January 2014 resulted in 97 middle school students and teachers being hospitalized. They inhaled toxic gas from sewage dumped by an auto repair factory.

Five days after the incident, the water quality was back to normal, and all 97 victims were discharged from hospital.

In April, a section of the Hanjiang River, which flows through Wuhan, the seat of the central province of Hubei, was found to contain an excessive concentration of ammonia and nitrogen.

The contamination was traced to an upstream city that had released flood water. It took two days for the water to be returned to a safe level.

In August, the Qianzhangyan Reservoir in southwest Chongqing—which supplies 50,000 people with drinking water—was polluted by waste from a mining company.

Huangchangping Mining Co. illegally began a trial production of pyrites, and dumped its untreated waste water on land near the plant. The toxic waste water seeped into ground water that flowed to the Qianzhangyan Reservoir, which is three kilometers away.

The company was fined one million yuan (160,600 U.S. dollars), and its manager was put into custody, according to the MEP.

8.7.1 REDUCING CHINA'S AIR POLLUTION MAY PREVENT ABOUT 900,000 CARDIOVASCULAR DEATHS BY 2030: STUDY

http://news.xinhuanet.com/english/2015-11/11/c_134803356.htm

Lowering air pollution to the 2008 Beijing Olympics level could prevent about 900,000 cardiovascular deaths in urban China by 2030, a study said in November.

To guarantee clean air for the 2008 Olympics, China temporarily closed factories, construction sites and limited auto traffic in Beijing.

In the new study, researchers from Beijing's Fuwai Hospital and other research agencies simulated two air quality improvement scenarios from 2015 to 2030, each achieved gradually over 10 years.

One simulation was of the air quality during the 2008 Beijing Olympics, which was a fine particle matter (PM2.5) level of 55 micrograms per cubic meter. The other was of the World Health Organization's recommendation of 10 micrograms per cubic meter.

For comparison, they also projected the effect of a 50 percent reduction in active and secondhand smoking and lowering systolic high blood pressure to 140 millimeters of mercury, each over 5 years.

They found achieving the 2008 Olympic air quality level would reduce stroke deaths by 2.7 percent and coronary heart disease deaths by 7.2 percent in urban China, including Beijing, from 2015 to 2030. That means 304,000 stroke deaths, 619,000 coronary heart disease deaths would be prevented in the next 15 years.

But the Olympics scenario would only gain life-years on the order of about a third of that projected for a 50 percent smoking reduction, and a fourth of that projected for systolic hypertension control, they said.

The more aggressive World Health Organization pollution goal, however, would yield greater life year gains than either tobacco or systolic blood pressure control.

"Air pollution is a leading cardiovascular risk factor in Beijing and all urban China," the researchers concluded in their paper. "We projected that lowering air pollution to Beijing Olympics level could prevent about 900,000 cardiovascular deaths and gain about 4.2 million life years in urban China by 2030."

The findings were presented in Nov. 10 at the American Heart Association's annual scientific meeting in Orlando, Florida.

8.8 GREEN VOLUNTEER ALLIANCE LAUNCHED

http://news.xinhuanet.com/english/china/2015-07/22/c_134435550.
htm

Shanghai's first environmental protection young volunteer alliance was established in July, and members of 69 volunteer organizations are expected to be its first members, the city's greenery authorities said.

The alliance aims to encourage more people to join in the city's garbage sorting plan, the Shanghai Greenery and Public Sanitation Bureau said. It will help to promote garbage sorting knowledge and host activities such as cycling, summer camping, and micro film competition related to garbage sorting to raise people's awareness.

A further 1 million households will be covered in the city's garbage sorting plan this year, and the target is to cover all residential communities within the middle ring road by the year end, the bureau said. By the end of last year, the plan covered 2.8 million households in the city.

8.9 CHINESE MAN INVENTS "GREEN FIRECRACKER" TO FIGHT SMOG

http://news.xinhuanet.com/english/china/2015-02/07/c_133977207.
htm

Chinese revelers may have the hard choice of deciding between protecting the environment or protecting tradition as they prepare fireworks displays for the upcoming Spring Festival, which falls on Feb. 19 this year.

But, a man from central China's Henan Province has devised an invention that could allow them to do both.

Wang Xinming, an oil company employee, created a non-polluting firecracker to help people protect the environment and enjoy festive atmosphere at the same time.

"My invention is not powered by explosives or electricity," the 29-year-old

Wang said,

Approved for patent in July, the firecracker uses a closed cavity which can be injected with air. Users then just need to press a button and the closed cavity will immediately open a small hole, through which, compressed air will discharge and produce an explosive sound.

It is more beautiful than normal firecrackers. If customers need, the firecracker can emit water mist and even fragrance, Wang said.

Chinese people traditionally light firecrackers and fireworks during the Spring Festival or Chinese Lunar New Year, based on the superstition that the noise will fend off evil spirits and bad luck.

However, this tradition has been blamed for dust, sulfur dioxide and lingering smog in recent years.

"My firecracker is safe and environmentally friendly," Wang said. Although the invention has not been mass produced, Wang sees great potential in the market.

It is mainly produced from plastic. With the manufacturing cost reaching about 150 yuan per unit (about 25 U.S. dollars), the selling price may be higher. But it can be reused, Wang said.

"Some ways of celebrating festivals may have drastic impact on our environment. If Wang's invention can be mass produced, it's another way for us to fight smog," said Chen Ying, a research fellow at the Institute for Urban and Environmental Studies under the Chinese Academy of Social Sciences.

Part 9

Poverty Relief High on China's 2016-2020 Government Agenda: Official

http://news.xinhuanet.com/english/2015-10/12/c_134705734.htm

Poverty alleviation will be a major task in China's 2016-2020 development plan, an official said at a press conference ahead of the 23rd International Day for the Eradication of Poverty on October 17, which also marked China's second National Poverty Relief Day.

Poverty relief remains a top priority for China and related work will be a major issue for a key meeting later this month to set the course for China's development over the next five years (2016-2020), said Hong Tianyun, deputy director of the State Council Leading Group Office of Poverty Alleviation and Development of China.

Beijing will host the Global Poverty Reduction and Development Forum on October 16, during which around 300 representatives will gather to share their experience in combating poverty.

President Xi Jinping will deliver a keynote speech at the forum, Hong said.

China has made remarkable progress in poverty relief. It was the first developing country to meet the Millennium Development Goals

(MDGs) target of reducing the population living in poverty by half ahead of the 2015 deadline.

In the past 15 years, China has lifted more than 600 million people out of poverty, accounting for about 70 percent of those brought out of poverty worldwide.

Despite this, China still had 70.17 million people in the countryside living below the country's poverty line of 2,300 yuan (376 U.S. dollars) in annual income at the end of last year.

Hong said it will be challenging for China to achieve its goal of lifting all people out of poverty by 2020.

He said the government will come up with a string of more effective and targeted measures to achieve the goal, including launching education campaigns, encouraging financial support and building public platforms to mobilize more people to join the fight.

While striving to reduce poverty domestically, China has also supported other developing countries in the cause.

Speaking to a United Nations summit last month, President Xi pledged an initial 2 billion U.S. dollars to establish an assistance fund to help developing nations reach the target.

9.1 MORE THAN 10 MLN CHINESE OVERCOME POVERTY IN 2014

http://news.xinhuanet.com/english/china/2015-01/30/c_133959852. htm

More than 10 million rural Chinese residents cast off the label of impoverished in 2014, another achievement for the world's second largest economy apart from GDP, official data showed in January.

The central authority and government in poverty-stricken regions increased their efforts to reduce poverty last year, finally beating the poverty-relief target of 10 million, Hong Tianyun, deputy director of the State Council Leading Group Office of Poverty Alleviation and Development, said during a press conference.

Hong said the governments dispatched around 430,000 officials, forming more than 100,000 work teams to help residents shake off poverty around the country.

China initiated a targeted help-the-poor program last year and identified 128,000 impoverished villages with 88.62 million people living under the poverty line.

9.2 CHINA'S RICH-POOR GAP NARROWS IN 2014

http://news.xinhuanet.com/english/china/2015-01/20/c_133932404.htm

The Gini coefficient, an index reflecting the rich-poor gap, dropped for the sixth consecutive year in China since a peak recorded in 2008, data showed in Janauary.

The index stood at 0.469 in 2014, dropping for six years in a row since the index hit its 0.491 high in 2008, the National Bureau of Statistics (NBS) said in a statement.

Last year, the average disposable income of Chinese residents rose 8 percent in real terms to 20,167 yuan (3,294 U.S. dollars), faster than a 7.4 percent economic growth, the NBS said.

The disposable income of rural residents increased 9.2 percent year on year, while that for urban residents rose 6.8 percent.

9.3 CHINA REALIZES UNIVERSAL POWER ACCESS

http://news.xinhuanet.com/english/2015-12/25/c_134949385.htm

China has realized universal power access when the last remote group of 39,800 people became able to light their homes with electricity.

The light came on Dec. 23 in Gomang and Changjiang villages in the northwestern Qinghai province, the last group in the country without power.

The 9,614 households are at an average altitude of more than 4,000 meters in the remote hinterland of the Qinghai-Tibet Plateau, said Shi Xueqian, Communist Party chief of Qinghai Electric Power Company under the State Grid.

The company spent 2.1 billion yuan (324 million U.S.dollars) and more than 5,000 workers were involved in the operation.

Two thirds of households are connected to the national grid while the rest use photovoltaic devices.

"This means Qinghai has provided power to its whole population and China has fulfilled its goal of providing electricity to all its people set out in the 12th five-year plan (2011-2015)," said Tan Rongyao, a senior official of the National Energy Administration (NEA).

NEW LIFE, NEW HOPE

"Now we have electricity, we no longer need to burn cow dung for heat or use oil lamps for lighting," said Hudong, a herder from Gomang village.

Burning cow dung won't get them through the long, bitter winter, so Hudong and other villagers had to cut forest trees and bring them from 30 km away.

His 16-year-old granddaughter, a junior middle school student, can read books in more light, he said. He bought a TV set several years ago, but it was just ornament before. Now, they can finally watch TV.

The grid access brings new life and hope for local people. Cering said he planned to buy a refrigerator and an electric machine to produce ghee to sell.

"We have been looking forward to having electricity for many years," said Jamyang, a herder. His village began to have power via a photovoltaic station in November.

"Now, at nights in our pasturing area, we can watch TV while drinking tea or eating, instead of going to sleep early as in the past," he added.

Since 2013, Huanghe (the Yellow River) Hydropower Development Co. Ltd has built 261 photovoltaic stations and distributed more than 40,000 household photovoltaic devices in the area, helping 185,000 people to get connected, said Wei Xiangui, deputy general manager of the company.

UNIVERSAL POWER ACCESS

At the end of 2012, China had 2.73 million people without electricity,mainly in Xinjiang, Sichuan, Tibet, Qinghai, Gansu and Inner Mongolia regions or provinces. Qinghai had about 470,000 people of them.

After two years, 2.73 million had dropped to 237,800 and all of them were in Sichuan and Qinghai.

In March, Chinese Premier Li Keqiang vowed to provide electricity to these last few before the end of the year.

In June, Sichuan province completed its task and 39,800 people in Qinghai became the last without power.

From 2013 to 2015, Qinghai spent 5.1 billion yuan on expanding power access. During the same period, the country invested 24.8 billion yuan (3.8 billion U.S. dollars) in extending power grids and building renewable energy facilities.

The country will upgrade rural grids to improve their operation stability and supply capabilities to meet demands, according to the NEA.

Part 10

China Pledges 3 Billion USD for Developing Countries to Fight Climate Change

http://news.xinhuanet.com/english/2015-09/26/c_134663232.htm

China pledged in September a 20-billion-yuan (3-billion U.S. dollars) fund to help other developing countries combat climate change.

The China South-South Climate Cooperation Fund will also enhance their capacity to access the Green Climate Fund (GCF), according to a China-U.S. joint presidential statement on climate change signed during Chinese President Xi Jinping's state visit to the United States.

China and the United States recognized the importance of mobilizing climate finance to support low-carbon, climate-resilient development in developing countries, particularly the least developed countries, small island developing states and African countries, according to the statement.

In this connection, the United States also reaffirmed its 3-billion-dollar pledge to the GCF.

In the statement, the Chinese and U.S. presidents reaffirmed determination to implement domestic climate policies, strengthen bilateral

coordination and cooperation, and to promote sustainable development and the transition to green, low-carbon as well as climate resilient
economies.

VISION FOR PARIS CLIMATE CONFERENCE

Xi and Obama stood together in Beijing in November, 2014 to make
the China-U.S. Joint Announcement on Climate Change, emphasizing
their personal commitment to a successful climate agreement in Paris.

The "historic" announcement "marked a new era of multilateral climate
diplomacy as well as a new pillar in their (China,and U.S.) bilateral
relationship," the presidential statement said.

China and the United States said in the statement they support the inclu-
sion in the Paris outcome of an enhanced transparency system to build
mutual trust and confidence and promote effective implementation.

"It should provide flexibility to those developing countries that need it
in light of their capacities," the statement said.

The two sides stressed that the Paris agreement should accord greater
prominence and visibility to adaptation, including by recognizing that it
is a key component of the long-term global response to climate change,
in terms of both preparing for the unavoidable impacts of climate
change and enhancing resilience.

The statement also underscored the importance of continued, robust
financial support beyond 2020 to help developing countries build
low-carbon and climate-resilient societies.

It urged continued support by developed countries to developing countries and encourage such support by other countries willing to do so.

Developed countries committed to a goal of mobilizing jointly 100 billion
dollars a year by 2020 to address the needs of developing countries and
that this funding would come from a wide variety of sources, public and
private, bilateral and multilateral, including alternative sources of finance.

China and the United States also recognized the crucial role of major technological advancement in the transition to green and low-carbon, climate-resilient and sustainable development and affirmed the importance of significant increases in basic research and development in the coming years both within their own economies and globally.

ADVANCING DOMESTIC CLIMATE ACTION

Both China and the United States are committed to achieving their respective post-2020 actions as announced in last November's joint announcement.

The presidential statement noted that the two countries have taken key steps toward implementation and are committed to continuing to intensify efforts, which "will substantially promote global investment in low-carbon technologies and solutions."

China has been making great efforts to advance ecological civilization and promote green, low carbon, climate resilient and sustainable development through accelerating institutional innovation and enhancing policies and actions.

According to the statement, among other endeavors, China will lower carbon dioxide emissions per unit of GDP by 60 to 65 percent from the 2005 level by 2030 and increase the forest stock volume by around 4.5 billion cubic meters on the 2005 level by 2030.

China will promote green power dispatch, giving priority, in distribution and dispatching, to renewable power generation and fossil fuel power generation of higher efficiency and lower emission levels.

China also plans to start in 2017 its national emission trading system, covering key industry sectors such as iron and steel, power generation, chemicals, building materials, paper-making and nonferrous metals.

ENHANCING BILATERAL, MULTILATERAL COOPERATION

In the presidential statement, China and the United States committed to further deepening and enhancing efforts to combat climate change through the U.S.-China Climate Change Working Group, the premier mechanism for facilitating constructive bilateral dialogue and cooperation on climate change.

The two countries also emphasize that businesses can play an important role in promoting low-carbon development, and will make continued efforts to encourage and incentivize actions by businesses.

China and the Untied States consider that their bilateral investments in other countries should support low carbon technologies and climate resilience and are committed to discussing the role of public finance in reducing greenhouse gas emissions.

Both sides are to use public resources to finance and encourage the transition toward low-carbon technologies as a priority, according to the statement.

China and the United States will also strengthen dialogue and cooperation to advance climate change related issues in relevant fora complementary to the UN Framework Convention on Climate Change, such as the G20, Montreal Protocol, the International Civil Aviation Organization and the World Trade Organization.

10.1 CLIMATE CHANGE MAINLY CAUSED BY HUMAN ACTIVITIES: CLIMATE REPORT

http://news.xinhuanet.com/english/2015-03/24/c_134090972.htm

The World Meteorological Organization (WMO) said in March that amidst increasing temperatures, extreme precipitations and flooding, a plethora of evidence continues to suggest that climate change is mainly a consequence of human activities and related greenhouse gases.

Coinciding with World Meteorological Day on March 23, WMO released a detailed statement on 2014's weather trends across the globe.

WMO Secretary-General Michel Jarraud stated that in light of the report and future predictions, "the cost of inaction is high and will become even higher" if significant steps to reduce greenhouse gas emissions are not taken.

Under WMO's "climate change for climate knowledge" theme, Jarraud also stressed that key improvements have enabled better predictions to be made, and that a deeper understanding of weather systems and man's effect on the climate can render climate change more manageable.

According to the Statement on the Status of the Climate in 2014, the mean global temperature increased by 0.57°C compared to the 1961-1990 average of 14°C, making it the warmest year to date. Surface melting of Greenland's ice sheet was also above the 1981-2010 average in June, July and August.

An increase in surface sea-temperature has also been noted, with major consequences for the future as the ocean absorbs 93 percent of excess heat. Mean precipitation remained close to its long-term average of 1,033 mm.

According to the report, the importance of the UN-led Global Framework for Climate Services (GFCS) spearheaded by the WMO and set up in 2009 remains tangible as over 70 countries lack basic climate services.

10.1.1 TOP METEOROLOGICAL OFFICIAL WARNS OF CLIMATE CHANGE RISKS

http://news.xinhuanet.com/english/2015-05/05/c_134212379.htm

A top Chinese meteorological official has warned that the increase of extreme weather in recent years is related to climate change and the country is facing rising risk.

Zheng Guoguang, head of China Meteorological Administration, said China had a higher magnitude of climate change than the global level, according to a recent report run by the Study Times, a weekly newspaper operated by the Party School of the Central Committee of the

Communist Party of China.

Zheng said China's average surface temperature rose by 1.38 degrees Celsius in the past 60 years, or 0.23 degrees every ten years, almost double that of the global level.

He suggested China deal with climate change as an issue of national security to boost China's sustainable development.

Zheng said rise of extreme weather in China such as typhoons, floods, droughts, heavy rain, hail and heat waves in recent years are "highly connected" to climate change.

Zheng also warned climate change is increasingly threatening the safety and stability of major projects such as the Qinghai-Tibet Railway, the power grid, the Three Gorges Dam, south-to-north water diversion project and other energy and ecology projects.

Such risks may also affect their operation efficiency, economical benefits, technical standards and construction, Zheng said without going into specifics.

He said climate change also added to the difficulty of China's fight against hazardous air quality.

Zheng said China is facing an uphill battle against climate change and in its push for energy conservation and emission reduction.

10.1.2 TIBET'S GLACIERS RETREAT, EVEN AS PROTECTION ADVANCES

http://news.xinhuanet.com/english/2015-04/22/c_134175297.htm

Since the 1950s, China's glaciers have retreated by about 7,600 square kilometers; around 18 percent. An average of 247 square kilometers of glacial ice has disappeared every year.

Even mountaineers on Mount Qomolangma seem surprised.

"Qomolangma base camp, 5,200 meters above sea level, had been covered by thick ice, but now there is nothing but stones," Zhang Mingxing, director of Tibet's mountaineering administration center, told Xinhua.

His view was echoed by Kang Shichang of the institute of Tibetan Plateau research, part of the Chinese Academy of Sciences (CAS). He calculates that glaciers around the mountain have shrunk by 10 percent since 1974, evidenced in the fact that a glacial lake downstream of the mountain is now 13 times bigger.

China has more than 46,000 glaciers, mainly on the Qinghai-Tibet Plateau, about 14.5 percent of the world's total. Glaciers are not only a major reservoir of fresh water but an important part of the climate system. "They are sources of life for China's western arid regions," said Kang.

The melting glaciers will inevitably lead to ecological and environmental change. Liu Shiyin, who led a survey of China's glaciers, told Xinhua that, in the short term, retreating glaciers will release meltwater and create lakes, leading to disaster. Glacial lakes in Tibet were breached 15 times between the 1930s and 1990s, causing floods and mudslides.

Glacial melt is closely related to climate change, and the regional government of Tibet is doing all it can to cut emissions. Enterprises which invest in green energy including solar, wind and methane can enjoy tax privileges for up to eight years.

In addition to cutting emissions, Tibet has spent heavily to protect its environment.

Jiang Bai from the regional environmental protection department believes local governments are committed to ensuring clean water and blue sky in Tibet. Back in 2009, the State Council invested 15.5 billion yuan (about 2.5 billion U.S. dollars) in protecting Tibet's environment, Jiang said.

Although the money helps, it is not enough to stop glaciers from retreating, said Kang Shichang.

Kang wants more research on glaciers and climate change, and better use of the meltwater. A warning system on glacier lakes is needed to protect local people.

"If glaciers do not have ice and mountains do not have snow, what will our lives become? Humans must make every effort to protect nature and co-exist with it," said monk Ngawang Doa from a monastery on the foot of Mount Qomolangma.

10.2 CHINA'S ENVIRONMENTAL PROTECTION EXPERIENCE COULD BENEFIT WORLD: GROUP

http://news.xinhuanet.com/english/2015-04/29/c_134197078.htm

A U.S.-based group said China's inroads in environmental protection can be of benefit to the countries linked by the Silk Road Economic Belt and the 21st Century Maritime Silk Road.

Speaking at a symposium held at Tsinghua University in April, president of the Environmental Defense Fund Fred Krupp said the Belt and Road initiative features great prospects for both economic and environmental progress.

The China-proposed initiative, which will combine its modernization with neighboring countries' infrastructure building, will be a vehicle to apply the lessons China has learned regarding sustainability and green process, he said.

Noting China's remarkable progress in this regard in recent years, Krupp said it should become an exporter of ideas as well as of capital. He added that ecological preservation was a common goal across the globe.

His words were echoed by Fang Li, assistant secretary-general of the China Council for International Cooperation on Environment and Development, an advisory body.

"Environmental protection is a shared consensus among all nation [...] As a developing country, we understand that in nations involved in the Belt and Road initiative there exists the contradictory mentality of environmental protection versus development," Fang said.

"We have rich experiences in this regard. We have learned our lessons, which we are willing to share," she said.

Meanwhile, Krupp also said Chinese social groups could play a larger role in future cross-border environmental protection endeavors.

He suggested that social organizations march toward the global platform and call for more international exchanges and cooperation in climate change and ecosystem protection.

The internationalization of Chinese NGOs could be an importance adjunct to China's Belt and Road initiative, he said.

10.3 SUSTAINABLE DEVELOPMENT AGENDA PURSUES ECONOMIC, SOCIAL PROGRESS WHILE HIGHLIGHTING ENVIRONMENT PROTECTION: UN OFFICIAL

http://news.xinhuanet.com/english/2015-08/07/c_134489499.htm

A sustainable development agenda the United Nations is in the process of defining pursues economic and social progress while highlighting environment protection, said UN Under-Secretary-General for Economic and Social Affairs Wu Hongbo.

"The so-called sustainable development is not just about economic growth," he told Xinhua. "It involves three dimensions — economic development, social progress and environment protection."

"Each one of them is indispensable," he added.

Negotiators from 193 UN member states agreed in August on a draft blueprint for sustainable development over the next 15 years which will be adopted at a United Nations Summit in late September at UN Headquarters in New York.

The agreement, called "Transforming our World: The 2030 Agenda for Sustainable Development," outlining 17 goals with 169 specific targets, basically redefines how the world works together to end poverty, promote prosperity, and combat climate change.

"The goals and targets can be categorized as People, Planet, Prosperity, Peace and Partnership," he said, adding that the five Ps have well explained the fundamental concerns of sustainable development.

Wu said the accord marks the first-ever global consensus that only focusing on GDP growth while ignoring environment protection or social justice is not the right path for development.

In this regard, he said the global community has agreed to ensure sustainable consumption and production patterns and at the same time address social as well as environmental problems, which is a "revolutionary" change.

"This will profoundly benefit the world for generations to come, "he added.

NO ONE SHOULD BE LEFT BEHIND

During the negotiation process of the draft agenda, the UN member states have been stressing that "no one should be left behind," Wu noted.

According to the document, the world has vowed to end poverty in all its forms everywhere, especially to eradicate extreme poverty for all people, currently measured as people living on less than 1.25 U.S. dollars a day.

"With this measurable indicator, countries as well as international community can work out policies and ways to lift these people out of poverty," said Wu.

"It is a tough task," he noted, adding that to achieve that goal, it needs joint efforts of the global community as well as strengthened partnerships like North-South cooperation.

In this regard, the document has asked the developed countries to implement fully their official development assistance commitments in support of developing countries, he mentioned.

"This reflects the appeal from the developing countries for the developed countries to show their good will to cooperate," he added.

STRONG POLITICAL FORCE BEHIND AMBITIOUS COMMITMENTS

The 2030 agenda is going to replace the retiring 15-year-old Millennium Development Goals (MDGs), a development plan that mainly targeted at developing countries from 2000 to 2015.

Wu noted that compared with the MDGs, which were proposed by a group of experts, the 2030 agenda has gathered member states, academia, civil society, among others to discuss its drafting for the global community as a whole.

"The document belongs to the world, to every country, which has laid a solid foundation for its implementation," he said.

Furthermore, the document has outlined means of implementation as well as follow-up and review mechanisms to track progress in implementing the goals and targets, he noted.

According to the document, the goals and targets will be followed-up and reviewed using a set of global indicators, and these will be complemented by indicators at regional as well as national levels which will be developed by member states.

"I think all these have made a complete development agenda for the international community," he said. "And we are more confident of its implementation."

10.4 RENEWABLE ENERGY SOURCES COST-COMPETITIVE: IRENA REPORT

http://news.xinhuanet.com/english/sci/2015-01/17/c_133926674.htm

The cost of generating power from renewable energy sources such as wind and solar energy has reached parity or dropped below the cost of fossil fuels, a new report released by the International Renewable Energy Agency (IRENA) showed in January.

Titled "Renewable Power Generation Costs in 2014," the IRENA's report said that the solar energy, wind energy or bio-thermal became cost-competitive compared to oil and gas applied to "many technologies and in many parts of the world."

The report was launched on the occasion of the two-day annual IRENA assembly which started in Abu Dhabi in January in its 5th edition.

The report showed that biomass, hydropower, geothermal and onshore wind are all competitive with or cheaper than coal, oil and gas-fired power stations, even without financial support and despite falling oil prices.

Dr. Adnan Z. Amin, director general of the 139-member state IRENA, said the new figures indicated a game-changer in producing energy from renewable sources.

"The plummeting price of renewables is creating a historic opportunity to build a clean, sustainable energy system and avert catastrophic climate change in an affordable way," said Amin.

Renewable energy is now cost-advantageous, especially when accounting for the cost of pollution and ill health, he added.

IRENA, a United Nations affiliated organization, supports the UN's "sustainable energy for all" objective which UN Secretary General Ban Ki-moon launched in 2012 and aims to provide access to alternative energies to every citizen in the world by 2030.

The report said individual wind projects are consistently delivering electricity for 0.05 U.S. dollars per kilowatt-hour (kWh) without financial support, compared to a range of 0.045 dollars to 0.14 dollars per kWh for fossil-fuel power plants.

The report also revealed that the average cost of wind energy ranges from 0.06 dollars per kWh in China and Asia to 0.09 per kWh in Africa.

"It has never been cheaper to avoid dangerous climate change, create jobs, reduce fuel import bills and protect our energy system with renewables," Amin said.

The two-day event brings together 1,069 delegates and 160 media representatives. A total of 151 countries plus the European Union states participate.

Appendix

I. Full Text: Integrated Reform Plan for Promoting Ecological Progress

The Communist Party of China (CPC) Central Committee and the State Council, or China's cabinet, published a reform plan for promoting ecological progress in the country. Following is the full text:

INTEGRATED REFORM PLAN FOR PROMOTING ECOLOGICAL PROGRESS

This plan has been formulated for putting systematic and complete systems for improving the ecosystem in place more quickly; achieving faster ecological progress; and making the reform for promoting ecological progress more systemic, more holistic, and better coordinated.

I. A GENERAL DESCRIPTION

1. The thinking behind the reform

It is crucial to fully implement the guiding principles from the 18th National Congress of the Communist Party of China (CPC) and the second, third, and fourth plenary sessions of the 18th CPC Central Committee; follow the guidance of Deng Xiaoping Theory, the Theory of the Three Represents, and the Scientific Outlook on Development; thoroughly put into practice the guiding principles from the major speeches of General Secretary Xi Jinping; act in accordance with the decisions and plans of the CPC Central Committee and the State Council; adhere to the fundamental state policy of conserving resources and protecting the environment; and give high priority to resource conservation, environmental protection, and the restoration of nature. Based on the fundamental context of China being in the primary stage of socialism and in the particular characteristics new to China in the present phase, and in order to build a beautiful China, handle correctly the relationship between humankind and nature, and solve serious ecological and environmental problems, it is essential to safeguard China's ecological security, improve the environment, ensure that resources are used more efficiently, and step up efforts to promote the formation of a new pattern of modernization in which humankind develops in harmony with nature.

2. The ideas

The idea is to:

Respect, protect, and stay in tune with nature. Ecological conservation is vital not only to sustained, healthy economic development, but also to political and social progress, and must therefore be given a position of prominence and incorporated into every aspect and the whole process of economic, political, cultural, and social development.

Integrate development and conservation. It is necessary to remain committed to the strategy of treating development as being of the utmost importance to China. Development is good only when it is green, circular, and low-carbon. There should be the right balance between development and conservation. The intensity of development should be brought under control on the basis of functional zoning and spatial planning should be adjusted to ensure that development and conservation are coordinated and reinforce each other so we leave behind a comfortable place that future generations can call home with blue skies, green lands, and clear waters.

Foster an understanding that lucid waters and lush mountains are invaluable assets. Fresh air, clean water sources, beautiful rivers and mountains, fertile land, and biological diversity form an ecological environment that is essential to human survival. As development is a top priority for China, it is imperative to protect forests, grasslands, rivers, lakes, wetlands, seas, and other natural ecosystems.

Cultivate respect for the value of nature and natural capital. Natural ecosystems have value; the protection of nature is a process of increasing the value of nature and the value of natural capital, and means the protection and development of the productive forces. Protection efforts should, then, be adequately rewarded and come with economic returns.

Seek equilibriums in China's territorial space. To move forward with development, it is necessary to find the right balance between population, economy, resources, and the environment and ensure that the population, the industrial structure, and the economic growth of a region do not surpass its environmental capacity and the carrying capacity of its water and land resources.

See that mountains, waters, forests, and farmlands are a community of life. Based on the integrity and systemic nature of ecosystems and the way they work, it is necessary to take into consideration all the elements of the natural ecosystem - both hills and their surrounding areas, both above and under the ground, both land and sea, both upper and lower river basins -and work to protect them in their entirety, restore them systematically, and take a comprehensive approach to their governance in order to preserve ecological balance by strengthening the ability of ecosystems to circulate.

3. The principles

Ensuring that the reform moves in the right direction. China's market mechanisms need to be improved, and the government should make better use of its leadership and regulatory roles. Those in the business sector should bring their own initiative into play and exercise self-restraint. Social organizations and the general public should participate and play a supervising role in ecological conservation.

Maintaining the public nature of natural resource assets. New property rights systems should be created for natural resources. Ownership rights should be clarified. There should be a distinction between ownership rights and the authority to manage. Powers and regulatory responsibilities of the central and local governments should be divided more appropriately. Everyone should be entitled to benefit from state-owned natural resource assets.

Integrating environmental governance for rural and urban areas. Continued efforts should be made to strengthen urban environmental protection and industrial pollution prevention and control. The rural coverage of ecological and environmental protection efforts should be expanded. Effective systems and mechanisms for rural environmental governance should be established. The development of pollution prevention and control facilities should be stepped up in rural areas, and related funding should be increased.

Attaching equal importance to incentives and restraints. It is imperative to develop interest-related mechanisms for promoting green, circular, and low-carbon development, and at the same time practice strict prevention at the source of pollution, strict regulation over operations, strict compensation for environmental damage, and accountability for those responsible in order to effectively restrain all types of market entities and, step by step, make ecological conservation efforts more market-, law-, and procedure-based.

Combining China's own independent efforts with international cooperation. Strengthening ecological conservation and environmental protection is something China is doing of its own accord, though at the same time it needs to deepen exchange and practical cooperation with other countries, borrow from their advanced technology and their valuable experience in institution building, take an active part in global environmental governance, and assume and perform its international responsibilities as a large developing country.

Integrating piloting first with overall coordination. It is necessary, in accordance with the unified plans of the CPC Central Committee and the State Council, to deal with the easier parts first, move forward step by step, and launch each reform when conditions are ripe to do so. On the basis of the fundamental direction laid out in this plan, encouragement should be given to local governments to explore and experiment boldly in light of their own local conditions.

4. The objectives

This reform is designed to establish a systematic and complete institutional framework composed of eight systems for promoting ecological progress with clearly defined property rights, diversified participation, and equal focus on incentives and restraints by 2020. It is also designed to modernize China's governance system and capacity for governance in the field of ecological progress and usher in a new era for socialist ecological progress. These eight systems include a system of property rights for natural resource assets, a system for the development and protection of territorial space, a spatial planning system, a system for regulating total consumption and comprehensive conservation of resources, a system for payment-based resource consumption and compensating conservation and protection efforts, the environmental governance system, the market system for environmental governance and ecological preservation, and the system for evaluating officials' ecological conservation performance and for holding those responsible for ecological damage to account.

A system of property rights for natural resource assets will be established, according to which ownership is clearly defined, powers and responsibilities are explicit, and regulation is effective, in order to ensure there are owners for natural resources and ownership is clear.

A system will be built on the basis of spatial planning for the development and protection of territorial space, drawing on regulation of its uses as the main approach, with a view to stopping the over-use of quality cropland and ecological space, ecological damage, and environmental pollution caused by disorderly, excessive, and scattered development.

A spatial planning system will be designed, with the main purpose of strengthening the spatial governance and improving its structure, which is nationally unified and better connected between different departments of government, and according to which management is divided between governments at multiple levels, in an effort to eliminate overlapping and conflicting spatial plans, the overlap and duplication of responsibilities between departments, and the issue of local authorities frequently changing their plans.

An effective, standardized,and strictly managed system that achieves complete coverage will be established for regulating total consumption and comprehensive conservation of resources, in order to address inefficiency and serious waste in resource consumption.

A system for payment-based resource consumption and compensating conservation and protection efforts will be established. The system will reflect market supply and demand, resource scarcity, the value of nature, and the need for intergenerational compensation, in order to address the problems of excessively low prices for natural resources and their products, the cost of production and development being lower than the social cost, and inadequate incentives for ecological conservation efforts.

An environmental governance system which is oriented toward improving the environment, and which incorporates unified regulation, strict law enforcement, and multi-party participation will be developed in an effort to deal with weak capacity for pollution prevention and control, overlapping regulatory functions between government departments, powers not being in accord with responsibilities, and the cost of law violations being too low.

A market system which allows economic levers to play a greater role in environmental governance and ecological conservation will be developed, with a view to addressing the slow development of market entities and market systems and low rates of public participation in ecological conservation.

An evaluation and accountability system will be developed to assess the performance of officials in ecological conservation and hold to account those responsible for ecological damage. This system will be designed to be fully reflective of resource consumption, environmental damage, and ecological benefits, and is to be built so as to correct the shortcomings in performance evaluations, narrow the gaps in responsibility systems, and improve poor accountability for ecological damage.

II. IMPROVING THE SYSTEM OF PROPERTY RIGHTS FOR NATURAL RESOURCE ASSETS

5. Establishing a unified system for determining and registering ownership

The owners of natural resource assets of all types throughout all Chinese territorial space will be determined in accordance with the principles that all natural resources in China are publicly owned and all property rights are legally prescribed. Ownership of all natural ecological spaces including water flows, forests, mountains, grasslands, uncultivated land, and tidal flats will, according to a unified system, be determined and registered. Clear lines will be gradually delineated to distinguish between assets owned by the whole people and assets collectively owned, ownership by the whole people and ownership operated by different levels of government, and between different collective owners. The rule of law will be strengthened in the determination and registration of ownership.

6. Establishing a system of property rights for natural resources within which rights and responsibilities are explicit

A list of rights will be developed to specify the rights of ownership for all types of natural resource assets. The relationship between ownership rights and use rights will be properly dealt with. New forms of collective ownership and ownership by the whole people will be created. With the exception of natural resources which are ecologically important, the ownership rights and use rights for all other natural resources can be separated. It will be made clear who has the right to possess, use, benefit from, or dispose of natural resources, and corresponding rights and responsibilities will be clarified. The right to sell, transfer, and rent out use rights, as well as the right to use them as collateral, as the basis of a loan guaranty, or to gain an equity stake, will all be suitably expanded. The roles of owners and users of land on which state-owned farms, forests, and pastures are located will be clearly defined. A complete system for sale will be established covering all types of natural resource assets owned by the whole people, while the uncompensated transfer of rights or their sale at excessively low a price are to be strictly forbidden. We will draw up an integrated plan for strengthening efforts to develop a natural resource asset exchange.

7. Improving the state system of management for natural resource assets

In accordance with the principles of separating owners from regulators and assigning the responsibility for one matter to one single department, the currently diffuse duties and responsibilities of ownership of natural resource assets owned by the whole people will be integrated, and one body will be established to carry out the unified exercise of ownership rights for all types of natural resources owned by the whole people, such as mineral deposits, water flows, forests, mountains, grasslands, uncultivated land, marine areas, and tidal flats, and take responsibility for the sale of these natural resources.

8. Exploring the establishment of a system for exercising ownership rights at different levels

Research will be conducted to explore how a system can be put into practice in which, in accordance with the type of resource and its importance in relation to the ecological environment, the economy, and national defense, the central and local governments act as the agents of the owners of natural resource assets owned by the whole people, in order to achieve both efficiency and equity. Resources and territorial space for which the ownership rights are owned by the whole people and directly exercised by the Central Government will be distinguished from those for which the ownership rights are owned by the whole people and exercised by local governments. The Central Government will primarily exercise directly the ownership rights for petroleum and natural gas, valuable and rare mineral resources, key state-owned forests, major rivers and lakes, trans-boundary rivers, ecologically important wetlands and grasslands, marine areas, tidal flats, rare and endangered species of wild fauna and flora, and some national parks.

9. Launching trials for determining property rights for water flows and wetlands

Explorations will be made into establishing a water ownership system. Trials will be carried out in determining ownership of bodies of water, coast lines, and other aquatic ecospace. On the basis of respecting the systematic nature and integrity of water ecosystems, the ownership rights, use rights, and allowable volumes for water resource use will be delineated. Trials will be launched in Gansu, Ningxia, and other areas for determining the ownership of wetlands.

III. ESTABLISHING A SYSTEM FOR THE DEVELOPMENT AND PROTECTION OF TERRITORIAL SPACE

10. Improving the functional zoning system

National- and provincial-level planning of functional zones will be coordinated. Regional policies which are based on the functional zones will be improved. On the basis of the different functions- urban areas, primary production areas for agricultural products, or key ecosystem service areas — adjustments and improvements to policies regarding finance, industry, investment, population flow, land to be used for construction, resource development, and environmental protection will be stepped up.

11. Improving the regulatory system for the use of territorial space

The top-down land-use indices control system will be simplified and the method of allocating indices based on administrative district and baselines for land use will be adjusted. Development intensity indices will be broken down and assigned to the county-level administrative districts as binding quotas to control the total amount of land used for construction purposes. Land use regulation will be extended to all natural ecological spaces, ecological redlines will be defined and strictly observed, and arbitrary changes to land use will be strictly prohibited. Efforts will be made to protect against ecological redlines being crossed by unreasonable development and construction activities. The monitoring system for all territorial space will be improved and a longitudinal approach will be used to monitor changes within China's territorial space.

12. Establishing a national park system

The protection of important ecosystems will be strengthened to ensure their sustainable use. The system of departments independently setting up their own nature reserves, historical and scenic sites, cultural and natural heritage sites, geological parks, and forest parks will be reformed. These protected areas will be reorganized by function and the scope of national parks will be determined as appropriate. National parks will be under more stringent protection: with the exception of improvements to the facilities used by local people in their everyday lives and work and nature-based research, education, and tourism which do not harm ecosystems, other types of development and construction will be prohibited so as to protect the authenticity and integrity of the natural ecological environment and natural and cultural heritage. Guidance on national park trials will be strengthened, and on the basis of these trials, research will be carried out into designing an overall plan for establishing a national park system. A permanent mechanism will be created for the protection of rare and endangered species of wild plants and animals.

13. Improving the system for regulating natural resources

Duties and responsibilities related to regulation of use, which are currently spread among different departments, will be gradually concentrated within a single department. This department will then perform all use-related regulatory duties and responsibilities for all territorial spaces.

14. Formulating plans for territorial space

All types of current spatial plans formulated by different departments will be integrated into unified spatial plans, which will be all-encompassing. The new plans will be the guide for the development of the country's territorial space, and the spatial blueprints for sustainable development; they will be the fundamental basis for all types of development and construction programs. Spatial plans will be divided into national, provincial, and municipal (or county) levels (spatial plans for cities which are divided into districts will be formulated for the district level). Research will be conducted into how to establish unified and standardized mechanisms for formulating spatial plans. An environmental impact assessment system will be set up to be used in spatial planning. Provincial-level spatial planning trials are encouraged. A spatial plan will be developed for the Beijing-Tianjin-Hebei region.

15. Integrating municipal-level (county-level) plans

Cities and counties will be supported in combining different types of plans into a single spatial plan, such that gradually, there will be one plan—one blueprint—per city or county. Municipal or county spatial plans should classify land using a unified standard, and, in accordance with the relevant functional zoningand the requirements of the provincial-level spatial plan, should delineate production space, living space, and ecological space, demarcate the development boundaries of urban construction areas, industrial areas, and rural living areas, as well as the boundaries of protected areas of arable land, woodlands, grasslands, rivers, lakes, and wetlands, and strengthen coordinated planning for urban subsurface space. More effective guidance will be given to cities and counties regarding their trials for plan integration. Research will be undertaken into developing guidelines and technical standards for the formulation of municipal-level (county-level) spatial plans, which will then serve as experience that can be applied elsewhere.

16. Developing new approaches for formulating municipal-level (county-level) spatial plans

We will explore how best to standardize procedures for formulating municipal-level (county-level)spatial plans, public participation will be expanded, and planning will be made more effective and transparent. Those areas piloting municipal-level (county-level) spatial plans are encouraged to integrate planning departments, making a single department responsible for formulating the spatial plan for that municipality or county; and they may form a planning appraisal committee of experts and representatives of the relevant fields. Prior to the formulation of a plan, a resource and environmental carrying capacity assessment must be carried out, and the results of the assessment should serve as the fundamental basis of planning. During the process of formulation, efforts should be made to solicit opinions of those from relevant sectors; the draft of the plan should be published in full so that the suggestions and comments of local residents can be extensively solicited. After evaluation and approval by the planning appraisal committee, the plan must be deliberated and passed by the local people's congress, then reported to the relevant government department at the next level up to be placed on record. The finalized plan should include the text of the plan along with precise maps and images, and should be made available to the public through websites and other forms of local news media. Local residents are to be encouraged to oversee the implementation of the plan and report any development and construction activities that violate it. The local people's congress and its standing committee will hear reports at regular intervals on the implementation of the plan, and will hold the local government accountable for violations of the plan.

V. IMPROVING THE SYSTEMS FOR TOTAL RESOURCE MANAGEMENT AND COMPREHENSIVE RESOURCE CONSERVATION

17. Improving the systems for providing the strictest possible protection for farmland and securing the economical and intensive use of land

The system for the protection of basic cropland will be improved and a redline below which the area of China' s permanent basic cropland must not fall will be established. To ensure that the area of basic crop-land are not diminished, its quality does not deteriorate, and it is not converted to any other uses, the duty of basic cropland protection will be assigned to farming households and every piece of this cropland will be captured through photo-imaging and entered into the national cropland protection database, and its strict protection will be enforced. With the exception of unavoidable cases as specified by law in which basic cropland has to be used as the site of key national projects, no basic cropland may be used for construction purposes. Efforts will be redoubled to grade and monitor as well as maintain and improve the quality of cultivated land. The system for offsetting the occupation of cultivated land for purposes other than cultivation will be improved. A cap will be set on total cultivated land that can be used for new construction projects. It will be made sure that equivalent land is offset ahead of occupation and that the replacement land is of equal or higher grade than the cultivated land to be occupied. A cap will also be on total land that can be occupied for construction purposes, management will be instituted to reduce the amount of cultivatable land that is used as such, and incentive and constraint mechanisms will be established to encourage more economical and intensive use of land. Reasonable annual plans will be made for the use of land, adjusting the structure of land used for different purposes and making the best use of land that has already been made available.

18. Improving the system for the strictest possible management of water resources

To give priority to saving water, achieve harmony between development and water conservation, carry out systemic governance, and ensure that both government and market play their respective roles, the system for controlling total water usage will be improved to ensure water security. Efforts will be accelerated to formulate water allocation plans for major river basins, strengthen coordination between provincial-level govern-ments, and improve the system of targets for control of total water usage at the provincial, municipal, and county levels. Effective mechanisms will be established to ensure economical and intensive water usage.

More work will be done to adjust the way water resources are used and improve their allocation. The system for evaluating the impact of plans and construction projects on water resources will be improved. Efforts will be made to draw principally on pricing and taxation to gradually establish systems for controlling and instituting quota-based management of the volume of water used in irrigation, and for controlling and instituting quota-based management of the planned water usage of high-water-consuming industrial enterprises. In regions seriously affected by water scarcity, water quotas will be used as a threshold for market entry and the development of high-water-consuming projects will be strictly controlled. The protection and environmental restoration of areas producing aquatic products will be strengthened, their aqua culture will be controlled, and mechanisms will be established for the protection of aquatic plant and animal life. Regulation of water functional zones will be improved and systems for promoting the utilization of alternative water resources will be established.

19. Establishing a system for total energy consumption management and energy conservation

High priority will be given to energy conservation, the control of energy intensity will be strengthened, and the responsibility system and the system of incentives for meeting energy conservation targets will be improved. Improvements will be made to the energy statistics system. The management system for energy conservation by major energy-consuming organizations will be improved, and a mechanism for making voluntary pledges on energy conservation will be implemented on an explorative basis. The system of energy conservation standards will be improved to make timely updates to energy efficiency standards for energy-consuming products, limits on energy consumption for energy-intensive industries, and energy efficiency standards for buildings. A reasonable target will be established for total national energy consumption and broken down and assigned to the provincial-level and major energy-consuming organizations. The mechanism for promoting the use of energy-saving, low-carbon products, technologies, and equipment will be improved and lists of technologies will be issued at regular intervals. Supervision over energy conservation will be strengthened. Stronger support will be provided for the development of renewable energy sources, and subsidies for all fossil fuels will be phased out. A system for controlling total national carbon emissions and a mechanism for breaking down the responsibility for implementation will be gradually established. A mechanism for effectively increasing forest, grassland, wetland, and ocean carbon sinks will be set up. China's involvement in international cooperation on responding to climate change will be strengthened. (more)

20. Establishing a system for protecting virgin forests

All virgin forests will be placed under protection. A national timber forest reserve system will be established. Government administration will be gradually separated from the management of state-owned forests, and the public benefit forest protection and management system will be improved for state-owned forestry farms drawing principally on service procurement. The collective forest tenure system will be improved. Tenure contracts for collective forests will be kept stable, the operations allowed under these contracts will be expanded, and the systems by which forest tenure rights are used as collateral for loans and tenure rights are transferred will be improved.

21. Establishing a system for protecting grassland

The system by which collective grassland is contracted out for operation to individual households will be kept stable and improved to ensure that the plot and area of every piece of grassland contracted out is measured accurately, contracts are signed, and contracting certificates are granted. Proper procedures will be introduced for the transfer of grassland under such contracts. A system for protecting basic grassland will be put into effect to ensure that the area of basic grassland does not diminish, its quality does not deteriorate, and it is not converted for any other use. The subsidy and award mechanisms for the ecological conservation of grassland will be improved. Grazing on certain areas of grassland will be banned or temporarily suspended, rotational paddock grazing will be introduced, and efforts will be made to strike a balance between grass and livestock. Oversight over there view and approval of grassland requisitions will be strengthened and the use of grassland for any purpose other than animal husbandry will be strictly controlled.

22. *Establishing a system for protecting wetlands*

All wetlands will be placed under protection, and the unauthorized requisition or occupancy of wetlands of international importance, and those of national importance,and wetland reserves will be banned. The services of wetlands will be determined, their protection and utilization will be standardized, and a mechanism for the ecological restoration of wetlands will be established.

23. *Establishing a system for closing off desertified land for protection*

Contiguous areas of desertified land for which conditions are not currently in place to carry out anti-desertification programs will be designated as closed-off protection zones. Systems for strict protection will be established, construction of infrastructure needed to close off and protect and manage such zones will be stepped up, desertified land governance will be strengthened, and vegetation will be increased. The appropriate development of the sand industry will be encouraged. The mechanisms for protection and management drawing principally on service procurement will be improved. New approaches that combine development with governance will be explored.

24. *Improving the system for developing and protecting marine resources*

Marine functional zones will be established, the major functions of offshore waters and islands will be determined, and efforts will be made to guide, control, and standardize behavior related to the use of oceans and islands. A system will be introduced to control total sea reclamation, imposing binding limits on the total area of ocean over which reclamation can take place. A system will be established for maintaining natural coastlines. The system for managing total marine fishery resources will be improved. The systems for instituting fishing off-seasons and bans on fishing will be strictly enforced. Limits on offshore fishing will be imposed. The scale of offshore and mudflat aquaculture will be controlled.

25. Improving the system for managing the development and utilization of mineral resources

A system for the investigation and evaluation of the development and utilization of mineral resources will be established. The ascertainment and registration of mineral resources and registration management of their pay-per-time occupation will be strengthened. A mechanism for the intensive development of mineral resources will be established, the concentration of enterprises in mining areas will be increased, and large-scale development is encouraged. National standards including those regarding the mining recovery rate of major mineral resources, ore dressing recovery rate, and the comprehensive utilization rate of mineral resources will be improved. The economic policies for encouraging better utilization of mineral resources will be refined. A system will be established to make available to the public information on whether mining enterprises are utilizing mineral resources efficiently and comprehensively, and a system will be set up for blacklisting those breaking mining operation rules. The mechanism for introducing industry-based approaches will be improved to support the recycling of major mineral resources. The systems for protecting the geological environment in mining areas and reclaiming deserted areas will also be improved.

26. Improving the system of resource recycling

An effective system will be established to record resource-output ratio statistics. The extended producer responsibility (EPR) system will be put into effect, pushing producers to perform their responsibilities for take-back and disposal of their end-of-life products. A system will be established to utilize farming, livestock, and aquaculture waste and achieve the organic integration and circular development of farming, husbandry, and aquaculture. The establishment of a system for making the separation of waste compulsory will be accelerated. A list of renewable resources to be recycled will be worked out and the mandatory recycling of composite packaging, batteries, agricultural plastic sheeting, and other low-value waste will be required. Efforts will be accelerated to develop standards for the recycling and reuse of resources by type. A system for promoting the use of products and raw materials made of recycled resources will be established to require enterprises consuming related raw materials to use a certain proportion of recycled products. The system for restricting the use of single-use disposable products will be improved. Taxation policies will be implemented and improved to promote the comprehensive utilization of resources and the development of the circular economy. A list of circular economy technologies will be formulated and policies such as priority government procurement and discounted interest on loans will be implemented.

VI. IMPROVING THE SYSTEM FOR PAYMENT-BASED RESOURCE CONSUMPTION AND COMPENSATING CONSERVATION AND PROTECTION EFFORTS

27. Accelerating price reform for natural resources and their products

In line with the principles of cost-benefit balancing and based on full consideration of society' s ability to tolerate price increases, a cost assessment mechanism for natural resource exploitation and consumption will be established to incorporate the interests of resource owners and any ecological and environmental damage into the pricing mechanism for natural resources and their products. Price regulation over natural monopolies will be strengthened. A system will be created for overseeing and reviewing the pricing cost and a mechanism will be established for making pricing adjustments. Procedures for decision-making on pricing and the information disclosure system will be improved. The overall price reform of water for agricultural purposes will be moved forward. A system of progressive pricing for water will be put into full practice for non-household water consumption that exceeds plans or quotas for water consumption, and a system of tiered pricing for urban household water consumption will be fully implemented.

28. Improving the payment-based system for land use

The scope of state-owned land that is operated on the basis of a payment-based use system will be expanded. The proportion of land for which use rights can be transferred through bidding, auction, or listing will be enlarged. Less land will be allocated for non-public use. Income and expenditures related to selling use rights for state-owned land will be incorporated into public budgeting. Industrial-land supply methods will be reformed and improved, with the implementation of flexible transfer periods, long-term leasing, lease-then-sell arrangements, and lease-and-sell arrangements being explored. The mechanisms for setting and appraising land prices will be improved. The system of grade-based pricing for land will be refined. The relationship of land-related transaction and lease expenses with taxes and fees will be straightened out. An effective regulatory mechanism will be put in place to achieve reasonable price parity between industrial-use and residential-use land. Prices of industrial-use land will be raised, and the proportion of industrial-use land will be reduced. Methods such as land contracting and leasing out will be explored to improve the payment-based use system for state-owned land for agricultural use.

29. Improving the payment-based system for mineral resource use

Improvements will be made to the system for the sale of mining rights, and means suited to a market economy and the nature of the mining industry will be established for the sale of prospecting and extraction rights. In principle, the sale of these rights will be market-oriented, and the income and expenditures related to the sale of state-owned mineral resources will be incorporated into public budgeting. The property rights of owners, investors, and operators during the processes of payment-based acquisition, possession, and exploitation will be clarified, and research will be conducted into the development of a system of national premiums for the use of mineral resources. Standard fees for the use of prospecting and extraction rights, and minimum investment in mineral prospecting will be adjusted. Progress will be made in building a nationally unified mining rights exchange, and efforts in information disclosure on the sale and transfer of such rights will be intensified.

30. Improving the payment-based system for use of sea areas and offshore islands

A mechanism will be created for adjusting use fees for sea areas and uninhabited islands. An effective system will be established for the sale of use rights for sea areas and uninhabited islands through bidding, auction, and listing.

31. Accelerating reform of resource and environmental taxes and fees

The taxes and fees for natural resources and their products will be straightened out, their respective purposes will be clarified, and the appropriate scope of taxation regulation will be defined. Faster progress will be made in introducing price-based on resources. The scope of resource taxes will be gradually expanded to cover the use of all kinds of ecological spaces. A trial reform will be carried out in parts of northern China to levy a resource tax on groundwater. The development of legislation on environmental protection tax will also be accelerated.

32. Improving the ecological compensation system

Explorations will be made into establishing a diversified compensation mechanism, transfer payments to major ecological functional zones will be increased step by step, and the incentive mechanism that links ecological protection performance with fund allocation will be improved. Measures will be drawn up for implementing a mechanism, principally for local compensation, and supported by additional funds from the central budget, by which local governments compensate each other for ecological or environmental damage and ecological conservation efforts. Local governments are encouraged to launch ecological compensation trials. Efforts will continue in carrying out the ecological compensation pilot initiative for the Xin' an River ecosystem. Help will be given to carry out trans-regional ecological compensation pilot initiatives in the Beijing-Tianjin-Hebei water source conservation area, in areas along the Jiuzhou River in Guangxi and Guangdong, and in areas along the Ting and Han rivers in Fujian and Guangdong. Explorations will be made into carrying out pilot ecological compensation initiatives in the Yangtze River basin- an environmentally sensitive region.

33. Improving the mechanism for utilizing ecological protection and restoration funds

Given the need for systematic governance of mountains, forests, farmland, rivers, and lakes, the measures for utilizing and managing relevant funds will be improved and existing policies and channels will be integrated. At the same time as efforts are being made to comprehensively improve the conditions of rivers throughout their entire drainage basins,more funds will be spent on the protection and restoration of national ecological-security shields, such as the Qinghai-Tibet Plateau ecological shield, the Loess Plateau-Sichuan-Yunnan ecological shield, the northeast China forest belt, the northern China desertification-prevention belt, and the southern China mountainous belt.

34. Creating a recuperation system for farmland, grasslands, rivers, and lakes

A recuperation plan will be formulated for farmland, grassland, rivers, and lakes, adjusting the use of farmland in areas where there is heavy pollution or where groundwater has been over-extracted. Basic agricultural activity from land sloped greater than 25 degrees, which is not suitable for, and the ecosystem of which is harmed by, cultivation, will be gradually excluded from classification as basic cropland. A permanent mechanism will be formulated to consolidate progress in returning farmland to forest and grassland and converting grazing land back into grassland. Pilot projects will be launched to return cultivated land to lakes and wetlands. Efforts will be made to move forward with the pilot initiative for the restoration of heavy-metal contaminated soil in the Changsha-Zhuzhou-Xiangtan region, as well as the pilot project to comprehensively deal with the over-extraction of groundwater in northern China.

VII. ESTABLISHING AN EFFECTIVE SYSTEM FOR
ENVIRONMENTAL GOVERNANCE

35. Improving the pollutant emissions permit system

A unified and fair business emissions permit system covering all fixed
pollution sources will be established quickly nationwide. Emissions permits will be issued in accordance with the law. Emission of pollutants
without a permit or in violation of a permit will be prohibited.

36. Establishing a mechanism for cooperation within a region in pollution prevention and control

Cooperative mechanisms for joint prevention and control of air pollution
will be improved in major areas such as the Beijing-Tianjin-Hebei region,
the Yangtze River Delta, and the Pearl River Delta. Regional cooperation
mechanisms will be established in other areas, taking into consideration
their geographical features, levels of pollution, distribution of urban space,
and patterns of pollutant transmission. Trials for creating new administrative systems for environmental protection will be held in some areas,
using unified plans, standards, environmental evaluations, monitoring,
and law enforcement. Trials will also be launched for the establishment
of environmental regulators and administrative law enforcement agencies
for river basins. A variety of cooperative mechanisms for protecting the
water environments of river basins as well as early-warning systems for
risk control will be put in place with the participation of the relevant
provincial-level water-related departments within each river basin. An
integrated mechanism for pollution prevention and control both on land
and at sea and a control system governing the total quantity of pollutants discharged into key marine areas will be set up. The mechanism for
responding to environmental emergencies will be improved and China'
s capacity for dealing with environmental emergencies of varying degrees
of severity and involving different pollutants will be strengthened.

37. Establishing systems and mechanisms for rural environmental governance

An eco-oriented system of agricultural subsidies will be created. Efforts to formulate and improve relevant technical standards and specifications will be accelerated. Reductions to the use of chemical fertilizers, pesticides, and plastic sheeting and the recycling or safe disposal of animal husbandry waste will be carried out quickly. The production and use of biodegradable plastic sheeting is encouraged. The system for comprehensively utilizing crop straw will be improved. Networks for recycling, storing, transporting, and processing plastic sheeting and chemical fertilizer and pesticide packaging will be improved. Development of environmental protection facilities, such as those for handling rural wastewater and refuse, will be bolstered by subsidies from governments and village collectives, fee payments from residents, and the participation of non-government capital. A variety of assistive measures, including government procurement of services, will be adopted to foster and develop market entities for the control of all types of agricultural pollution from non-point sources and for the handling of rural wastewater and refuse. County- and township-level governments will carry greater responsibility for environmental protection, and efforts to build their capacity for environmental regulation will be boosted. In allocating government funds for supporting agriculture, full consideration should be given to improving overall agricultural production capacity and to preventing and controlling rural pollution.

38. Improving systems for public disclosure of environmental information

Extensive efforts will be made to ensure public availability of environmental information pertaining to the atmosphere, water, and so on, to businesses that emit pollution, and to regulatory bodies. The mechanism for the public release of environmental impact evaluations for development projects will be improved. The environmental spokesperson system will be refined. Efforts will be made to promote awareness for environmental protection among the general public, the system of public participation will be improved, and more work needs to be done to ensure that the people exercise oversight over the environment in a legal and orderly way. An online platform and system will be created for the reporting of offenses related to environmental protection, and systems for offense-reporting, hearings, and public opinion-based oversight will be improved.

39. Strictly implementing compensation systems for ecological and environmental damage

Manufacturers' legal responsibilities for environmental protection will be tightened, and the cost of illegal activities will be significantly increased. Legal provisions concerning environmental damage compensation, methods for appraising damage, and mechanisms for enforcing compensation will be improved. In accordance with the law, penalties will be meted out to those who violate environmental laws and regulations, compensation for ecological and environmental damage will be determined by the extent of damage and other factors, and when violations result in serious adverse consequences, criminal liability will be pursued.

40. Improving the administrative system for environmental protection

An effective administrative system for environmental protection will be established to strictly regulate the emissions of all pollutants. Duties and responsibilities for environmental protection, which are currently spread across departments, will be assigned to one single department, progressively creating a system whereby one department is responsible for unified regulation and administrative law enforcement over urban and rural environmental protection work. Regulatory authority from different fields and departments and at different levels will be systemically organized to create a unified and authoritative system for environmental law enforcement, strengthen the ranks of law enforcement, and provide those tasked with environmental law enforcement the necessary conditions and means to enforce the law. The mechanisms linking administrative law enforcement and environmental judicial work will be improved.

VIII. IMPROVING THE MARKET SYSTEM FOR ENVIRONMEN-
TAL GOVERNANCE AND ECOLOGICAL CONSERVATION

41. Fostering market entities for environmental governance and ecological conservation

Systems, mechanisms, policies, and measures that encourage energy efficient and environmentally friendly industries will be adopted. Regulations and practices that hinder fair competition and the creation of a nationally unified market will be discontinued, and all types of investment will be encouraged to enter the environmental protection market. Non-government investors may participate in the development and operation of any environmental governance or ecological conservation program where cooperation between government and non-government investment is viable. By means of government procurement of services and other methods, more support will be provided for third-party governance of environmental pollution. The transformation of organizations in charge of the operation and management of wastewater and refuse treatment facilities into companies that exercise independent accounting and management will be accelerated. Companies that take investment from or are operated with state capital will be set up or created through reorganization in order to encourage greater investment of state capital into environmental governance and ecological conservation. Support will be given to state-owned firms in fields of ecological and environmental protection to reform toward a mixed-ownership system.

42. Promoting the trading of energy-use rights and carbon emissions rights

Combined with efforts to see that major energy-consuming organizations increase energy efficiency and to subject new projects to energy reviews, the trading of energy saved on projects will be allowed, and will progressively move toward the trading of energy-use rights based on the cap system for energy consumption. A trading system and a measurement and verification system for energy-use rights will be established. Energy performance contracting will be promoted. Trials of carbon emissions rights trading will be deepened, a national exchange for carbon emissions rights will be progressively created, and a national plan for setting the total trade and quota allocation of carbon emissions rights will be formulated. The carbon trading registration system will be improved and a regulatory system will be established for the carbon emissions rights exchange.

43. *Promoting the trading of pollution rights*

On the basis of the cap system for enterprise pollution emissions, improvements will be made as quickly as possible to the granting of initial pollution rights, and coverage will be expanded to include more pollutants. Working from the foundations provided by the current mechanism for granting pollution rights to administrative regions, and on the basis of the best industry-wide levels of pollution emissions, the mechanism will be gradually strengthened to ensure the cap system for enterprise pollution emissions is implemented and the trading of pollution rights creates incentives for emissions reductions at the level of the individual enterprise. In key river basins and key areas for air pollution, implementation of pollution rights trading across administrative regions will be carried out as appropriate. Trials for the payment-based use and trading of pollution rights will be expanded to include more areas where conditions are appropriate. Efforts will be stepped up to improve the pollution rights exchange. Regulations will be developed on granting pollution rights, collecting and using pollution rights use fees, and setting trading prices.

44. *Promoting the trading of water rights*

Combined with efforts to establish an effective mechanism for compensating the expenses of water ecosystem protection and conservation, water-related rights will be appropriately defined and allocated and ways of trading water rights between regions, between river basins, between the lower and upper reaches of rivers, between industries, and between water users will be explored. Research will be conducted into formulating regulations concerning the trading of water rights, to clearly define the scope and types of tradable water rights, the trading entities and time frames, the mechanisms for determining trading prices, and the rules for the operation of the exchange. An exchange for water rights will be developed.

45. Establishing a green finance system

Green credit will be promoted, with research being undertaken into adopting methods such as government interest subsidies to boost the level of support. All types of financial institutions are encouraged to step up grants of green loans. Requirements for the due diligence of borrowers as well as their legal responsibilities concerning environmental protection will be clarified. Efforts will be stepped up to further develop the systems related to capital markets. Research will be conducted to explore the establishment of a green stock index and the development of relevant investment products, and studies will be undertaken to explore the issuance of green bonds by banks and enterprises, encouraging the securitization of green credit assets. Support will be given for the launch of multiple types of green development funds, the operations of which will be market-based. A mechanism will be established for the mandatory release of environmental protection information by listed companies. Guaranty mechanisms for energy-efficient, low-carbon, and environmentally friendly projects will be improved, and the level of risk compensation increased. A compulsory liability insurance system for environmental pollution will be established in sectors involving high environmental risks. A green rating system as well as a non-profit system for calculating environmental costs and evaluating environmental impact will be established. Cooperation of all types with other countries will be promoted in green finance.

46. Establishing a unified system for green products

Products that are licensed as environmentally friendly, energy-efficient, water-saving, circular, low-carbon, recyclable, or organic will be uniformly classified as green products, and standardized green product standards, certifications, and logos will be established for them. Improvements will be made to policies on fiscal and tax support and government procurement for the research and development, production, transport, delivery, purchase, and use of green products.

IX. IMPROVING ECOLOGICAL CONSERVATION PERFOR-
MANCE EVALUATION AND ACCOUNTABILITY SYSTEMS

47. Establishing ecological conservation targets

Research will be conducted into developing practicable and visually representable indicators for assessing green development. Measures will be put in place to evaluate the attainment of ecological conservation targets, and indicators for resource consumption, environmental damage, and ecological benefit will be incorporated into a comprehensive evaluation system for economic and social development. Different performance evaluation criteria will be applied to different regions on the basis of their functional zoning.

48. Establishing monitoring and early-warning mechanisms for environmental and resource carrying capacity

Research will be undertaken into developing indicators and applying the right technology for monitoring and producing early warnings about resource and environmental carrying capacity. Monitoring and early-warning databases and IT platforms will be created for resources and the environment. Reports on monitoring and early-warning about resource and environmental carrying capacity will be prepared at regular intervals, and warnings will be issued and measures taken to place restrictions on regions which have exceeded or are approaching their carrying capacity in terms of resource consumption and environmental capacity.

49. Exploring the creation of balance sheets for natural resource assets

Guidelines will be formulated on preparing balance sheets for natural resource assets. Asset and liability accounting methods will be developed for use with water, land, forest, and other types of resources; accounts will be established for accounting natural resources in physical terms; classificatory criteria and statistical standards will be clearly laid out; and changes in natural resource assets will be regularly assessed. The preparation of balance sheets for natural resource assets will take place on a trial basis at the municipal (county) level, with physical accounts of major natural resource assets being assessed and results released.

50. Auditing outgoing officials' management of natural resource assets

On the basis of the preparation of balance sheets for natural resource assets and making reasonable allowance for objective natural factors, active efforts will be made to explore the objectives, content, methods, and appraisal indicators for auditing outgoing officials' management of natural resource assets. Based on the changes in natural resource assets within their area of jurisdiction during their term of office, through auditing, an objective evaluation will be carried out of the outgoing official' s management of natural resource assets; an official' s liability will be determined in accordance with the law, and auditing results will be put to better use. Trials for preparing balance sheets for natural resource assets and for audits of the management of natural resource assets by outgoing officials will be conducted in the cities of Hulun Buir in Inner Mongolia, Huzhou in Zhejiang, Loudi in Hunan, Chishui in Guizhou, and Yan' an in Shaanxi.

51. Establishing a lifelong accountability system for ecological and environmental damage

Leaders of local CPC committees and governments will be responsible for both economic development and ecological progress. On the basis of the results of the natural resource asset audits of outgoing officials and ecological and environmental damage, the circumstances under which the principal leaders of local CPC committees and governments, related leaders, and departmental leaders will be held accountable and the procedures for confirming accountability will be made clear. Those responsible for ecological and environmental damage will, on the basis of the severity of misconduct, be reprimanded, required to make a public apology, or dealt with through organizational, Party, or disciplinary action. For circumstances which constitute a criminal act, criminal liability will be pursued in accordance with the law. A system of lifelong accountability will be put into effect for major ecological and environmental damage which becomes apparent after an official has left office and for which he or she is found liable. A national supervision and inspection system for environmental protection will be established.

X. ENSURING SUCCESSFUL IMPLEMENTATION OF THE REFORM TO PROMOTE ECOLOGICAL PROGRESS

52. Strengthening leadership over the reform to promote ecological progress

All local governments and departments need to study the central leadership' s guiding principles on making ecological progress and carrying out reform to this effect, develop a deep understanding of the tremendous significance of this reform, and strengthen their sense of responsibility, sense of purpose, and sense of urgency over its implementation. Local governments and departments need to do their utmost to put into effect the policy decisions and arrangements of the CPC Central Committee and the State Council and see to it that all objectives contained within this reform plan are carried out quickly. In accordance with the requirements set out in this plan, all government departments concerned should promptly draw up plans for implementing each item of the reform, delegate responsibility and set time frames, and through close cooperation and collaboration with others create a concerted reform effort.

53. Launching pilot initiatives and explorative projects

Both the central and local governments will play an active role. All local governments are encouraged, in line with the direction of reform set out in this plan, to proactively explore and move forward with the reform to promote ecological progress,treating their local conditions as their point of departure and the solving of serious ecological and environmental problems as their target. Reforms that require legal authorization should be handled in accordance with statutory procedures. Comprehensive pilot initiatives for achieving ecological progress being conducted independently by different government departments will be incorporated into national pilot initiatives and explorative projects and will receive guidance and encouragement from those authorities whose own functions put them in a position to provide such support.

54. Improving laws and regulations

Legislative support will be provided for the reform to promote ecological progress through the development of effective laws and regulations on property rights for natural resource assets, the development and protection of territorial space, national parks, spatial planning, seas, responses to climate change, protection of cropland quality, water conservation and groundwater management, grassland and wetland preservation, pollutant emission permits, and compensation for ecological and environmental damage.

55. Improving guidance on public communication

Publicity both in China and abroad on efforts to promote ecological progress and carry out the reform to this effect will be stepped up. This will require coordinated planning and accurate interpretations of each of the systems and the direction of reform-all designed to promote ecological progress. It should cultivate and popularize eco-culture, raise public awareness about ecological progress, and advocate a green lifestyle, thereby creating a positive social atmosphere in which efforts to promote eco-progress are viewed with respect, and which will help to promote ecological progress and the reform designed to bring about it.

56. Exercising stricter supervision over reform implementation

The office of the Central Leading Group for Comprehensively Deepening Reform and the leading group' s Reform Taskforce for the Promotion of Economic Development and Ecological Progress should strengthen its overall coordination, carry out follow-up analyses and supervisory inspections over the implementation of this plan, accurately interpret and promptly resolve any problems arising during its implementation, and promptly report any major issues to the CPC Central Committee and the State Council.

II. Full Text: Enhanced Actions on Climate Change: China's Intended Nationally Determined Contributions

Climate change is today's common challenge faced by all humanity. Human activities since the Industrial Revolution, especially the accumulated carbon dioxide emissions from the intensive fossil fuels consumption of developed countries, have resulted in significantly increasing the atmospheric concentration of greenhouse gases, exacerbated climate change primarily characterized by global warming. Climate change has significant impacts on global natural ecosystems, causing temperature increase and sea level rise as well as more frequent extreme climate events, all of which pose a huge challenge to the survival and development of the human race.

Climate change is a global issue that requires the collaboration of the international community. For years, in accordance with the principles of equity and common but differentiated responsibilities and respective capabilities, the Parties to the United Nations Framework Convention on Climate Change (hereinafter referred to as the Convention) have been working to enhance cooperation and achieved positive progress in the implementation of the Convention. To further enhance the full, effective and sustained implementation of the Convention, negotiations and consultations are now under way on enhanced actions beyond 2020, so as to reach an agreement at the Conference of the Parties to the Convention in Paris at the end of 2015. This will open up a new prospect for green and low-carbon development across the globe and promote sustainable development worldwide.

As a developing country with a population of more than 1.3 billion, China is among those countries that are most severely affected by the adverse impacts of climate change. China is currently in the process of rapid industrialization and urbanization, confronting with multiple challenges including economic development, poverty eradication, improvement of living standards, environmental protection and combating climate change. To act on climate change in terms of mitigating greenhouse gas emissions and enhancing climate resilience, is not only driven by China's domestic needs for sustainable development in ensuring its economic security, energy security, ecological security, food security as well as the safety of people's life and property and to achieve sustainable development, but also driven by its sense of responsibility to fully engage in global governance, to forge a community of shared destiny for humankind and to promote common development for all human beings.

In accordance with relevant decisions of the Conference of the Parties to the Convention, China hereby presents its enhanced actions and measures on climate change as its nationally determined contributions towards achieving the objective set out in Article 2 of the Convention, which represent its utmost efforts in addressing climate change, and contributes its views on the 2015 agreement negotiations with a view to making the Paris Conference a great success.

I. ENHANCED ACTIONS ON CLIMATE CHANGE

China attaches great importance to addressing climate change since long, making it a significant national strategy for its social and economic development and promoting green and low-carbon development as important component of the ecological civilization process. It has already taken a series of climate actions which represent a significant contribution to combating the global climate change. In 2009, China announced internationally that by 2020 it will lower carbon dioxide emissions per unit of GDP by 40% to 45% from the 2005 level, increase the share of non-fossil fuels in primary energy consumption to about 15% and increase the forested area by 40 million hectares and the forest stock volume by 1.3 billion cubic meters compared to the 2005 levels. In this connection, China has enacted and implemented the National Program on Climate Change, the Work Plan for Controlling Greenhouse Gas Emissions during the 12th Five-Year Plan Period, the Comprehensive Work Plan for Energy Conservation and Emission Reduction for the 12th Five Year Plan Period, the 12th Five Year Plan for Energy Conservation and Emission Reduction, the 2014-2015 Action Plan for Energy Conservation, Emission Reduction and Low-Carbon Development, and the National Plan on Climate Change (2014-2020). China has accelerated the adjustment of its industry and energy structures and invested great efforts in improving energy efficiency, lowering carbon emissions and enhancing the ecosystem. China has initiated carbon emission trading pilots in 7 provinces and cities and low-carbon development pilots in 42 provinces and cities to explore a new mode of low-carbon development consistent with its prevailing national circumstances. By 2014 the following has been achieved:

- Carbon dioxide emissions per unit of GDP is 33.8% lower than the 2005 level;
- The share of non-fossil fuels in primary energy consumption is 11.2%;
- The forested area and forest stock volume are increased respectively by 21.6 million hectares and 2.188 billion cubic meters compared to the 2005 levels;
- The installed capacity of hydro power is 300 gigawatts (2.57 times of that for 2005);
- The installed capacity of on-grid wind power is 95.81 gigawatts (90 times of that for 2005);
- The installed capacity of solar power is 28.05 gigawatts (400 times of that for 2005); and

- The installed capacity of nuclear power is 19.88 gigawatts (2.9 times of that for 2005).

China is accelerating the implementation of the National Strategy for Climate Adaptation, and improving its capacity to respond to extreme climatic events and making positive progress in key areas of climate change adaptation. Capacity building on combating climate change is further strengthened. Supports in terms of science and technology are further enhanced by implementing China's Science and Technology Actions on Climate Change.

Looking into the future, China has defined as its strategic goals to complete the construction of a moderately prosperous society in an all-round way by 2020 and to create a prosperous, strong, democratic, culturally developed and harmonious modern socialist country by the middle of this century. It has identified transforming the economic development pattern, constructing ecological civilization and holding to a green, low-carbon and recycled development path as its policy orientation. New industrialization, urbanization, informatization, agricultural modernization and greenisation will be promoted in a coordinated manner. Resource conservation and environmental protection have become the cardinal national policy, placing mitigation and adaptation on equal footing, promoting innovation in science and technology and putting in place the necessary management and regulatory mechanisms and systems. China will accelerate the transformation of energy production and consumption and continue to restructure its economy, optimize the energy mix, improve energy efficiency and increase its forest carbon sinks, with a view to efficiently mitigating greenhouse gas emissions. China is making efforts to embark on a sustainable development path that is in line with its national circumstances and leads to multiple wins in terms of economic development, social progress and combating climate change.

Based on its national circumstances, development stage, sustainable development strategy and international responsibility, China has nationally determined its actions by 2030 as follows:

- To achieve the peaking of carbon dioxide emissions around 2030 and making best efforts to peak early;

- To lower carbon dioxide emissions per unit of GDP by 60% to 65% from the 2005 level;

- To increase the share of non-fossil fuels in primary energy consumption to around 20%; and

- To increase the forest stock volume by around 4.5 billion cubic meters on the 2005 level.

Moreover, China will continue to proactively adapt to climate change by enhancing mechanisms and capacities to effectively defend against climate change risks in key areas such as agriculture, forestry and water resources, as well as in cities, coastal and ecologically vulnerable areas and to progressively strengthen early warning and emergency response systems and disaster prevention and reduction mechanisms.

II. POLICIES AND MEASURES TO IMPLEMENT
ENHANCED ACTIONS ON CLIMATE CHANGE

A one-thousand-mile journey starts from the first step. To achieve the nationally determined action objectives on climate change by 2030, China needs, building on actions already taken, to make a sustained effort in further implementing enhanced policies and measures in areas such as regime building, production mode and consumption pattern, economic policy, science and technology innovation and international cooperation.

A. Implementing Proactive National Strategies On Climate Change

- To strengthen laws and regulations on climate change;

- To integrate climate-change-related objectives into the national economic and social development plans;

- To formulate China's long-term strategy and roadmap for low-carbon development;

- To implement the National Program on Climate Change (2014-2020) and provincial climate programs; and

- To improve the overall administration of climate-change-related work and to make carbon-emission-related indicators play guiding role, by subdividing and implementing climate change targets and tasks, and improving the performance evaluation and accountability system on climate change and low-carbon development targets.

B. Improving Regional Strategies on Climate Change

- To implement regionalized climate change policies to help identify differentiated targets, tasks and approaches of climate change mitigation and adaptation for different development-planning zones;

- To strictly control greenhouse gas emissions in Urbanized Zones for Optimized Development;

- To enhance carbon intensity control in Urbanized Zones for Focused Development and to accelerate green and low-carbon transformation in old industrial bases and resource-based cities;

- To enhance the control of development intensity, to limit large-scale industrialization and urbanization, to strengthen the planning and construction of medium-and-small-sized towns, to encourage moderate concentration of population and to actively push forward the appropriate scale production and industrialization of agriculture in Major Agricultural Production Zones;

- To define ecological red lines, to formulate strict criteria for industrial development and to constrain the development of any new carbon intensive projects in Key Ecological Zones; and

- To introduce a withdrawal mechanism for those industries that do not match with functions of development-planning zones and to develop low-carbon industries in line with local conditions and circumstances.

C. Building Low-Carbon Energy System

- To control total coal consumption;
- To enhance the clean use of coal;

- To increase the share of concentrated and highly-efficient electricity generation from coal;

- To lower coal consumption of electricity generation of newly built coal-fired power plants to around 300 grams coal equivalent per kilowatt-hour;

- To expand the use of natural gas: by 2020, achieving more than 10% share of natural gas consumption in the primary energy consumption and making efforts to reach 30 billion cubic meters of coal-bed methane production;

- To proactively promote the development of hydro power, on the premise of ecological and environmental protection and inhabitant resettlement;

- To develop nuclear power in a safe and efficient manner;

- To scale up the development of wind power;

- To accelerate the development of solar power;

- To proactively develop geothermal energy, bio-energy and maritime energy;

- To achieve the installed capacity of wind power reaching 200 gigawatts, the installed capacity of solar power reaching around 100 gigawatts and the utilization of thermal energy reaching 50 million tons coal equivalent by 2020;

- To enhance the recovery and utilization of vent gas and oilfield-associated gas; and

- To scale up distributed energy and strengthen the construction of smart grid.

D. Building Energy Efficient and Low-Carbon Industrial System

To embark on a new path of industrialization, developing a circular economy, optimizing the industrial structure, revising the guidance catalogue of the adjustment of industrial structure, strictly controlling the total expansion of industries with extensive energy consumption and emissions, accelerating the elimination of outdated production capacity and promoting the development of service industry and strategic emerging industries;

- To promote the share of value added from strategic emerging industries reaching 15% of the total GDP by 2020;

- To promote low-carbon development of industrial sectors, implementing Action Plan of Industries Addressing Climate Change (2012-2020) and formulating carbon emission control target and action plans in key industries;

- To research and formulate greenhouse gas emission standards for key industries;

- To effectively control emissions from key sectors including power, iron and steel, nonferrous metal, building materials and chemical industries through energy conservation and efficiency improvement;

- To strengthen the management of carbon emissions for new projects and to actively control greenhouse gas emissions originating from the industrial production process;

- To construct a recycling-based industrial system, promoting recycling restructure in industrial parks, increasing the recycling and utilization of renewable resources and improving the production rate of resource;

- To phase down the production and consumption of HCFC-22 for controlled uses, with its production to be reduced by 35% from the 2010 level by 2020, and by 67.5% by 2025 and to achieve effective control on emissions of HFC-23 by 2020;

- To promote the low-carbon development in agriculture, making efforts to achieve zero growth of fertilizer and pesticide utilization by 2020;

- To control methane emissions from rice fields and nitrous oxide emissions from farmland;

- To construct a recyclable agriculture system, promoting comprehensive utilization of straw, reutilization of agricultural and forestry wastes and comprehensive utilization of animal waste; and

- To promote low-carbon development of service industry, actively developing low-carbon business, tourism and foodservice and vigorously promoting service industries to conserve energy and reduce carbon emissions.

E. Controlling Emissions from Building and Transportation Sectors

- To embark on a new pattern of urbanization, optimizing the urban system and space layout, integrating the low-carbon development concept in the entire process of urban planning, construction and management and promoting the urban form that integrates industries into cities;

- To enhance low-carbonized urbanization, improving energy efficiency of building and the quality of building construction, extending buildings' life spans, intensifying energy conservation transformation for existing buildings, building energy-saving and low-carbon infrastructures, promoting the reutilization of building wastes and intensifying the recovery and utilization of methane from landfills;

- To accelerate the construction of low-carbon communities in both urban and rural areas, promoting the construction of green buildings and the application of renewable energy in buildings, improving low-carbon supporting facilities for equipping communities and exploring modes of low-carbon community operation and management;

- To promote the share of green buildings in newly built buildings of cities and towns reaching 50% by 2020;

- To develop a green and low-carbon transportation system, optimizing means of transportation, properly allocating public transport resources in cities, giving priority to the development of public transportation and encouraging the development and use of low-carbon and environment-friendly means of transport, such as new energy vehicle and vessel;

- To improve the quality of gasoline and to promote new types of alternative fuels;

- To promote the share of public transport in motorized travel in big-and-medium-sized cities reaching 30% by 2020;

- To promote the development of dedicated transport system for pedestrians and bicycles in cities and to advocate green travel; and

- To accelerate the development of smart transport and green freight transport.

F. Increasing Carbon Sinks

- To vigorously enhance afforestation, promoting voluntary tree planting by all citizens, continuing the implementation of key ecological programs, including protecting natural forests, restoring forest and grassland from farmland, conducting sandification control for areas in vicinity of Beijing and Tianjin, planting shelter belt, controlling rocky desertification, conserving water and soil, strengthening forest tending and management and increasing the forest carbon sink;

- To strengthen forest disaster prevention and forest resource protection and to reduce deforestation-related emissions;

- To strengthen the protection and restoration of wetlands and to increase carbon storage capacity of wetlands; and

- To continue to restore grassland from grazing land, to promote mechanism of maintaining the balance between grass stock and livestock, to prevent grassland degradation, to restore vegetation of grassland, to enhance grassland disaster prevention and farmland protection and to improve carbon storage of soil.

G. Promoting the Low-Carbon Way of Life

- To enhance education for all citizens on low-carbon way of life and consumption, to advocate green, low-carbon, healthy and civilized way of life and consumption patterns and to promote low-carbon consumption throughout society;

- To encourage public institutes to take the lead to: advocate low-carbon government buildings, campuses, hospitals, stadiums and military camps, advocate moderate consumption, encourage the use of low-carbon products and curb extravagance and waste; and

- To improve waste separation and recycling system.

H. Enhancing Overall Climate Resilience

- To improve safe operation of infrastructure of water conservancy, transport and energy against climate change;

- To properly develop and optimize the allocation of water resources, implementing the strictest water management regulation, building water-saving society in all aspects and intensifying the development and utilization of unconventional water resources, including recycled water, desalinated sea water and rain and flood water;

- To improve the construction of water conservation facilities for farmlands, to vigorously develop water-saving agricultural irrigation and to cultivate heat-resistant and drought-resistant crops;

- To enhance resistance to marine disasters and management of coastal zones and to improve the resilience of coastal areas against climatic disasters;

- To track, monitor and assess the impact of climate change on biodiversity;

- To strengthen the construction of forestry infrastructure;

- To properly lay out functional zones in cities, to make overall arrangements in developing infrastructure and to effectively safeguard city lifeline system;

- To formulate contingency plan for public health under the impacts of climate change and to improve the capacity of public medical services to adapt to climate change;

- To strengthen comprehensive assessment and risk management of climate change and to improve the national monitoring, early warning and communication system on climate change;

- To take full consideration of climate change in the planning, engineering and construction of the distribution of productive forces, infrastructures and major projects;

- To improve the emergency response mechanism for extreme weather and climatic events; and

- To strengthen the development of disaster reduction and relief management system.

I. Innovating Low-Carbon Development Growth Pattern

- To advance low-carbon pilots in provinces and cities;

- To conduct low-carbon cities (towns) pilots as well as low-carbon industrial parks, low-carbon communities, low-carbon business and low-carbon transport pilots;

- To explore diversified patterns of low-carbon growth;

- To research on effective approaches to control carbon emissions in different regions and cities;

- To facilitate the emerging of low-carbon cities with rational space distribution, intensive utilization of resources, low-carbon and efficient production and livable green environment; and

- To research on and establish carbon emission accreditation and low-carbon honor system, to carry out low-carbon certification pilots and promotion of selected products.

J. Enhancing Support in terms of Science and Technology

- To improve the fundamental research into climate change, conducting research on climate change monitoring and forecasting and strengthening research on the mechanisms and assessment methodology of climate change impacts and risks;

- To strengthen research and development (R&D) and commercialization demonstration for low-carbon technologies, such as energy conservation, renewable energy, advanced nuclear power technologies and carbon capture, utilization and storage and to promote the technologies of utilizing carbon dioxide to enhance oil recovery and coal-bed methane recovery;

- To conduct R&D on early warning systems for extreme weather;

- To develop technologies on biological nitrogen fixation, green pest and disease prevention and control and protected agriculture;

- To strengthen R&D on technologies for water saving and desalination of sea water; and

- To improve the technical supporting system for addressing climate change, to establish a mechanism that effectively integrates government, industries and academic and research institutes and to strengthen professional personnel training for addressing climate change.

K. Increasing Financial and Policy Support

- To further increase budgetary support;

- To actively innovate the application of funds and explore new investment and financing mechanisms for low-carbon development, such as public-private partnerships;

- To implement preferential taxation policies for promoting the development of new energy and to improve mechanisms of pricing, grid access and procurement mechanisms for solar, wind and hydro power;

- To improve green government procurement policy systems including that on procurement of low-carbon and energy-conservation products;

- To advance the reform in the pricing and taxation regime for energy-and-resource-based products;

- To improve the green credit mechanisms, to encourage and guide financial institutions to operate energy-efficiency crediting business and to issue asset-securitized products for green credit assets; and

- To improve disaster insurance policy against climate change.

L. *Promoting Carbon Emission Trading Market*

- To build on carbon emission trading pilots, steadily implementing a nationwide carbon emission trading system and gradually establishing the carbon emission trading mechanism so as to make the market play the decisive role in resource allocation; and

- To develop mechanisms for the reporting, verifying and certificating of carbon emissions and to improve rules and regulations for carbon emission trading to ensure openness, fairness and justice in the operation of the carbon emission trading market.

M. *Improving Statistical and Accounting System for GHG Emissions*

- To further strengthen the work on statistics of climate change;

- To improve greenhouse gas emission statistics covering areas including energy activity, industrial process, agriculture, land-use change, forestry and waste treatment;

- To improve the statistical indicator systems for climate change, to strengthen personnel training and to constantly improve the quality of data;

- To strengthen the work on greenhouse gas emission inventory accounting;

- To prepare greenhouse gas inventories at the national and provincial level on a regular basis;

- To establish a greenhouse gas emission reporting mechanism for key enterprises;

- To formulate greenhouse gas emission accounting standards for enterprises in key sectors; and

- To build a fundamental statistics and accounting system for greenhouse gas emissions at national, subnational and enterprise levels.

N. *Broad Participation of Stakeholders*

- To enhance the responsibility of enterprises for low-carbon development and to encourage them to explore low-carbon development modes that are resource-saving and environment-friendly;

- To strengthen the role of public supervision and participation in low-carbon development;

- To use platforms such as National Low Carbon Day to raise public awareness of low-carbon development throughout society;

- To encourage voluntary actions of the public to combat climate change;

- To let media play the role of supervision and guidance; and

- To enhance related education and training and to fully utilize the function of schools, communities and civil organizations.

O. Promoting International Cooperation on Climate Change

As a responsible developing country, China will stand for the common interests of all humanity and actively engage in international cooperation to build an equitable global climate governance regime that is cooperative and beneficial to all. Together with other Parties, China will promote global green low-carbon transformation and development path innovation. China will adhere to the principles of equity and common but differentiated responsibilities and respective capabilities and urge developed countries to fulfill their obligations under the Convention to take the lead in substantially reducing their emissions and to provide support of finance, technology and capacity building to developing countries, allowing developing countries more equitable access to sustainable development and more support of finance, technology and capacity building and promoting cooperation between developed and developing countries. China will take on international commitments that match its national circumstances, current development stage and actual capabilities by enhancing mitigation and adaptation actions and further strengthening south-south cooperation on climate change. It will establish the Fund for South-South Cooperation on Climate Change, providing assistance and support, within its means, to other developing countries including the small island developing countries, the least developed countries and African countries to address climate change. China will thereby promote mutual learning, mutual support and mutual benefits as well as win-win cooperation with other developing countries. China will engage in extensive international dialogue and exchanges on addressing climate change, enhance policy coordination and concrete cooperation in related areas, share positive experiences and good practice, promote climate friendly technologies and work together with all Parties to build a beautiful homeland for all human beings.

III. CONTRIBUTIONS TO 2015 AGREEMENT NEGOTIATION

China is committed to the full, effective and sustained implementation of the Convention and to working with other Parties to achieve a comprehensive, balanced and ambitious agreement at the Paris Conference. In this connection, China submits its views regarding the process and outcome of the 2015 agreement negotiation as follows:

A. General View

The negotiation on the 2015 agreement shall be under the Convention and guided by its principles, aiming at enhancing the full, effective and sustained implementation of the Convention in order to achieve the objective of the Convention. The outcomes of negotiation shall be in accordance with the principles of equity and common but differentiated responsibilities and respective capabilities, taking into account differentiated historical responsibilities and distinct national circumstances, development stages and the capabilities of developed and developing countries. It should reflect all elements in a comprehensive and balanced way, including mitigation, adaptation, finance, technology development and transfer, capacity building and transparency of action and support. The negotiation process should be open, transparent, inclusive, Party-driven and consensus-based.

B. Mitigation

The 2015 agreement shall stipulate that the Parties, in accordance with the provisions of the Convention, shall formulate and implement programs and measures to reduce or limit greenhouse gas emissions for the period 2020-2030 and promote international cooperation on mitigation. Developed countries shall, in accordance with their historical responsibilities, undertake ambitious economy-wide absolute quantified emissions reduction targets by 2030. Developing countries shall, in the context of sustainable development and supported and enabled by the provision of finance, technology and capacity building by developed countries, undertake diversifying enhanced mitigation actions.

C. Adaptation

The 2015 agreement shall stipulate that the Parties shall, in accordance with the provisions of the Convention, strengthen international cooperation on adaptation as well as the implementation of adaptation plans and projects at both regional and national levels. Developed countries shall provide support for developing countries to formulate and implement national adaptation plans as well as other related projects. Developing countries will identify their adaptation needs and challenges in their national adaptation plans and take enhanced actions. A subsidiary body on adaptation to climate change should be established. The linkage between adaptation and finance, technology and capacity building shall be strengthened. The Warsaw International Mechanism on Loss and Damage shall also be strengthened.

D. Finance

The 2015 agreement shall stipulate that developed countries shall, in accordance with the provisions of the Convention, provide new, additional, adequate, predictable and sustained financial support to developing countries for their enhanced actions. It shall provide for quantified financing targets and a roadmap to achieve them. The scale of financing should increase yearly starting from 100 billion U.S. dollars per year from 2020 which shall primarily come from public finance. The role of the Green Climate Fund (GCF) as an important operating entity of the financial mechanism of the Convention shall be strengthened. The GCF shall be under the authority of, guided by and accountable to the Conference of the Parties to the Convention.

E. Technology Development and Transfer

The 2015 agreement shall stipulate that developed countries shall, in accordance with the provisions of the Convention, transfer technologies and provide support for the research, development and application of technologies to developing countries based on their technology needs. The function of the existing technology mechanism shall be strengthened to help address the intellectual property right issue and assess technology transfer performance, and its linkage with the financial mechanism shall be enhanced, including creating a window for technology development and transfer in the GCF.

F. Capacity Building

The 2015 agreement shall stipulate that developed countries shall, in accordance with the provisions of the Convention, provide support to developing countries in capacity building in all areas. An international mechanism on capacity building shall be established to develop and implement action plans for capacity building and to enhance capacity building for climate change mitigation and adaptation in developing countries.

G. Transparency of Action and Support

The 2015 agreement shall stipulate that the Parties shall, in accordance with the provisions of the Convention and relevant COP decisions, improve the transparency of enhanced actions of all Parties. Developed countries shall, in accordance with the provisions of the Convention as well as relevant provisions of the Kyoto Protocol, enhance the transparency of their actions through existing reporting and review systems. Rules on enhancing the transparency of finance, technology and capacity-building support by developed countries as well as the relevant review shall further be elaborated. Developing countries shall, with support by developed countries in terms of finance, technology and capacity building, enhance the transparency of their enhanced actions through existing arrangements on transparency and in a way that is non-intrusive, non-punitive and respecting national sovereignty.

H. Legal Form

The 2015 agreement shall be a legally binding agreement implementing the Convention. It can take the form of a core agreement plus COP decisions, with mitigation, adaptation, finance, technology development and transfer, capacity building and transparency of action and support being reflected in a balanced manner in the core agreement and relevant technical details and procedural rules being elaborated in COP decisions. The nationally determined contributions by developed and developing countries can be listed respectively and separately in the Paris outcome.

www.ingramcontent.com/pod-product-compliance
Lightning Source LLC
Chambersburg PA
CBHW060325200326
41519CB00011BA/1841